COLLINS DESIGN
An Imprint of HarperCollins *Publishers*

CREATIVITY 39

For additional information, or to learn how your work may be submitted to the CREATIVITY INTERNATIONAL AWARDS
for possible inclusion in subsequent Annuals, please address inquiries to:

CREATIVITY INTERNATIONAL AWARDS
2410 Frankfort Avenue
Louisville, KY 40206
PHONE: 502.893.7899
FAX: 502.896.9594
EMAIL: info@creativityawards.com.
WEBSITE: www.creativityawards.com

HarperCollins books may be purchased for educational, business, or sales promotional use.
For information, please write: Special Markets Department, HarperCollins*Publishers*,
10 East 53rd Street, New York, NY 10022.

First published in 2010 by:
CREATIVITY INTERNATIONAL AWARDS
2410 Frankfort Avenue
Louisville, KY 40206
PHONE: 502.893.7899
FAX: 502.896.9594
EMAIL: info@creativityawards.com
WEBSITE: www.creativityawards.com

Distributed throughout the world by:
HarperCollins*Publishers*
10 East 53rd Street
New York, NY 10022
Fax: (212) 207-7654

Book design by SW!TCH Studio • www.switchstudio.com
Photography, scanning & pre-press services provided by FCI Digital • www.fcidigital.com

Library of Congress Number: 2010926089

ISBN 978-0-06-199786-0

Produced by CREATIVITY ANNUAL AWARDS, Louisville, KY

Printed in China by Everbest Printing Company.

First Printing, 2010

contents

contents

acknowledgments

A HUGE thank you to the 2009 judges for donating their time, expertise and humor! Ana Rodrigues - Nielsen Business Media; Alberto March - GrafMarc; Ben Williams - AKQA, New York; Burkey Belser - Greenfield Belser Ltd.; Craig Brimm - Culture Advertising Design; James Pietruszynski - Optima Soulsight; Jeremy Carrus - WHOISCARRUS; John McCafferty - McCafferty & Company; Keith Steimel - Cornerstone Strategic Branding, Inc.; Lisa Fargo - Fargo Design Co.; Peter "Hula Hooper" Klueger - 1919 Creative Studio; Solana Crawford - DESIGNaboutTOWN.com; Will Burke - Brand Engine; William McMillian - McMillian Design. The competition could not happen without the dedicated staff of Creativity International and Crescent Hill Books so thank you for your long hours and smiling faces.

medal designations

 This symbol designates a PLATINUM AWARD winning design. Our most prestigious award is reserved for the best in category. Only one design is awarded per category.

 This symbol designates a GOLD AWARD winning design. The top 10% of designs in each category are selected for the GOLD AWARD.

 This symbol designates a SILVER AWARD winning design. The top 25% of designs in each category are selected for the SILVER AWARD

foreword

Elephants are known to be one of the smartest animals on earth. They are able to communicate over great distances and supposedly "never forget." My grandfather would sit with me as a child and he would teach me to draw elephants. It wasn't until I was an adult that I realized the powerful symbol of the elephant and the deeper meaning in my quest to draw the perfect elephant.

Being creative is very similar to the symbolic meaning of the elephant. Maybe it was unintentional (or brilliance) but my grandfather realized that to be successfully creative you need to be brave, determined and loyal. In addition, you also need to be able to express sensitivity. This is a lesson I will never forget.

As a judge for the 39th Creativity Awards Annual, the process of distilling through thousands of entries with colleagues from every area of the creative industry was illuminating and inspiring. The vast array of submissions from around the world illustrated the universal language of design and its ability to connect on a level far greater than words alone.

We are an international community of creative individuals that come together to share our creative executions. The 39th Creativity Awards Annual celebrates the differences in our creative diversity and the bravery it takes to stand out in a competitive world.

In many ways, the creative phenomenon parallels the wisdom and intelligence of the elephant. When we are strong and brave, our creative values and wisdom become very powerful. We are able to communicate around the world and if we are lucky, our work will never be forgotten.

James Pietruszynski
Soulsight®
Principal // Creative Director

REGISTER ONLINE AT

creativityawards.com

CREATIVE CATEGORY
print

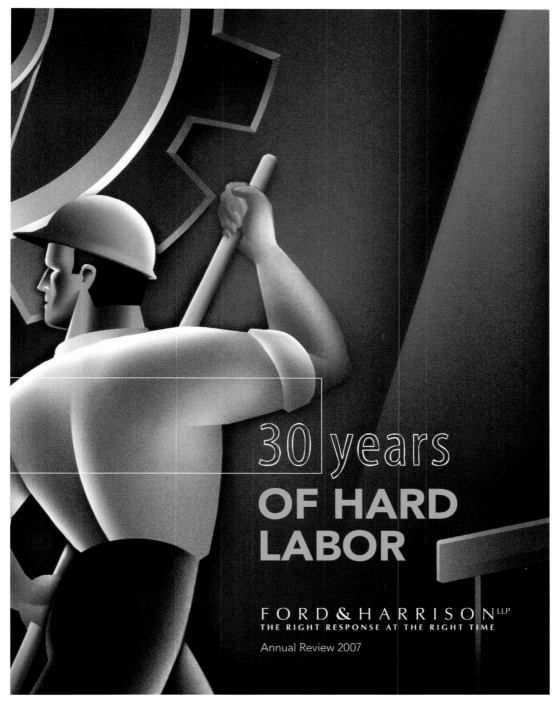

 PLATINUM

Creative Firm: Greenfield/Belser Ltd. -
Washington, D.C.

Creative Team: Erika Ritzer – Director of Client
Services; Margo Howard – Designer; Burkey Belser –
Creative Director; Mark Ledgerwood – Art Director;
Joe Walsh – Creative Director; Jaime Chirinos –
Production Artist

Client: Ford & Harrison LLP

An Easy Read

For its first-ever annual review, labor and employment law firm Ford & Harrison wanted to address the state of the economy in graphic form. Marketing firm Greenfield/Belser took the familiar style of Depression-era WPA illustrations and updated them using current graphic techniques under the banner, "30 years of hard labor." "Most annuals we've seen present a tsunami of words that defeats even the most dedicated readers," says the Washington, D.C.-based agency. "Our goals were simple: Tell stories that are enjoyable and easy to follow, and position the firm as important, confident and a leader." By inverting the usual word-image ratio, the overall book seamlessly focuses on important business issues through the years, while the sidebars trace the firm's geographical expansion and growth in numbers.

1

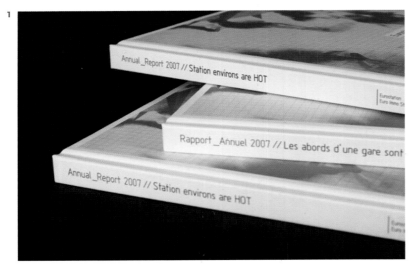

2

3

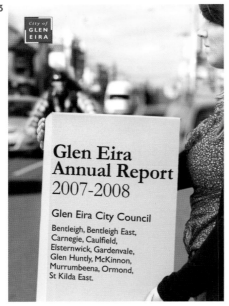

1 Creative Firm: LUON - Overijse, Belgium **Creative Team:** Onno Hesselink – Creative Director; Els Vandecan – Graphic Designer; Sophie Baras – Account **Client:** Eurostation **2 Creative Firm:** Q-Plus Design Pte Ltd. - Singapore **Creative Team:** Dillon Devan – Creative Director; Lisar Sng – Senior Design Consultant **Client:** China Hongxing Sports Limited **3 Creative Firm:** housemouse - Melbourne, Australia **Client:** City of Glen Eira

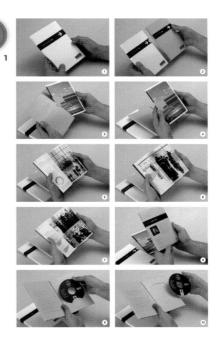

1 Creative Firm: Finar Kurumsal - Istanbul, Turkey **Creative Team:** Teoman Fiçicioglu – Creative Director; Mustafa Kirarslan – Art Director; Süheyla Acar - Copywriter; Talha Hosgör – Illustrator; Mustafa Cosan – Assistant Copywriter; Grasiela Bardavit Giritli – Account Manager **Client:** TAV Airports Holding **2 Creative Firm:** Splash Productions Pte Ltd - Singapore **Creative Team:** Norman Lai – Art Director; Terry Lee - Copywriter; Serene See – Copywriter; Joshua Tan – Photographer; Zaki Razak – Illustrator; Yiling Lui – Illustrator **Client:** Media Development Authority Singapore **URL:** www.mda.gov.sg **3 Creative Firm:** MFG Baden-Württemberg mbH - Public Innovation Agency for ICT and Media - Stuttgart, Germany **Creative Team:** Klaus Haasis – CEO; Silke Ruoff – Manager Communication/Marketing; Matthias Holzner – Project Manager International Affairs/Marketing; Jürgen Gerhardt – Graphical Designer/Design Partner; Tom Philippi – Photographer; Matthias Malpricht - Photographer **Client:** MFG Baden-Württemberg mbH **URL:** www.mfg-innovation.com

1 Creative Firm: VSA Partners · Chicago, IL **Creative Team:** Jeff Walker – Principal/Creative Director; Thom Wolfe – Associate Partner/Design Director; Melissa Schwister – Associate Partner/Account Director; Kyle Pof – Designer; Anne-Marie Rosser – Associate Partner/Strategist **Client:** McDonald's **2 Creative Firm:** Kirchhoff Consult AG / Red Cell Werbeagentur GmbH · Gütersloh, Germany **Creative Team:** Stefanie Wulf – Director Annual Reports; Claudia Weithase – Art Director **Client:** Bertelsmann AG

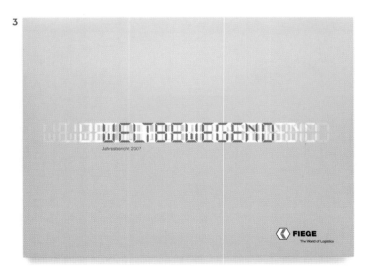

1 Creative Firm: Credence Partnership Pte Ltd - Singapore **Creative Team:** Wong Zhihong – Art Director; Sim Francis – Design Director **Client:** Engro Corporation Limited
2 Creative Firm: Vertex Pharmaceuticals Incorporated - Cambridge, MA **Creative Team:** Robert McKelvey – Manager; Ilana Robbins – eBusiness Design Manager; Theron Wallis – Graphic Designer; Diana Picariello – Web Designer; Jonathan Kirk – Graphic Designer; Zachry Barber – Writer **Client:** Vertex Pharmaceuticals Incorporated **3 Creative Firm:** RTS Rieger Team Werbeagentur GmbH - Duesseldorf, Germany **Creative Team:** Yvonne Wicht – Senior Account Executive; Daniela Schäfer – Senior Art Director; Luisa Lueg – Junior Art Director; Marc Fielers – Copywriter **Client:** Fiege Stiftung & Co. KG

1

2

G

3

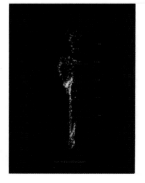

1 Creative Firm: Stan Gellman Graphic Design, Inc. - St. Louis, MO **Creative Team:** Teresa Thompson – Vice President; Britni Eggers – Designer **Client:** UniGroup, Inc.
2 Creative Firm: Randi Wolf Design - Glassboro, NJ **Creative Team:** Randi Wolf – Designer/Creative Director; Donna Midili – Client/Director; Kim Wallace – Client/Supervisor **Client:** Robins' Nest **3 Creative Firm:** DesignLab - Pacific Palisades, CA **Creative Team:** Scott Lambert – Creative Director/Art Director; Jeff Corwin – Photographer, location; Rick Brian – Photographer, studio; Tim Richardson – Photographer, charts; Shannon Dean – Writer **Client:** California Water Service Group

1

3

---

1 **Creative Firm:** Nesnadny + Schwartz - Cleveland, OH **Creative Team:** Mark Schwartz – Creative Director; Cindy Lowrey – Designer; Michelle Moehler – Designer; Keith Pishnery – Designer; Caleb Charland – Photographer; Glenn Renwick – Writer **Client:** The Progressive Corporation 2 **Creative Firm:** Please Touch Museum - Philadelphia, PA **Creative Team:** Christie Morrison – Graphic and Web Designer **Client:** Please Touch Museum 3 **Creative Firm:** Q-Plus Design Pte Ltd. - Singapore **Creative Team:** Dillon Devan – Creative Director; Mark Sidwell – Art Director **Client:** Singapore Press Holdings Limited

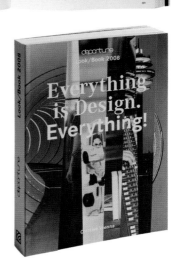

1 Creative Firm: Rosebud, Inc. - Vienna, Austria **Creative Team:** Ralf Herms – Creative Direction (Rosebud, Inc.); Raphael Drechsel – Art Direction (Rosebud, Inc.); Marlene Leichtfried – Project Management (Rosebud, Inc.); Heinz Wolf – Strategic Planning; Martin Stöbich – Photography; Dorothea Köb – Text **Client:** departure wirtschaft, kunst und kultur gmbh **2 Creative Firm:** Cosmic Ltd. - Pembroke, Bermuda **Creative Team:** Sean Collier – President **Client:** Sovereign Risk Insurance Ltd. **3 Creative Firm:** VSA Partners - Chicago, IL **Creative Team:** Dana Arnet – Principal/Creative Director; Melissa Schwister – Associate Partner/Account Director; Luke Galambos – Design Director; Conor McFerran – Designer; Jarrod Ryha – Designer; Andy Blakenburg – Associate Partner/Writer **Client:** Harley-Davidson

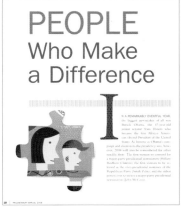

1 Creative Firm: Object 9 - Baton Rouge, LA **Client:** Baton Rouge Area Chamber (BRAC). **2 Creative Firm:** Tom Dolle Design - New York, NY **Creative Team:** Tom Dolle – Creative Director; Cheryl Loe – Project Director; Chris Riely – Designer **Client:** Foundation Center

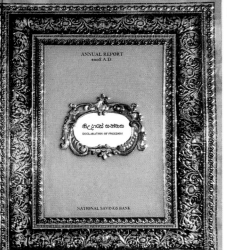

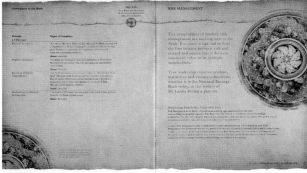

New Standards in Precision

1 **Creative Firm:** Smart Media - Colombo, Sri Lanka **Client:** National Savings Bank 2 **Creative Firm:** Smart Media - Colombo, Sri Lanka **Client:** DIMO

1

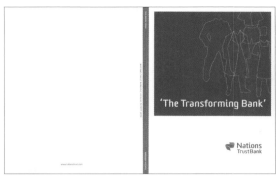

3

2

1 Creative Firm: Smart Media - Colombo, Sri Lanka **Client:** Nations Trust Bank **2 Creative Firm:** Coal Creative Consultants Pte Ltd - Singapore **Creative Team:** Yong Yau Goh – Account Director/Copy Editor; Lwin Mun Tin Thein – Creative Director; Eng Teck Tan – Art Director **Client:** Competition Commission of Singapore **3 Creative Firm:** Smart Media - Colombo, Sri Lanka **Client:** Sri Lanka Association of Printers

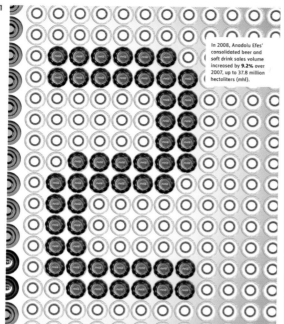

In 2008, Anadolu Efes' consolidated beer and soft drink sales volume increased by **9.2%** over 2007, up to 37.8 million hectoliters (mhl).

2008 Activities

Vuosikertomus 2008

Yli 140 maata,
135 000 asiantuntijaa

Ernst & Young on johtava, maailmanlaajuinen tilintarkastuksen, verokonsultoinnin, yritys-järjestelyiden, liikkeenjohdon konsultoinnin ja liikejuridiikan asiantuntija.

As the world gets smaller, we're thinking bigger.

Sisältö

1 Creative Firm: Finar Kurumsal - Istanbul, Turkey **Creative Team:** Teoman Fiçicioglu – Creative Director; Mustafa Kirarslan – Art Director; Süheyla Acar – Copywriter; Talha Hosgör – Illustrator; Mustafa Cosan – Assistant Copywriter; Grasiela Bardavit Giritli – Account Manager **Client:** Anadolu Efes Biracilik ve Malt Sanayi A.S. **2 Creative Firm:** Zeeland Oy - Helsinki, Finland **Creative Team:** Teija Himberg – Art Director; Anni Jaakkola – Project Manager **Client:** Ernst&Young

1

2

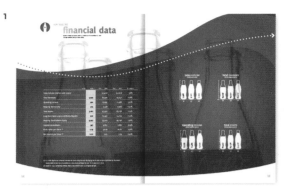

Life On BlackBerry

1 Creative Firm: SIGNI - Mexico **Creative Team:** René Galindo – Art Director; Odette Edwards – Designer **Client:** Coca-Cola Femsa **2 Creative Firm:** Coal Creative Consultants Pte Ltd - Singapore **Creative Team:** Yong Yau Goh – Account Director/Copy Editor; Lwin Mun Tin Thein – Creative Director; Eng Teck Tan – Art Director **Client:** Singapore Sports Council **3 Creative Firm:** RWI - New York, NY **Creative Team:** Michael DeVoursney – Art Director/Designer **Client:** Research in Motion

1

3

1 Creative Firm: Suka - New York, NY **Creative Team:** Brian Wong – Creative Director; Rob Saywitz – Art Director **Client:** YMCA of Greater New York **2 Creative Firm:** Suka - New York, NY **Creative Team:** Brian Wong – Creative Director; Matthew Carl – Designer; Dave Caputo – Designer **Client:** GLSEN (Gay/Lesbian and Straight Education Network) **3 Creative Firm:** Suka - New York, NY **Creative Team:** Brian Wong – Creative Director; Matthew Carl – Designer **Client:** GLSEN (Gay/Lesbian and Straight Education Network)

1

2

3

1 Creative Firm: Edelman - Chicago, IL **Creative Team:** John Avila SVP – US Design Director; Ginny Tevere – Art Director **Client:** Burger King **2 Creative Firm:** Zeesman Communications, Inc. - Beverly Hills, CA **Creative Team:** John Taylor – Creative Director; Ryan Powell – Sr. Graphic Designer **Client:** National Council of Jewish Women Los Angeles **3 Creative Firm:** Rassman Design - Denver, CO **Creative Team:** Jonathan Wheeler – Designer; John Rassman – Creative Director **Client:** Brownstein Hyatt Farber Schreck

 **PLATINUM**

Creative Firm: Campbell-Ewald - Warren, MI

Creative Team: Bill Ludwig – Vice Chairman/Chief Creative Officer; Mark Simon; Debbie Karnowsky; Mike Conboy; Jo Herringer; Charlie Noback; Marge Bornais; Neville Anderson; Woo Tom; Dawn Manza; Cindy Kuretski; Jamie Levey; David Sullivan; Chip Kettering; John Dolab; Angela Zepeda; Jennifer Bittner; Matt Clark; Ali Forgeron; Darlene Hodge;

Client: Kaiser Permanente

1

2

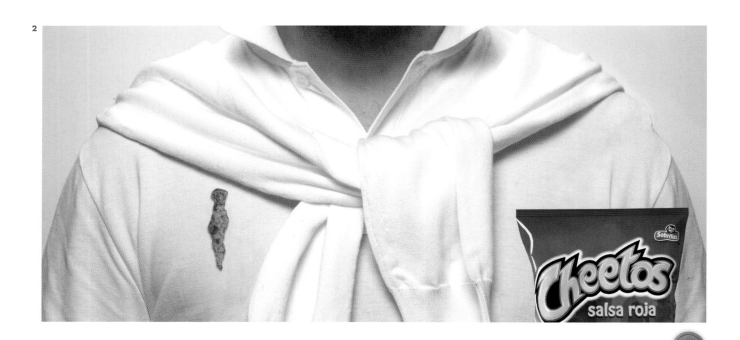

1

The Goddess of Ice Creams
is here to bless your tastebuds !

Special
Sitaphal Flavour
from

2

**NEW UNDER COVER PARKING
THAT COULDN'T BE
ANY CLOSER**

**SYDNEY INTERNATIONAL AIRPORT
7 DAYS FOR JUST $132**

This price only online at **sydneyairport.com**

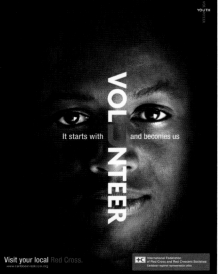

PLATINUM

Creative Firm: Inglefield, Ogilvy & Mather
Caribbean Ltd. - Port of Spain, Trinidad & Tobago

Creative Team: David Gomez – Executive Creative
Director; Rory Moses – Associate Creative Director;
Tricia Dukhie – Graphic Artist; Monica Kanhai – Senior
Account Executive

Client: Red Cross

Who Can Volunteer? You Can.

The Red Cross wanted to promote volunteerism, and Inglefield, Ogilvy & Mather Caribbean Ltd., Port of Spain, Trinidad & Tobago, helped them with their mission by making their billboard campaign one hundred percent volunteer-produced. "No matter what your talent or skill, you can play a role," says senior copywriter Paula Obe. "All work for this campaign—from production, modeling, photography, copywriting and design—were done by people giving their talent, time and skills for free for the bigger picture."

Typographically, the word *VOLUNTEER* and the copy intersect to echo the cross from the organization's logo. The U is red in order to stand out and focus on the target market, which Obe describes as "each and every person." Capturing the essence of each of those persons posed a challenge. "The closeup of the 'volunteers' facial expression had to evoke many emotions," says Obe. "The eyes of the models needed to capture in one glimpse that they have the power to uplift a society."

1

1 Creative Firm: Launch Creative Marketing - Chicago, IL **Creative Team:** Amy Zwikel – Art Director; Sarah Wielusz – Associate Art Director **Client:** Sara Lee Corporation

BARBIE 50TH CELEBRATION
fashion week, new york - advertising

Barbie

WHEN YOU MAKE AN ENTRANCE, ALWAYS MAKE IT GRAND

Barbie™ Runway Show 2009, Mercedes-Benz Fashion Week

barbie.com/BarbieStyle

TOMORROW, I'M CELEBRATING MY FIRST LOVE...

FASHION

Barbie
Runway Show 2009
Mercedes-Benz Fashion Week

I'D LIKE TO TAKE A MOMENT TO THANK ALL THE BIG PEOPLE

I'M SIMPLY PLASTIC WITHOUT YOU

Barbie
Runway Show 2009
Mercedes-Benz Fashion Week

BARBIE 50TH CELEBRATION
promotional doll & new york fashion show giftbox

BARBIE 50TH CELEBRATION
retail branding, new york

dylan's candy bar, new york   sephora, new york   bloomingdale's, new york

PLATINUM

Creative Firm: Mattel, Inc. - El Segundo, CA
Creative Team: Mattel, Inc.

An Icon Turns 50

To celebrate the 50th anniversary of the Barbie doll, Mattel brought the past, present and future together in a fun and playful way—with a lot of pink, of course. To enhance the emotional connection shared each generation of consumers, collectors and fans, Mattel's in-house agency in El Segundo, California used existing images of Barbie through the years, starting with her 1959 debut and through the '60s, '70s, '80s, '90s and 2000s. "Everyone has a Barbie story," Mattel says. "The campaign celebrated the continuing influence and

impact that Barbie has had on girls around the world for the past 50 years."

As part of the festivities, the foot-tall fashionista opened New York Fashion Week at Bryant Park for the first time ever, as over 50 designers created outfits especially with Barbie in mind. The accompanying lobby display welcomed visitors to a series of events spotlighting Barbie's signature style, which included promotional tie-ins from retailers such as Sephora and Bloomingdale's.

1 Creative Firm: Mattel, Inc. - El Segundo, CA **Creative Team:** Mattel, Inc. **2 Creative Firm:** Mani & Company - New York, NY **Creative Team:** Dino Maniaci – Art Director; Chris Bartick – Designer **Client:** Spawoof **3 Creative Firm:** YARD - New York, NY **Creative Team:** Stephen Niedzwiecki – Creative Director; Sarah Evans – Designer; Jennifer Carter-Campbel – Producer; April Hughes – Stylist; Herve Bernard – Hair and Make Up Artist **Client:** LeSportsac

1

2

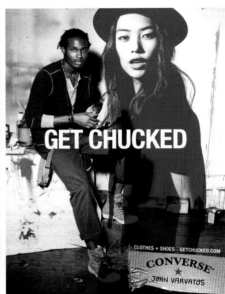

3

1 Creative Firm: Planet Ads and Design P/L - Singapore **Creative Team:** Hal Suzuki – Creative Director; Suzanne Lauridsen – Senior Copywriter; Patrick Jabillo – Art Director; Hironori Kawaguchi – Art Director; John Loke – Graphic Designer; Octa Lesmana – Graphic Designer **Client:** Paris Miki **2 Creative Firm:** YARD - New York, NY **Creative Team:** Stephen Niedzwiecki – Creative Director; Tyer Ochs – Art Director; David Calderley – Art Director; Jennifer Carter-Campbell – Producer; Kate Lanphear – Stylist **Client:** Converse and John Varvatos **3 Creative Firm:** Goble & Associates - Chicago, IL **Creative Team:** Ryan Van Pelt – VP/Account Supervisor; Carmela Wegworth – Account Director; Dave Raube – EVP/Creative Director; Brooke Claussen – Group Creative Director; Karen MacShane – Creative Director; Natalie Greer – Senior Writer **Client:** Upsher-Smith Laboratories

1 PACKAGING, CROCKERY AND
PRINT

PACKAGING, CROCKERY AND
PRINT

2

3

1 Creative Firm: Storm Corporate Design - Auckland, New Zealand **Creative Team:** Rehan Saiyed – Design Director/Designer/Typographer **Client:** Noora's Mediterranean Kitchen, Auckland, New Zealand **2 Creative Firm:** Goble & Associates - Chicago, IL **Creative Team:** Nancy Finigan – EVP/Account Group Director; Brooke Sellars – Account Director; Chris Gavazzoni – Account Supervisor; Dave Raube – EVP/Creative Director; Johnny Murawski – Creative Director; Denis O'Keefe – Copy Supervisor **Client:** Ikaria **3 Creative Firm:** Max2o - Atlanta, GA **Creative Team:** Jessica Mullis – Designer **Client:** Atlanta Film Festival

1

SIGNAGE, INTERIOR AND
ENVIRONMENT

PACKAGING AND PRINT

2

3

1 Creative Firm: Storm Corporate Design - Auckland, New Zealand **Creative Team:** Rehan Saiyed – Designer/Design Director **Client:** Cheetal Foods Limited/Auckland/ New Zealand **2 Creative Firm:** design systemat - Makati, Phillipines **Creative Team:** Angel Bunag – President; Ma. Pilar Bunag - Creative Director; Stefano Paolo Bunag – Designer/Artist; Geronimo Santos – Designer/Artist **Client:** Roxas Holdings, Inc. **3 Creative Firm:** Merchan-Design - Sao Paulo, Brazil **Creative Team:** Marcelo Lopes; Volleyball Team **Client:** Bernardinho - Coach of Brazilian Volleyball Team

38

1 Creative Firm: Rassman Design - Denver, CO **Creative Team:** Lyn D'Amato – Designer; John Rassman – Creative Director **Client:** Denver Botanic Gardens **2 Creative Firm:** Merchan-Design - Sao Paulo, Brazil **Creative Team:** Marcelo Lopes; Yael Sonia **Client:** Yael Sonia Art Jewelry

1

display ad

classified ad

banner ad

1 Creative Firm: Silver Creative Group - South Norwalk, CT **Creative Team:** Paul Zullo – Creative Director; Suzanne Petrow – Art Director; Stephanie Trainor – Designer; Scott Weiner – Programmer/Flash Animation; David Rodman – Programmer/Website; David Paler – Photographer **Client:** TF Cornerstone **URL:** 455w37.com

1

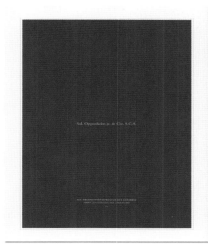
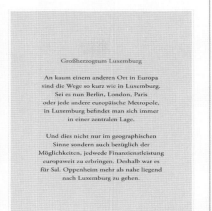

Großherzogtum Luxemburg

An kaum einem anderen Ort in Europa
sind die Wege so kurz wie in Luxemburg.
Sei es nun Berlin, London, Paris
oder jede andere europäische Metropole,
in Luxemburg befindet man sich immer
in einer zentralen Lage.

Und dies nicht nur im geographischen
Sinne sondern auch bezüglich der
Möglichkeiten, jedwede Finanzdienstleistung
europaweit zu erbringen. Deshalb war es
für Sal. Oppenheim mehr als nahe liegend
nach Luxemburg zu gehen.

2

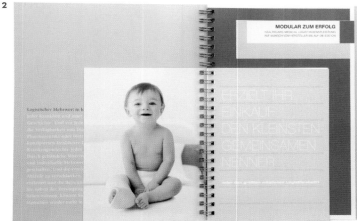

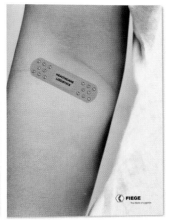

1 **Creative Firm:** Simon & Goetz Design GmbH & Co. KG - Frankfurt, Germany **Creative Team:** Bernd Vollmöller – Creative Direction/Art Direction **Client:** Sal. Oppenheim jr. & Cie. S.C.A. **2 Creative Firm:** RTS Rieger Team Werbeagentur GmbH - Duesseldorf, Germany **Creative Team:** Yvonne Wicht – Senior Account Executive; Daniela Schäfer – Senior Art Director; Luisa Lueg – Junior Art Director; Marc Fielers – Copywriter **Client:** Fiege Stiftung & Co. KG

1 **Creative Firm:** Goble & Associates - Chicago, IL **Creative Team:** Nancy Finigan – EVP/ Account Group Director; Chris Gavazzoni – Account Supervisor; Brooke Claussen – Group Creative Director; Terry Lawrence – Senior Art Director; Denis O'Keefe – Copy Supervisor **Client:** Hospira 2 **Creative Firm:** Object 9 - Baton Rouge, LA **Client:** Arkeel 3 **Creative Firm:** Finished Art Inc. - Atlanta, GA **Creative Team:** Donna Johnston – Creative Director; Gretchen Chern – Designer **Client:** Coca-Cola

1

2

3

1 **Creative Firm:** American Specialty Health - San Diego, CA **Client:** American Specialty Health **2 Creative Firm:** American Specialty Health - San Diego, CA **Client:** American Specialty Health **3 Creative Firm:** SIDES & Associates - Lafayette, LA **Creative Team:** Larry Sides – President; Kathy Ashworth – Executive Vice President; Donny Gallagher – Interactive and Design Director **Client:** Slack | Alost Development

"I didn't fail ten thousand times,
I successfully eliminated ten
thousand times, materials and
combinations which wouldn't work."

— Thomas Edison

efore Thomas Edison, the process of inventing was a solitary pursuit. Edison, the world's most prolific inventor, also invented the modern process for inventing. He brought together the best minds he could find to work as a team to help develop and refine each other's ideas. They would work diligently, never letting failure stop them from achieving their goals. That spirit lives on at C/S. Our talented designers and engineers not only work together, but also with architects and builders to help refine their good ideas. This culture of collaboration has led to many breakthroughs. Construction Specialties holds over 350 patents worldwide. Let's work together to make buildings better.

DESSO
The Floor is Yours

Around the World in 80 Days with DESSO

1 Creative Firm: Brian J. Ganton & Associates - Cedar Grove, NJ **Creative Team:** Brian Ganton Jr. – Creative Director/Copywriter; Mark Ganton – Art Director; Pat Palmieri – Designer **Client:** Construction Specialties **2 Creative Firm:** ELCAMEDIA BV - Hoofddorp, Netherlands **Client:** Carpet Manufacturer Desso

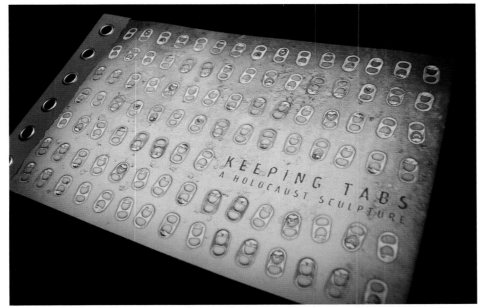

PLATINUM

Keeping Tabs

Creative Firm: Fitting Group - Pittsburgh, PA
Creative Team: Travis Norris – Creative Director; Andrew Ellis – Designer
Client: Community Day School
URL: www.fittingroup.com

Six million is a staggering number—so large, it must be seen to be believed. The students of Pittsburgh's Community Day School set out more than ten years ago to collect that many soda can tabs in order to illustrate the magnitude of the Holocaust and its six million Jewish victims. After a decade of perseverance and dedication, the school's project attracted the attention of an architect who promised to donate his time to design a sculpture, but the project needed money to get off the ground. To raise funds, the school approached local firm Fitting Design to put together a brochure that would generate interest and secure donations. "This entailed two things:

creating a special 'voice' that would tell the story, and a look that would be full of impact, tasteful and true to the theme," says Fitting. The resulting publication, "Keeping Tabs, A Holocaust Sculpture" emerged, imploring potential donors "Don't discard the truth" and to bring life to a magnificent memorial. The sculpture, arranged in a giant Star of David, encapsulated 6,250 tabs in each of 960 glass blocks. Adds the firm: "There is no way to describe the groundwork so many children did for this project, or the eventual goal. We were just proud to be a part of it—proud to have been chosen to create this piece, proud of its powerful outcome."

1

2

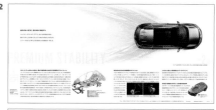

1 **Creative Firm:** E-graphics Communications - Tokyo, Japan **Creative Team:** Tomohira Kodama – Executive Creative Director; Yasuyuki Nagato – Creative Director; Junichi Yokoyama – Art Director; Naoya Miki – Designer; Dan Kazaana – Copywriter; One or Eight Graphic – Copywriter **Client:** Nissan Motor Company 2 **Creative Firm:** E-graphics Communications - Tokyo, Japan **Creative Team:** Tomohira Kodama – Executive Creative Director; Seiichi Yamasita – Creative Director; Hiroshi Kanda – Art Director; Keiichi Tuda – Art Director; Masao Kumagami – Copywriter **Client:** Nissan Motor Company

1

2

1 Creative Firm: E-graphics Communications - Tokyo, Japan **Creative Team:** Tomohira Kodama – Executive Creative Director; Yasuhiko Yoshida – Creative Director; Yoshi-hiro Mimura – Creative Director; Chieko Izumi – Art Director; Inter-wave – Designer; Hiroyuki Arai – Copywriter **Client:** Nissan Motor Company **2 Creative Firm:** E-graphics Communications - Tokyo, Japan **Creative Team:** Tomohira Kodama – Executive Creative Director; Yoshihiro Mimura – Creative Director; Ryuji Ishimatsu – Art Director; Nobuko Murakami – Designer; Nobuhiro Yamaguchi – Copywriter **Client:** Nissan Motor Company

1

2

3

1 **Creative Firm:** E-graphics Communications - Tokyo, Japan **Creative Team:** Tomohira Kodama – Executive Creative Director; Seiichi Yamasita – Creative Director; Ryuji Ishimatsu – Art Director; Nobuko Murakami – Designer; Nobuhiro Yamaguchi – Copywriter **Client:** Nissan Motor Company **2 Creative Firm:** E-graphics Communications - Tokyo, Japan **Creative Team:** Tomohira Kodama – Executive Creative Director; Yoshihiro Mimura – Creative Director; Masaya Okamoto – Art Director; Shigeharu Sugiyama – Designer; Mao Takahashi – Copywriter **Client:** Nissan Motor Company **3 Creative Firm:** E-graphics Communications - Tokyo, Japan **Creative Team:** Tomohira Kodama – Executive Creative Director; Toshiaki Yoshioka – Creative Director; Junichi Kanbara – Art Director; Yumiko Kawashima – Designer; Takanori Utsumi – Copywriter **Client:** Mitsubishi Motors

1

2

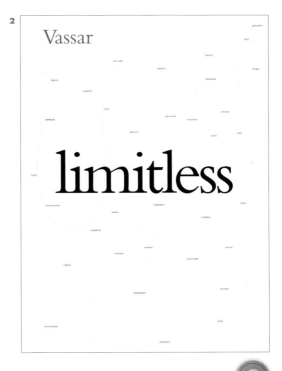

3

1 Creative Firm: VSA Partners - Chicago, IL **Creative Team:** Dana Arnett – Principal/Creative Director; Karolynn Earl – Account Director; Jonathan Turitz – Writer; John Foust – Senior Designer; Ken Quinn – Strategist; Laura Netz – Strategist **Client:** Sappi Fine Paper North America **2 Creative Firm:** Nesnadny + Schwartz - Cleveland, OH **Creative Team:** Mark Schwartz – Creative Director; Shawn Beatty – Designer; Cindy Lowrey – Designer; Keith Pishnery – Designer; Russell Monk – Photographer; Julia Van Develder – Writer **Client:** Vassar College **3 Creative Firm:** VSA Partners - Chicago, IL **Creative Team:** Dana Arnett – Principal/Creative Director; Melissa Schwister – Associate Partner/Account Director; Jason McKean – Design Director; Katie Kowaloff – Account Coordinator; Joe Grimberg – Writer; Conor McFerran – Designer **Client:** Harley-Davidson

1

2

3

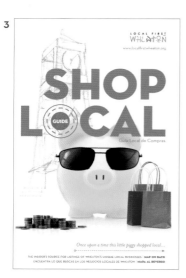

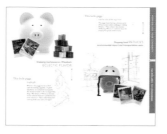

1 Creative Firm: VSA Partners - Chicago, IL **Creative Team:** Dana Arnett – Principal/Creative Director; Luke Galambos – Design Director; Melissa Schwister – Associate Partner/Account Director; Joe Grimberg – Writer; Jarrod Ryhalv – Designer; Conor McFerran - Designer **Client:** Harley-Davidson **2 Creative Firm:** Hornall Anderson Design Works - Seattle, WA **Creative Team:** John Rousseau – Art Director; Leo Raymundo – Designer; Erin Crosier – Account Director; Cindy Chin – Production Designer; Amy Bosch – Copywriter; Young Lee – Photographer **Client:** PDS **3 Creative Firm:** Nana Design - Silver Spring, MD **Creative Team:** Polina Pinchevsky; Shira Pepper **Client:** Local First Wheaton

1

3

1 Creative Firm: LFG-Group - Wuerzburg, Germany **Creative Team:** Jens Gutermann – Creative Director **Client:** von Wangenheim-Luxury Watches **2 Creative Firm:** Hornall Anderson Design Works - Seattle, WA **Creative Team:** Lisa Cerveny – Creative Director; Kathy Saito – Art Director; Yuri Shvets – Designer; Holly Craven – Designer; Pamela Mason Davey – Copywriter **Client:** Children's Hospital of Orange County

1 Creative Firm: Jacob Tyler Creative Group - San Diego, CA **Creative Team:** Les Kollegian – Creative Director; Gordon Tsuji – Art Director; Adam Roop – Senior Designer **Client:** AIGA San Diego **2 Creative Firm:** Primary Design, Inc. - Haverhill, MA **Creative Team:** Liz Fedorzyn – Senior Art Director; David Vadala – Senior Graphic Designer **Client:** AvalonBay Communities **3 Creative Firm:** Cognetix - Charleston, SC **Creative Team:** Jessica Crouch – Art Director/Designer; Holger M. E. Obenaus – Photographer **Client:** Charlestowne Hotels

1

2

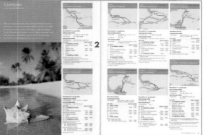

2

3

1 Creative Firm: Hornall Anderson Design Works - Seattle, WA **Creative Team:** Lisa Cerveny – Art Director; Julie Lock – Art Director; Leo Raymundo – Designer; Lauren DiRusso – Designer; Belinda Bowling – Designer; Jeff Wolff – Production Designer **Client:** Holland America **2 Creative Firm:** Hornall Anderson Design Works - Seattle, WA **Creative Team:** Lisa Cerveny – Art Director; Julie Lock – Art Director; Lauren DiRusso – Designer; Belinda Bowling – Designer; Beckon Wyld – Production Designer; Paula Cox – Production Designer **Client:** Holland America **3 Creative Firm:** KNOCK inc. - Minneapolis, MN **Creative Team:** Victoria Aksamit – Designer; Jill Milbery – Designer; Rachel Nybeck – Designer; Meenal Patel – Designer; Todd Paulson – Creative Director; Sara Nelson – Design Director **Client:** Children's Theatre Company

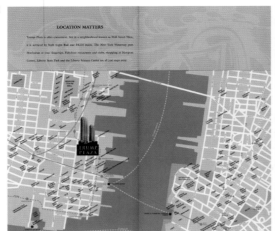

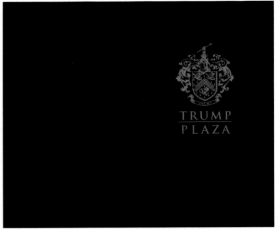

1 Creative Firm: Sherman Advertising/Mermaid, Inc. - New York, NY **Creative Team:** Sharon McLaughlin – Creative Director; Stephen Morse – Retoucher **Client:** Trump Plaza **2 Creative Firm:** Sherman Advertising/Mermaid, Inc. - New York, NY **Creative Team:** Sharon McLaughlin – Creative Director; Ted Gamble – Art Director; Stephen Morse – Retoucher **Client:** Trump Tower Philadelphia **3 Creative Firm:** Sherman Advertising/Mermaid, Inc. - New York, NY **Creative Team:** Sharon Mclaughlin – Creative Director; Stephen Morse – Retoucher **Client:** crystal point

1

2

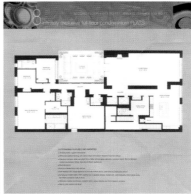

3

1 Creative Firm: Mattel, Inc. - El Segundo, CA **Client:** Mattel, Inc. **2 Creative Firm:** Sherman Advertising/Mermaid, Inc. - New York, NY **Creative Team:** Sharon McLaughlin – Creative Director; Stephen Morse – Retoucher **Client:** infinity flats **3 Creative Firm:** Mattel, Inc. - El Segundo, CA **Client:** Mattel, Inc.

1

2

3 Urška Drofenik is a fashion designer known for unique
lace gowns – her brochures are unique as well.
Each of them has a different lace on its cover.

1 Creative Firm: MultiCare Health Systems - Seattle, WA **Creative Team:** Jenny Davidson – Project Manager; Robin Pederson – Art Director; Julie Smith – Copywriter
Client: MultiCare Health Systems **2 Creative Firm:** MultiCare Health Systems - Seattle, WA **Creative Team:** Jenny Davidson – Project Manager; Robin Pederson – Art
Director; Julie Smith – Copywriter **Client:** MultiCare Health Systems **URL:** www.multicare.org **3 Creative Firm:** Futura DDB d.o.o. - Ljubljana, Slovenia **Creative Team:** Zare
Kerin – Creative Director; Dado Banovsek – Graphic Designer; Sasa Deu Bajt – Account Manager **Client:** Urska Drofenik

1 Creative Firm: Five Visual Communication & Design - Mason, OH **Creative Team:** Rondi Tschopp – Creative Director/Designer; Melissa Feldhaus – Graphic Designer; Laura Broermann – Graphic Designer **Client:** Miami University of Ohio

 **PLATINUM**

Creative Firm: KNOCK inc. - Minneapolis, MN

Creative Team: KNOCK inc. – Design Firm;
Meenal Patel – Designer; Todd Paulson – Creative
Director; Sara Nelson – Design Director; Creighton
King – Production

Client: KNOCK inc.

Knocked Out Of The Park

Minneapolis design agency KNOCK had been using a wood grain motif in their self-promotional pieces for some time (KNOCK on wood!), and when they decided to create an identity system to truly represent their personality as an agency—especially their three-dimensional retail environment—the idea emerged of making the business cards look like geometric logs that could pop and lock into a 3-D shape. However, unlike regular wood logs, keeping these little paper logs solid proved to be a challenge. "Card construction proved difficult, especially ensuring the cards would indeed pop up and stay that way," says director of special projects Leslie Yunis.

The cards also resisted reflattening for portability's sake, but trial and error led to the right paper stock for the pieces, which also could double as nametags in meet-ings. Despite the apparent homogeny of the cards/nametags, KNOCK's personality came through as they invited each employee to design the interior of his or her own card. "This offered more insight into each employee, and provided an additional surprise for the viewer, deepening their connection to the agency," says Yunis.

1

InWorld Solutions Business Cards

2

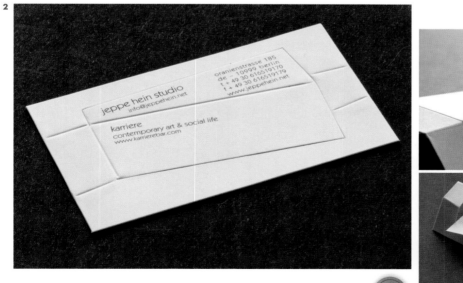 

---

1 **Creative Firm:** Gee + Chung Design - San Francisco, CA **Creative Team:** Earl Gee – Creative Director/Designer/Illustrator **Client:** InWorld Solutions 2 **Creative Firm:** Green Wave International Development - Hong Kong **Creative Team:** Sasha Sagan – Director; Alan Lee – Art Director **Client:** Jeppe Hein

1

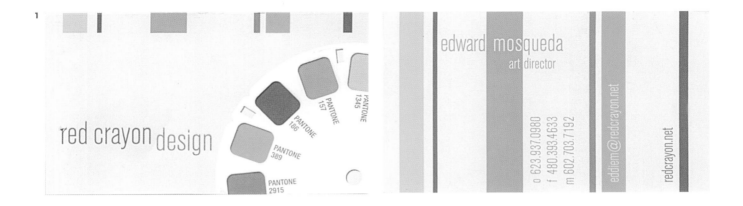

2

1 Creative Firm: Red Crayon Design, LLC - Glendale, AZ **Creative Team:** Randall Cajthaml – Creative Director **Client:** Red Crayon Design, LLC **2 Creative Firm:** Humana, Inc - Louisville, KY **Creative Team:** Karen Gahafer – Creative Developer/Art Director; Grant Harrison VP, Consumer Innovation; Greg Matthews Director, Social Networking **Client:** Greg Matthews - Social Networking

PLATINUM

Creative Firm: Health New England/HNE -
Springfield, MA

Creative Team: Leslie Bercume – Manager of
Marketing & Advertising

Client: Spirit of Springfield

Zen Is In The Details

Each year, the town of Springfield, Massachusetts puts on the biggest holiday light display in the western part of the state, Bright Nights at Forest Park, and local organization Spirit of Springfield helps keep the lights on by hosting a formal gala. Springfield agency Health New England took a Zen approach to designing the invitations for 2008's Asian-inspired theme, "Teahouse of the Autumn Moon."

"Because it is black tie and connected to a whimsical attraction I always try to take my design way beyond traditional," the designer says, "and I spent a lot of time listening to Asian music and researching Japanese culture before I ever sat down

to begin the design process." To evoke that Far Eastern sense of mystery, the cards became an exercise in unfolding the event information: Inside each of 550 hand-folded origami envelopes was a "tea bag" with details of the gala. "Precise measuring had to be well thought out for each element of the piece. I had to hand cut several prototypes before I was able to arrive at the right design/dimensions for the invitation carrier." While Spirit of Springfield brought a bit of the Orient to the Bay State, for now that's the closest many attendees—including the designer—could get. "I have never had the pleasure yet to have traveled there in person—yet!"

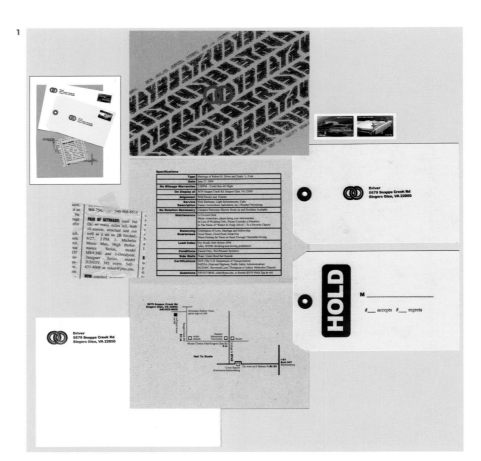

1 Creative Firm: TLC Design - Singers Glen, VA **Creative Team:** Trudy L. Cole – Graphic Designer/Illustrator/Writer **Client:** Robert Driver and Trudy Cole **2 Creative Firm:** Julia Tam Design - Palos Verdes Estates, CA **Creative Team:** Julia Tam – Creative Director **Client:** Team 7 International **3 Creative Firm:** Jacob Tyler Creative Group - San Diego, CA **Creative Team:** Les Kollegian – Creative Director; Gordon Tsuji – Art Director; Jessica Recht – Designer/Copywriter **Client:** Jacob Tyler

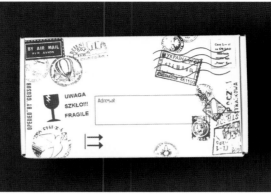

1 Client: www.awantgarde.pl **2 Creative Firm:** Gee + Chung Design - San Francisco, CA **Creative Team:** Earl Gee – Creative Director/Designer/Illustrator **Client:** DCM
3 Creative Firm: Crabtree + Company - Falls Church, VA **Creative Team:** Susan Angrisani – Creative Director; Rodrigo Vera – Art Director; Forrest Dunnavant – Production Artist; Lisa Suchy – Production Manager **Client:** Texas State Society

1

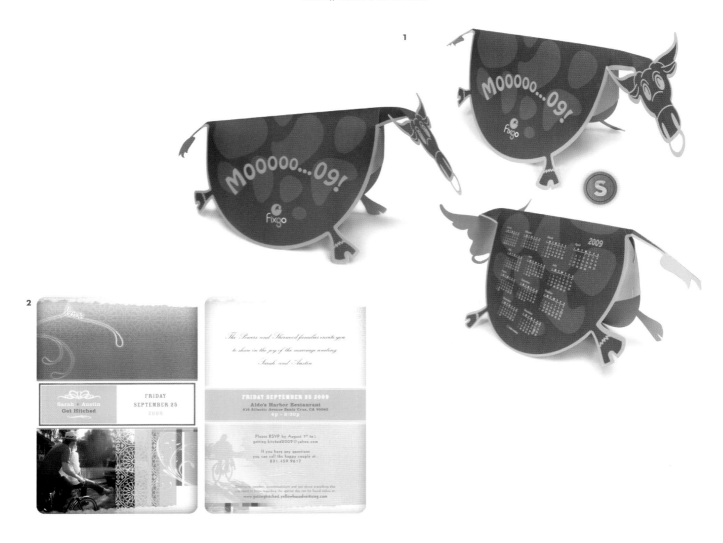

2

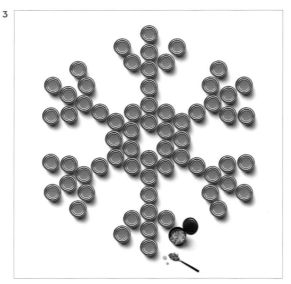

3

The start of a new year is a time to give thanks to those who made the past year special (that's you!) and to remember those who need our help.

In lieu of gifts to our friends and business partners this year, we are making a sizable donation to Food Bank for New York to help fight the growing hunger problem. We hope that you will join us in celebrating the good fortune we have and in sharing it with those less fortunate.

❄

from Tom, Chris, Mary, Eulie, and George at
TOM DOLLE DESIGN

HERE'S WISHING YOU A HAPPY AND HEALTHY 2009

1 Creative Firm: Fixgo Advertising (M) Sdn Bhd - Subang Jaya, Malaysia **Creative Team:** CK Chua – Creative Director; Aaron Liau – Art Director; Eugene Soh – Copywriter **Client:** Fixgo Advertising (M) Sdn Bhd **2 Creative Firm:** CJ Design - Santa Cruz, CA **Creative Team:** Chris Mark – Graphic Designer **Client:** Sherwood Wedding **3 Creative Firm:** Tom Dolle Design - New York, NY **Creative Team:** Tom Dolle – Creative Director; Chris Riely – Designer **Client:** Tom Dolle Design

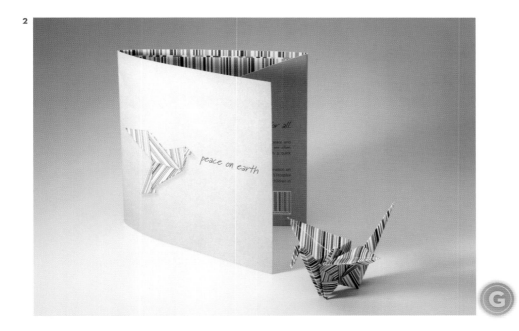

1 Creative Firm: HBO Off-Air Creative Services - New York, NY **Creative Team:** Venus Dennison – Creative Director; Christian Martillo – Design Manager; Katerina Tsioros – Designer; Jen McDearman – Copywriter **Client:** HBO Media Relations **2 Creative Firm:** Cline Davis and Mann LLC - New York, NY **Creative Team:** Ben Ingersoll – Managing Partner/Creative Director; Debra Polkes – Associate Partner/Creative Director; Rebecca Kuperberg – Art Supervisor; Emily Abessinio – Copy Supervisor **Client:** Cline Davis and Mann **3 Creative Firm:** Optima Soulsight - Highland Park, IL **Creative Team:** Aaron Funke – Designer **Client:** Ronald McDonald House Charities

1 **Creative Firm:** Hitchcock Fleming & Associates Inc. - Akron, OH **Creative Team:** Nick Betro – Executive Creative Director; Kim Bruns – Writer **Client:** Akron Art Museum
2 **Creative Firm:** Hitchcock Fleming & Associates Inc. - Akron, OH **Creative Team:** Nick Betro – Executive Creative Director; Lenny Spengler – Art Director; Kim Bruns – Writer; Greg Pfiffner – Writer; Andy Hagat – Computer Graphics Specialist/Artist **Client:** University of Akron

1

1 Creative Firm: Coal Creative Consultants Pte Ltd - Singapore **Creative Team:** Yong Yau Goh – Account Director/Copy Editor; Lwin Mun Tin Thein – Creative Director; Eng Teck Tan – Art Director **Client:** Singapore Sports Council **2 Creative Firm:** Design Nut - Kensington, MD **Creative Team:** Brent Almond – Designer/Illustrator **Client:** Design Nut

1

VIVER DESIGN EM SÃO PAULO
São Paulo Cityhall INVITATION

Translation
The Municipal Secretariat of International Relations hosts
A cocktail party to launch a week of activities of KM M MM –
Viver Design em São Paulo.

November 3, 2008, at 7:30p.m.
Museu da Casa Brasileira
Av. Brigadeiro Faria Lima, 2.705

During the event, the 5th Exhibition on Good Environmental
Practices will be presented, featuring the exposition
"I'm no longer just plastic, I'm sustainable and profitable."

A show by Barbara Marques

R.S.V.P
(11) 3118 8811 or 3113 8514

Invitation admits two

Brief:
CREATE AN INVITATION FOR THE COCKTAIL PARTY OFFICIALLY LAUNCHING THE SÃO PAULO
LIVE DESIGN WEEK ORGANIZED BY THE INTERNATIONAL RELATIONS SECRETARY OF THE
CITY OF SÃO PAULO.

Main challenges and goals:
ILLUSTRATE THE FIVE VERBS THAT REPRESENT THE WEEK-LONG EVENT AND CREATE A
LASTING IMAGE OF THE CITY OF SÃO PAULO, POSSIBLY THE FUTURE BRAZILIAN CAPITAL OF
DESIGN.

Describe how you arrived at the final design:
THE COVER OF THE INVITATION INCORPORATES THE GRAPHIC DRAWINGS FOUND ON THE
SIDEWALKS OF THE CITY OF SÃO PAULO, WHICH REPRESENT THE SHAPE OF THE STATE OF
SÃO PAULO.
THE BLUE DOT INDICATES THE LOCATION OF THE CITY IN THE RELATION TO THE STATE.
THE EVENT WAS REALIZED IN PUBLIC PLACES AROUND THE CITY TO STRESS THE NEED FOR
DOMOCRATIC DESIGN. THE ENVELOPES WERE CREATED IN THE COLORS OF THE FIVE
DESIGNATED DESIGN VERBS(WEAR DESIGN, LIVE DESIGN, COMMUNICATE DESIGN, and USE
DESIGN AND THINK DESIGN).
THE SURPRISE ELEMENT COMES WHEN OPENING THE ENVELOPES CONTAINING THE DESIGN
VERBS.

2

3

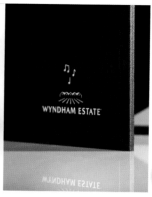

4

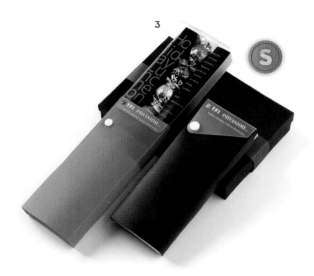

---

1 Creative Firm: Merchan-Design - Sao Paulo, Brazil **Creative Team:** Marcelo Lopes; Viver Design em Sao Paulo **Client:** City Hall - International Relations Secretary
2 Creative Firm: Design Nut - Kensington, MD **Creative Team:** Brent Almond – Designer/Art Director; Alphonse Mucha – Illustrator **Client:** The Choral Arts Society of
Washington **3 Creative Firm:** TFI Envision, Inc. - Norwalk, CT **Creative Team:** Elizabeth P. Ball **Client:** TFI Envision, Inc. **4 Creative Firm:** Grain Creative Consultants -
Surry Hills, Australia **Creative Team:** Jure Leko – Creative Director; Rikki Avenaim – Designer **Client:** Wyndham Estate

PLATINUM

Creative Firm: SIGNI - Mexico

Creative Team: René Galindo – Art Director; Felipe Salas – Designer

Client: Grupo Editorial Expansion

Beautiful And Functional

Every year, Expansion Editorial Group (GEE), a leading magazine publishing group in Mexico, produces a media kit as a marketing tool to sell advertising space in its seventeen magazines and four commercial Web sites. The kit also includes corporate and pricing information as well as specifications for preparing and delivering files for printing. Signi, a design studio in Mexico City, translated all these components into a tangible object by putting the kit in a slipcovered, custom-made binder featuring a new and attractive material that GEE's representatives would enjoy using and taking with them on sales calls.

Signi's designers presented the kit's information in a clear and organized manner, highlighted with metallic inks, gloss and dull varnishes. Gatefold brochures and bold tabs help the user expand the kit and find desired information easily. Later, Signi adapted the design to other collateral, such as folders, promotional gifts and templates for electronic presentations. Says the designer: "The project was a challenge in its own, but the solution is a testament that good design goes beyond pure beauty. Form and function merge effectively to achieve a solution that is cost efficient and memorable."

1

2

1 Creative Firm: LUON - Overijse, Belgium **Creative Team:** Onno Hesselink – Creative Director; Katrien Malfroid – Graphic Designer; Jos Moers – Graphic Designer; Katrien De Smedt – Account **Client:** Brepols **2 Creative Firm:** Zeesman Communications, Inc. - Beverly Hills, CA **Creative Team:** John Taylor – Creative Director; Anna Turchinsky – Graphic Designer **Client:** Barco Uniforms, Inc.

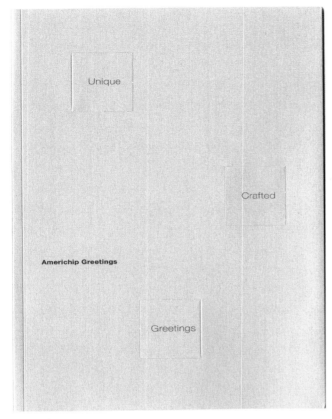

The finest craftsmen from around the globe have come together to create a series of exceptionally beautiful and unique greeting cards.

PLATINUM

Creative Firm: DesignLab - Pacific Palisades, CA

Creative Team: Scott Lambert – Creative Director/ Art Director/Writer; Keith Skelton – Photographer/ Location; Rick Brian – Photographer/Studio

Client: Americhip

Corporate Holiday Cards Get A Makeover

Americhip is already known in the advertising world for its high-tech components such as LED lights and audio chips—but greeting cards? "[It was] a tall order," says Scott Lambert, principal and creative director at DesignLab in Pacific Palisades, California, "to enter a retail environment with a product where they had no brand equity." Aimed at the corporate client market, however, the Americhip-greeting card market seemed an easy fit. "Corporations spend large amounts [of money] on holiday cards, " says Lambert. "Most have mediocre graphics and do not support the company's image."

By incorporating unusual paper techniques such as die-cut windows that open to reveal the message and high-quality pages featuring metallic and coated satin stocks, DesignLab's mission to highlight the cards' detail was the icing on the cake. Macro photographs provide viewers with a close-up view of the quality craftsmanship—each card resulting in what Lambert calls "a hand-assembled work of art." Even the black-and-white photographs show the real deal: As the art director and photographer scouted potential shooting areas, they saw the perfect pair of hands, belonging to a paper engineer in his seventies. "This single image captured the soul of Americhip greeting cards," says Lambert.

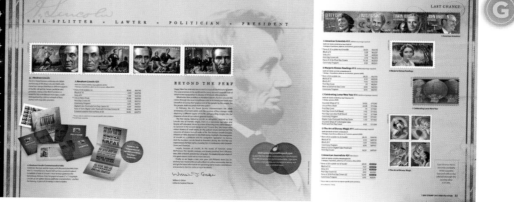

1 **Creative Firm:** United States Postal Service - Arlington, VA **Creative Team:** William Gicker – Creative Director; Journey Group – Designer **Client:** United States Postal Service 2 **Creative Firm:** United States Postal Service - Arlington, VA **Creative Team:** William Gicker – Creative Director; Journey Group – Designer **Client:** United States Postal Service

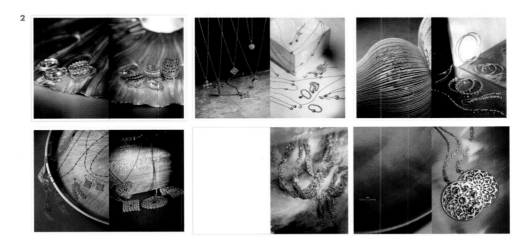

1 Creative Firm: Dreamedia Studios - Little Rock, AR **Creative Team:** Kyle Holmes – Designer/Creative Director; Jack Melton – Photographer; Steven Walenta – Photographer **Client:** Gary Hendershott Museum Consultants **2 Creative Firm:** omdr co., ltd. - Tokyo, Japan **Creative Team:** Osamu Misawa - Creative Director/Art Director; Mamaoru Takeuchi - Designer; Toshitaka Niwa - Photographer **Client:** World Co., Ltd

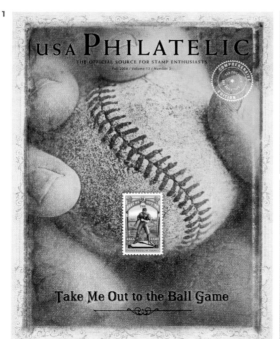

1 Creative Firm: United States Postal Service - Arlington, VA **Creative Team:** William Gicker – Creative Director; Journey Group – Designer **Client:** United States Postal Service **2 Creative Firm:** United States Postal Service - Arlington, VA **Creative Team:** William Gicker – Creative Director; Journey Group – Designer **Client:** United States Postal Service **3 Creative Firm:** Interrobang Design Collaborative, Inc. - Richmond, VT **Creative Team:** Lisa Sylvester – Creative Director/Designer **Client:** Nova Natural Toys and Crafts

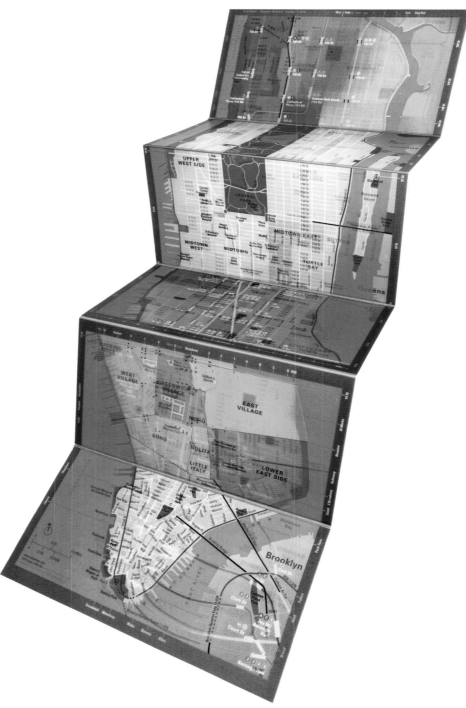

 **PLATINUM**

Creative Firm: Urban Mapping, Inc. -
San Francisco, CA

Creative Team: Ian White – CEO/Art Director; Christopher Cannon – Designer, Isotope 221

Client: Urban Mapping, Inc.

See Manhattan In A New Way

Everyone knows Manhattan, but not everyone *knows* Manhattan. To aid the tourist, traveler and anyone who doesn't normally venture outside the home neighborhood, Urban Mapping Inc. in San Francisco put together a fun, durable guide with a unique twist: the Panamap. The unique printing technology used to produce the Panamap "allows three different spatially-configured data sets to be displayed on a thin sheet of plastic," explains Urban Mapping. Depending on the angle of viewing, the Panamap reveals neighborhoods, streets or subway networks. The effort and research required to develop this compelling map were extensive, but the final product is both highly interactive and distinctly low-tech.

³ IMAGE NOT
AVAILABLE

1 Creative Firm: Van Vechten Creative - San Diego, CA **Creative Team:** Charles Van Vechten – Creative Director; Kathy McGraw – Senior Designer; Kristen Lucci – Designer **Client:** Terranea Resort **2 Creative Firm:** Van Vechten Creative **Creative Team:** Charles Van Vechten – Creative Director; Kathy McGraw – Senior Designer; Kristen Lucci – Designer **Client:** Terranea Resort **3 Creative Firm:** Purple, Rock, Scissors - Orlando, FL **Creative Team:** Bobby Jones – Creative Director; Aaron Drath – Illustrator; Aaron Harvey – Copywriting; Oslin Print – Printer **Client:** Northland, A Church Distributed **4 Creative Firm:** Alcone Marketing - Irvine, CA **Creative Team:** Chad Lasota – Digital Designer; Paul Ulloa – Digital Designer; Carlos Musquez – Creative Director; Cameron Young – Copywriter; Luis Camano – VP/Creative Director **Client:** Foster's Wine Estates

1

3

2

4

1 **Creative Firm:** Thompson Creative - Greensboro, NC **Creative Team:** Rob Bodle – Copywriter; Carrie Hughes – Art Director; Gary Thompson – Creative Director **Client:** Häfele 2 **Creative Firm:** CMg Design, Inc. - Pasadena, CA **Creative Team:** John Ewan – Art Director/Designer; Julie Markfield – Creative Director/Principal **Client:** Parsons Corporation 3 **Creative Firm:** American Specialty Health - San Diego, CA **Client:** American Specialty Health 4 **Creative Firm:** John Kneapler Design - New York, NY **Creative Team:** Nicole Audette – Graphic Designer; John Kneapler – President **Client:** Cornerstone Communications

1

S

2

3

4

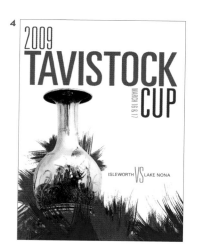

2009
TAVISTOCK
CUP
MARCH 16 & 17

ISLEWORTH VS LAKE NONA

1 Creative Firm: Bridgepoint Education - San Diego, CA **Creative Team:** Marc Riesenberg – Creative Director; David Dickey Sr. – Graphic Designer; Lizzie Wann – Copywriter; Lowell Tindell – Photographer **Client:** Ashford University **2 Creative Firm:** Bridgepoint Education - San Diego, CA **Creative Team:** Marc Riesenberg – Creative Director; David Dickey Sr. – Graphic Designer; Lizzie Wann – Copywriter; Alex Speaks – Photographer **Client:** Ashford University **3 Creative Firm:** Torre Lazur McCann - Parsippany, NJ **Creative Team:** Christian Gorrie – VP/Associate Creative Director, Art; Lin Betancourt – VP/Associate Creative Director, Copy; Ying Wong – Art Director; Scott Kraus – Copywriter; Donna Parano – VP/ Management Supervisor; Karin Pilaar – Account Supervisor; Kelly Dudeck – Sr. Account Executive **Client:** Reckitt Benckiser **4 Creative Firm:** Tavistock Group - Orlando, FL **Creative Team:** Kelly Lafferman – Vice President of Marketing; Karl Dinkler – Graphic Designer; Tina Holmes – Graphic Designer **Client:** Tavistock Cup

1

2

1 Creative Firm: Simon & Goetz Design GmbH & Co. KG - Frankfurt, Germany **Creative Team:** Bernd Vollmöller – Creative Direction/Art Direction; Christina Schirm – Art Direction **Client:** Sal. Oppenheim jr. & Cie. **2 Creative Firm:** Nana Design - Silver Spring, MD **Creative Team:** Polina Pinchevsky **Client:** Center to Advance Palliative Care

1 Creative Firm: Tom Dolle Design - New York, NY **Creative Team:** Cheryl Loe – Editor; Tom Dolle – Creative Director; Chris Riely – Designer; Rich Lillash – Illustrator **Client:** Foundation Center **2 Creative Firm:** Cleveland State University - Cleveland, OH **Creative Team:** Rob Spademan – Assistant V.P. Marketing; Karen Jewell-Kett – Senior Graphic Designer; Nancy Carlucci Smith – Writer/Account Representative; flourishphoto – Photographer; Bill Rieter – Senior Photographer **Client:** Cleveland State University **3 Creative Firm:** Leibowitz Communications - New York, NY **Creative Team:** Rick Bargmann – Creative Director; Courtney Dolloff – Art Director; Claudia Mark – Designer **Client:** First Eagle Funds **4 Creative Firm:** Berry Design Inc - Alpharetta, GA **Creative Team:** Berry Design; Berry Design Team **Client:** Popeyes

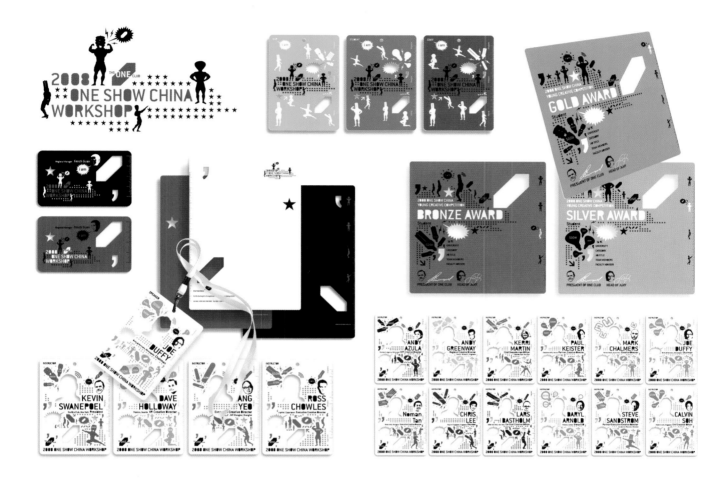

 **PLATINUM**

Creative Firm: Eric Cai Design Co. - Beijing, China
Creative Team: Eric Cai Shi Wei – Creative Director/
Art Director/Designer; Esther Tan Yan – Copywriter;
Duan Lian – Illustrator
Client: One Club China

Creativity For Creatives

The international advertising award presenters The One Club have been leading educational competitions and workshops in China since 2001, and it has become one of the most important international advertising educational activities in China. In order to extend the image and create an attractive visual brand incorporating the core value of The One Show event, Beijing's Eric Cai Design Co. incorporated a variety of elements in its accompanying collateral. "We used a [stylized light] bulb as the visual element to represent the inspiration of creativity, and the strong body graphics add

a more interesting and vivid atmosphere," says Cai. "The elements are extended to all the objects—instead of paper, synthetic glass goes together with artistic carvings, which make simple things [put] out endless creativity." Instructors and students from around the world proudly bring home the collateral—which includes notepads, ID cards and program covers—so long after the event, the brand continues to reach to a greater audience.

1

2

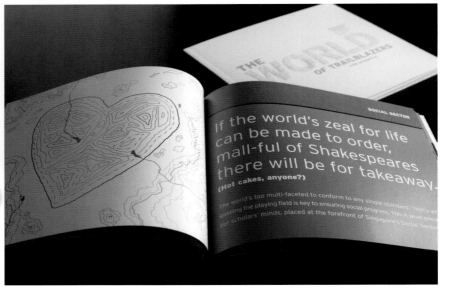

1 Creative Firm: IridiumGroup, Inc. - New York, NY **Creative Team:** Yison Ko – Art Director; Anne Foley – Designer **Client:** United Nation Federal Credit Union
2 Creative Firm: Splash Productions Pte Ltd - Singapore **Creative Team:** Stanley Yap – Art Director/Photographer; Serene See – Copywriter; Terry Lee – Copywriter
Client: Public Service Commission **URL:** www.pscscholarships.gov.sg

1

2

1 Creative Firm: Studio Fuse - Pasadena, CA **Creative Team:** Jennifer Logan – Creative Director; Scott Luberda – Senior Designer/Illustrator **Client:** Grand Performances
2 Creative Firm: Vision Design Studio - Long Beach, CA **Creative Team:** Carl Dene – Visionary; Sam Eames – Designer; Noah Pollock – Senior Creative Writer; David Arias – Web Designer **Client:** The Art Institute of Phoenix **URL:** www.aiportfolioshow.com/nt

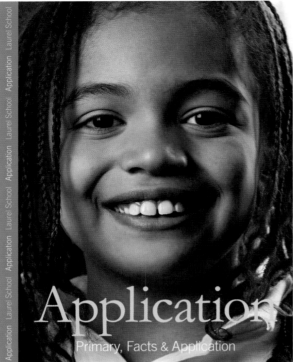

1 Creative Firm: Nesnadny + Schwartz - Cleveland, OH **Creative Team:** Mark Schwartz – Creative Director; Shawn Beatty – Designer; Cindy Lowrey – Designer; Gina Moraco – Designer; Julie Donahue – Writer; Roger Mastroianni – Photographer **Client:** Laurel School **2 Creative Firm:** Jacob Tyler Creative Group - San Diego, CA **Creative Team:** Les Kollegian – Creative Director; Gordon Tsuji – Art Director **Client:** Ossur

POSTER

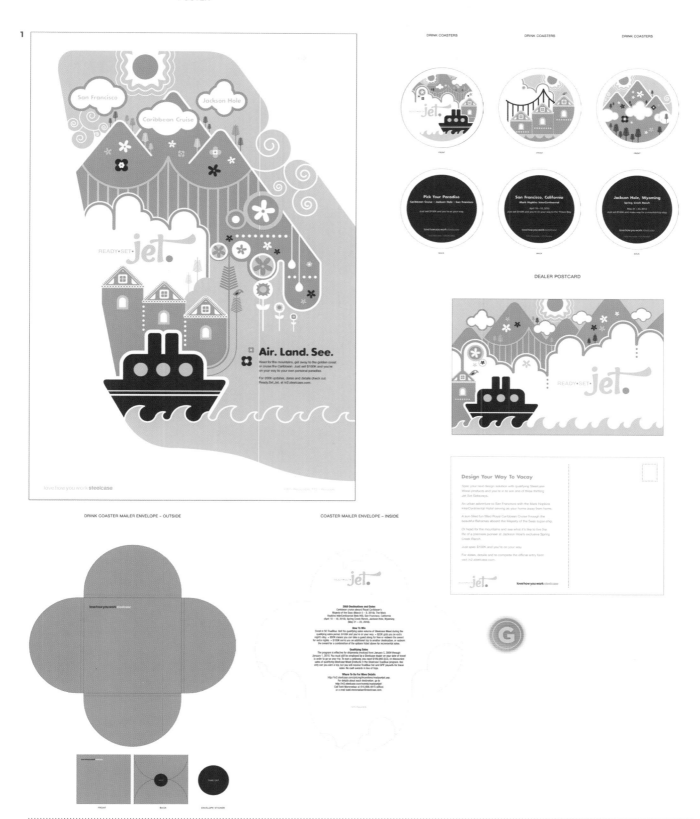

1 Creative Firm: Kantorwassink - Grand Rapids, MI **Creative Team:** Dave Kantor; Wendy Wassink; Tim Calkins **Client:** Steelcase

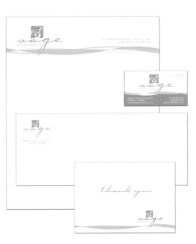

1 Creative Firm: Group Fifty-Five Marketing - Detroit, MI **Creative Team:** Heather Sowinski – Art Director; Jennifer Rewitz – Art Director **Client:** Beztak Properties
2 Creative Firm: Hitchcock Fleming & Associates Inc. - Akron, OH **Creative Team:** Nick Betro – Executive Creative Director; Milissa Shrake – Art Director; Tony Fanizzi – Writer; Scott Kristoff – Animator; Jeff Stager –Computer Graphics Specialist/Artist **Client:** Goodyear Tire & Rubber Co

1 Creative Firm: Coal Creative Consultants - Singapore **Creative Team:** Lwin Mun Tin Thein – Creative Director; Yong Yau Goh – Account Director **Client:** Coal Creative Consultants Pte Ltd **2 Creative Firm:** ds+f - Washington, D.C. **Creative Team:** ds+f Creative Team **Client:** ASIS International **3 Creative Firm:** Suka - New York, NY **Creative Team:** Brian Wong – Creative Director; Maria Belfiore – Art Director **Client:** American Friends of The Hebrew University

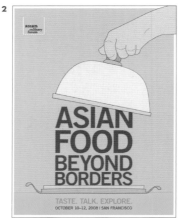

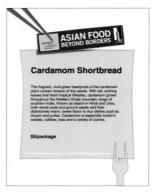

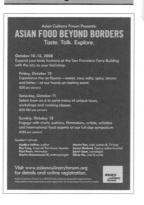

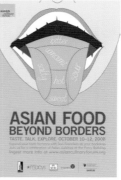

1 **Creative Firm:** Launch Creative Marketing - Chicago, IL **Creative Team:** Michelle Morales – Creative Director; Erin Pearson – Associate Creative Director **Client:** ConAgra Foods 2 **Creative Firm:** Tajima Creative - San Francisco, CA **Creative Team:** Elaine Tajima – Creative Director; Byron Del Rosario – Art Director/Designer; Komal Dedhia – Designer **Client:** Asian Culinary Forum

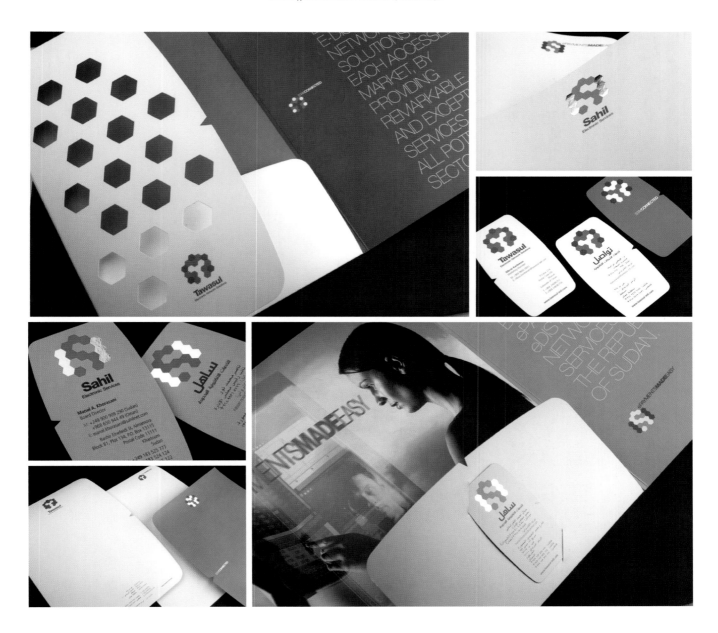

Creative Firm: Storm Corporate Design - Auckland, New Zealand

Creative Team: Rehan Saiyed – Designer/ Design Director

Client: Tawasul Electronic Network Solutions/ Muscat/Oman

Global Identity Expansion

The leading electronic point-of-sale provider in the Middle East and North Africa wanted to rebrand itself in order to develop the identity with a clear vision in anticipation of future expansion. With this in mind, Storm Corporate Design in Auckland, New Zealand sought to create consistency in the graphic elements for the growing brand structure under two different names—one for each of Tawasul Electronic Network Solutions' major markets. According to Storm, "visual similarity relat[ing] to each other but at the same time different enough so have their own individuality" guided the design.

Design elements tied into the idea of the client's system, with hexagons figuring prominently across the logos. "Connecting hexagons creates the illusion of networking," the agency explains. "The construction is further simplified to represent more meaningful concept and simplified geometry creates a visually more interesting, memorable and strong identity."

1

Powerful thinking advances the cure.

2

MARKETING SUCCESS STARTS WITH U™

---

1 Creative Firm: Guard Dog Brand Development - Malverne, NY **Creative Team:** Maria Casini – Co-President/Managing Partner; Camille DeSantis – Co-President/Managing Partner; Jeff Chen – Designer **Client:** Multiple Myeloma Research Foundation **2 Creative Firm:** RainCastle Communications - Newton, MA **Creative Team:** Paul Regensburg – President/Creative Director; Ji Lee – Senior Designer; Rotem Meller – Senior Designer **Client:** Unica Corporation

1 **Creative Firm:** Hornall Anderson Design Works - Seattle, WA **Creative Team:** Jack Anderson – Creative Director; David Bates – Art Director; Javas Lehn – Designer; Laura Jakobsen – Strategy Director; Julie Lock – Illustrator **Client:** Mammoth Mountain Ski Area 2 **Creative Firm:** IE Design + Communications - Hermosa Beach, CA **Creative Team:** Marcie Carson – Creative Director; Jane Lee – Art Director; Nicole Bednarz – Senior Designer **Client:** SteamDot Alaskan Air Roasted Coffee

1 **Creative Firm:** Joaquim Cheong Design - Macau, China **Creative Team:** Kuokwai Cheong – Creative Director/Designer **Client:** Agnes Lam/Iok Fong 2 **Creative Firm:** IE Design + Communications - Hermosa Beach, CA **Creative Team:** Marcie Carson – Creative Director; Jane Lee – Art Director; Nicole Bednarz – Senior Designer **Client:** Salzman Design 3 **Creative Firm:** Rule29 - Geneva, IL **Creative Team:** Justin Ahrens – Principal/Creative Director; Kara Ayaram – Designer **Client:** MacDonald Photography

1

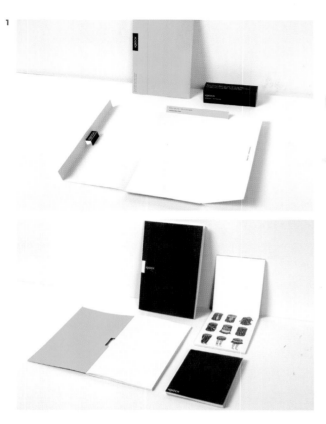

2

3

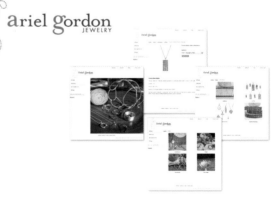

1 Creative Firm: KNOCK inc. - Minneapolis, MN **Creative Team:** KNOCK inc. Design Firm; Meenal Patel – Designer; Todd Paulson – Creative Director; Sara Nelson – Design Director; Creighton King – Production; Dan Black – Illustration **Client:** KNOCK inc. **2 Creative Firm:** Mel Lim Design - San Diego, CA **Creative Team:** Mel Lim – Designer **Client:** Ariel Gordon Jewelry **URL:** www.arielgordonjewelry.com **3 Creative Firm:** Impel Creative - Lakewood, OH **Creative Team:** Stacie Ross – Designer; Doug Crouch – Art Director **Client:** Red Apple Digital, Inc.

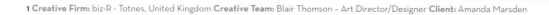

1 **Creative Firm:** biz-R - Totnes, United Kingdom **Creative Team:** Blair Thomson – Art Director/Designer **Client:** Amanda Marsden

PLATINUM

Creative Firm: Interrobang Design Collaborative, Inc. - Richmond, VT

Creative Team: Mark D Sylvester – Creative Director/ Designer; Robert Packert – Photographer

Client: Interrobang Design Cllbtv./Packert Photography

Quirky Styles Stand Out

Michael Albor of The Loft Salon and Spa in Boston wanted to showcase his hairstyling ability for a series of photos to be entered in a national competition, and to optimize his presentation he enlisted local photographer Bob Packert. The resulting images, embellished and turned into cards by Interrobang Design Collaborative in Richmond, Vermont, brought an unexpected whimsy to the competition in synch with the collection's name, Cirque du Quirk.

"Michael and Bob had developed the rough outline of a circus or carnival theme for the shoot before Bob contacted me to act as art director," says Interrobang's Mark

Sylvester. "These culminated into a stylebook that was sent around to the overall creative team and used to brief the models and stylists on the day of the shoot. I had included typographic references as well to grease the wheels for the postcard project. As long as the hair looked good, we could do whatever we wanted within the theme. The broad range of props"—including a six-foot albino python and multiple parrots—"clothing, makeup and talent we had available kept the day fluid and productive." Cirque du Quirk's "cast of characters" reflected the goal of creating a collection of elegant, yet still accessible, hairstyles in a fun, non-mainstream medium.

1

2

3

4

1 **Creative Firm:** Levine & Associates - Washington, D.C. **Creative Team:** John Vance – Managing Director; Monica Snellings – Creative Director; Lena Markley – Senior Art Director; Greg Sitzmann – Art Director; Jennie Jariel – Art Director; Scott Miller – Designer **Client:** Levine & Associates **2 Creative Firm:** Pareto - Toronto, ON, Canada **Creative Team:** Egon Springer – Creative Director/Designer/Copywriter; Jennifer Truong – Art Director; Denis Asllani – Print Production **Client:** Pareto **3 Creative Firm:** Joni Rae and Associates - Encino, CA **Creative Team:** Joni Rae Russell – Creative Director; Beverly Trengove – Art Director/Graphic Designer **Client:** Joni Rae and Associates **4 Creative Firm:** Grain Creative Consultants - Surry Hills, Australia **Creative Team:** Jure Leko – Creative Director **Client:** Grain Creative

1

2

3

4

1 **Creative Firm:** Purple, Rock, Scissors - Orlando, FL **Creative Team:** Bobby Jones – Chief Creative Officer; Shayne Bruno – Creative Director; Aaron Drath – Illustrator **Client:** Purple, Rock, Scissors 2 **Creative Firm:** Rule29 - Geneva, IL **Creative Team:** Justin Ahrens – Principal/Creative Director; Tim Damitz – Designer; Kerri Liu – Senior Designer **Client:** Rule 29 3 **Creative Firm:** Hitchcock Fleming & Associates Inc. - Akron, OH **Creative Team:** Nick Betro – Executive Creative Director; Greg Pfiffner – Writer; Todd Moser – Art Director **Client:** Hitchcock Fleming & Associates Inc 4 **Creative Firm:** Wallace Church, Inc. - New York, NY **Creative Team:** Stan Church – Creative Director/Designer; Tom Davidson – Illlustrator; Rich Rickaby – Project Manager **Client:** Wallace Church, Inc.

1

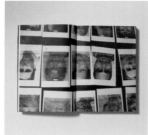 

2

3

4

1 Creative Firm: People Design Inc - Grand Rapids, MI **Creative Team:** Kevin Budelmann – Creative Director; Yang Kim – Creative Director; Jessica Lee – Designer **Client:** People Design **2 Creative Firm:** Eclipse Marketing Services, Inc. - Morristown, NJ **Creative Team:** Barbara Johnston – Creative Director; Amparo Pikarsky – Copywriter; Charles Borgerding – Designer/Illustrator; Karen Habib – Director, Hispanic Marketing **Client:** Eclipse Marketing Services **3 Creative Firm:** Julia Tam Design - Palos Verdes Estates, CA **Creative Team:** Julia Tam – Creative Director **Client:** Julia Tam Design **4 Creative Firm:** Torre Lazur McCann - Parsippany, NJ **Creative Team:** Christopher Bean –VP/Group Creative Director, Art; Mark Oppici – VP/Group Creative Director, Copy; Kristy Caraballo – VP/Management Supervisor **Client:** Torre Lazur McCann

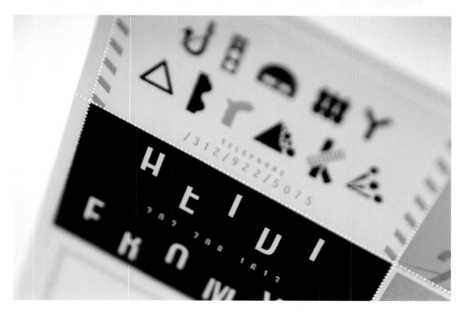

1 Creative Firm: Mauseth Design, LLC - Hoboken, NJ **Creative Team:** Ted Mauseth – Graphic Designer; Darren Farrell – Copywriter **Client:** Mauseth Design, LLC

1 **Creative Firm:** Alcone Marketing - Irvine, CA **Creative Team:** Luis Camano – VP/Creative Director; Kevin Kleber – Creative Director; Carlos Musquez – Creative Director; Shivonne Miller – Sr. Art Director **Client:** Mike's Hard Lemonade 2 **Creative Firm:** Pareto - Toronto, ON, Canada **Creative Team:** Egon Springer – Creative Director/Designer/Copywriter; Jennifer Truong – Art Director; Denis Asllani – Print Production **Client:** Pareto

1 Creative Firm: Alcone Marketing - Irvine, CA **Creative Team:** Luis Camano – VP/Creative Director; Carlos Musquez – Creative Director; Paul Ulloa – Digital Designer; Kevin Kleber – Copywriter; Cameron Young – Copywriter; Chad Lasota – Digital Designer **Client:** LG

 **PLATINUM**

Creative Firm: Foodmix - Westmont, IL
Creative Team: Foodmix Creative/Production Team
Client: Surlean Foods

Chow's On!

Surlean Foods wanted to make some noise about their custom, kettle-cooked products at select restaurant chains, and the creative team at Foodmix Marketing Communications delivered by ringing the dinner bell— an actual chuck wagon-style triangle in a mailer. The Elmhurst, Illinois agency's copy incorporates Surlean's company identity as a provider of affordable, customizable cuisine for their customers, and the dimensional mailer struck a responsive chord with chain decision makers, opening doors and helping to close sales.

 100

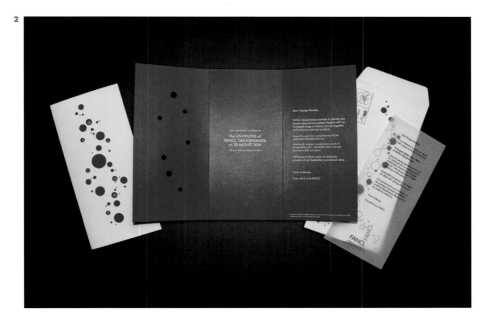

1 Creative Firm: Nesnadny + Schwartz - Cleveland, OH **Creative Team:** Mark Schwartz – Creative Director; Cindy Lowrey – Designer; Keith Pishnery – Designer; Russell Monk – Photographer; Julia Van Develder – Writer; Susan DeKrey – Writer **Client:** Vassar College **2 Creative Firm:** Planet Ads and Design P/L - Singapore **Creative Team:** Hal Suzuki – Creative Director; Suzanne Lauridssen – Senior Copywriter; Edwin Enero – Art Director **Client:** FANCL

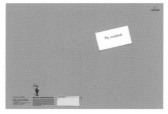

1 Creative Firm: Zeeland Oy - Helsinki, Finland **Creative Team:** Riina Pyöttiö – Project Manager; Juuso Enala – Designer; Tiina Viljakainen – Art Director; Paula Puikko – Copywriter; Mikko Vaija – Graphic Designer/Package **Client:** Hämeen kirjapaino and Zeeland Society Oy **2 Creative Firm:** Purple Focus Pvt. Ltd. - Indore, India **Creative Team:** Aarish Nandedkar – Copywriter; Jeetendra Rampuria – Designer; Praveen Karpe – Art Director **Client:** Eicher Trucks and Buses

1

L´ANNÉE DE LA FRANCE AU BRÉSIL

2

Brief:
Create a promotional institutional design piece that pays homage to the year of France in Brazil, to the 120 years of the salto factory, today's arjowiggins and the coincidence that it be the 120 years of the Eifel tower as well.

Main challenges and goals:
Send a message that touches the sentiments, moves and promotes positive feelings in people's everyday life; emotion design.
The challenge was in creating a three-dimensional project, the client did not want a message and image simply printed on a card.

Describe how you arrived at the final design:
We united the icons of two countries.
The Eifel tower within the Brazilian flag represents the year of france in brazil.
We chose the eifel tower as simbol of its 120 years, the same age as our client's factory.
The acrylic ball and the Eifel Tower was illuminated with led´s lamp.
We illuminated it to reflect paris'fame as the city of lights.

3

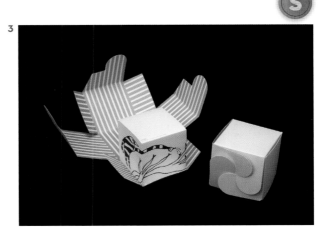

1 Creative Firm: Merchan-Design - Sao Paulo, Brazil **Creative Team:** Marcelo Lopes; L´ année de la France au Brésil **Client:** Arjowiggins **2 Creative Firm:** Greenfield/Belser Ltd. - Washington D.C. **Creative Team:** Leigh George – Account Executive; Aaron Thornburgh – Senior Designer; Donna Greenfield – Principal; Burkey Belser – Creative Director **Client:** The Montana Academy **3 Creative Firm:** Zuan Club - Tokyo, Japan **Creative Team:** Akihiko Tsukamoto – Design/Art Direction; Harumi Kimura – Illustration **Client:** ARJOWIGGINS K.K.

1

2

3

4

1 Creative Firm: Sherman Advertising/Mermaid, Inc. - New York, NY **Creative Team:** Sharon McLaughlin – Creative Director; Ted Gamble – Art Director **Client:** PowerHouse **2 Creative Firm:** EURO RSCG - Suresnes, France **Client:** Dainik Bhaskar **3 Creative Firm:** Liquified Creative - Annapolis, MD **Creative Team:** Shawn Noratel – Creative Director; Stephanie Moyer – Creative Copywriter; Denise Benoit – Account Executive **Client:** Goodstone Inn & Estate **4 Creative Firm:** HBO Off-Air Creative Services - New York, NY **Creative Team:** Venus Dennison – Creative Director; Christian Martillo – Design Manager; Carlos Tejeda – Art Director; Mary Tchorbajian – Art Director; Maria Marcial – Designer; Jen McDearman – Copywriter **Client:** HBO Marketing

 **PLATINUM**

Creative Firm: IE Design + Communications - Hermosa Beach, CA

Creative Team: Marcie Carson – Creative Director; Nicole Bednarz – Senior Designer

Client: Bob Stevens Photography

1

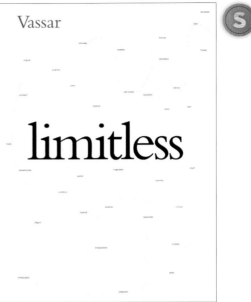

2

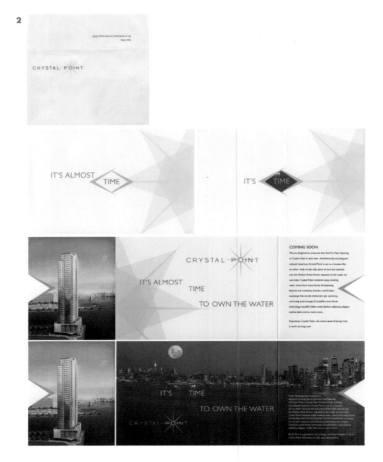

3

1 Creative Firm: Nesnadny + Schwartz - Cleveland, OH **Creative Team:** Mark Schwartz – Creative Director; Shawn Beatty – Designer; Cindy Lowrey – Designer; Keith Pishnery – Designer; Russell Monk – Photographer; Julia Van Develder – Writer **Client:** Vassar College **2 Creative Firm:** Sherman Advertising/Mermaid, Inc. - New York, NY **Creative Team:** Sharon Mclaughlin – Creative Director; Ted Gamble – Art Director; Stephen Morse – Retoucher **Client:** Crystal Point **3 Creative Firm:** Fitting Group - Pittsburgh, PA **Creative Team:** Travis Norris – Creative Director **Client:** University of Pittsburgh School of Law

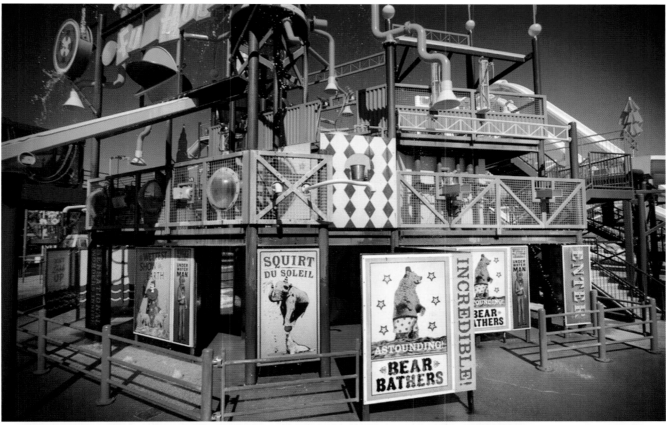

PLATINUM

Creative Firm: Rassman Design – Denver, CO
Creative Team: Andy Schneider – Designer;
John Rassman – Creative Director
Client: Water World

A Day At The Circus

Denver's Rassman Design and Water World in nearby Federal Heights have had a long relationship, and as the water park has grown into one of the nation's largest, Rassman has been right there with them. After Water World added a new family area called The Big Top, the adjacent FunH2Ouse attraction needed a facelift to better match the new circus theme. After the park retrofitted the existing structure with new plumbing and other infrastructural improvements, Rassman stepped in with the cosmetic enhancements, starting with a new color palette for the existing structure and a series of 27 waterproof posters inspired by early 20th century circus and movie advertisements on the outside walls. The firm also designed an additional 92 custom-routed polymer panels to help guide adventurers through the watery maze inside. As Rassman puts it, "The approach included the use of nostalgic graphics, large patterns and retro typesetting to breathe new life into one of the park's most popular attractions." Dive in.

barbie shanghai, china
wall murals

barbie shanghai, china
design center & inspiration wall

barbie shanghai, china
café

barbie shanghai, china
building glass façade, staircase and candy wall

PLATINUM

Creative Firm: Mattel, Inc. - El Segundo, CA
Creative Team: Slade Architecture
Client: Mattel, Inc.

The Barbie Experience

Barbie is an international brand, and Mattel's flagship Barbie store in downtown Shanghai brings together the world's largest and most comprehensive collection of Barbie dolls and lifestyle products, a special couture section featuring a young adult range—and everything in between. "Shanghai was the ideal choice for the inaugural Barbie flagship store," says Mattel, whose in-house agency created the look and feel of the 40,000-square-foot, six-floor store. "A progressive and modern city, it is cosmopolitan and outward looking and brings together cultural influences from around the world."

From the whimsical façade to the Design Center, which lets girls design their own doll and create a design portfolio like a true fashion designer—and even walk a runway in fashions from "the ultimate Barbie closet"—followed by lunch at one of the store's two restaurants and a manicure at a Barbie-themed spa, the store is "unapologetically all girl." Says Mattel, "Barbie Shanghai is a modern, fun, playful interpretation of the brand that pays homage to Barbie past, present and future."

1

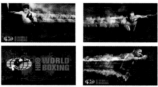

2

3

Ball Park 2009 Dew Tour Stage

1 **Creative Firm:** HBO Off-Air Creative Services - New York, NY **Creative Team:** Venus Dennison – Creative Director; Christian Martillo – Design Manager; Carlos Tejeda – Art Director; Jen McDearman – Copywriter **Client:** HBO Enterprises 2 **Creative Firm:** HBO Off-Air Creative Services - New York, NY **Creative Team:** Venus Dennison – Creative Director; Christian Martillo – Design Manager; Carlos Tejeda – Art Director; Jen McDearman – Copywriter **Client:** HBO Marketing 3 **Creative Firm:** Launch Creative Marketing- Chicago, IL **Creative Team:** David Lind – Creative Director; Sarah Wielusz – Associate Art Director **Client:** Sara Lee Corporation

1

2

1 Creative Firm: Ralph Appelbaum Associates - New York, NY **Creative Team:** Ralph Appelbaum - Principal in Charge; James Cathcart - Co-Project Director Design; Co-Project Director Content - Francis O'Shea; Carlos Rodriquez – Designer; Wes Kull - Graphic Design; Caitlin Mennen - Content Coordinator; Nikki Amdur - Copy Editor; George Robertson, Sean Pattison – Renderings **Client:** Rock & Roll Hall of Fame Annex NYC **2 Creative Firm:** Ralph Appelbaum Associates - New York, NY **Creative Team:** Ralph Appelbaum - Principal in Charge; Tim Ventimiglia – Project Director/Lead Designer; Arturo Padilla - Project Manager/Senior Exhibit Designer; Jande Wintrob - Senior Exhibit Designer; Lourdes Bernard, Helene Kenny, Buke Kumyol - Exhibit Designers; Mia Beurskens – Senior Graphic Designer; Tommy Matthews - Graphic Designer; Madeline Chinnici – Content Developer; Donna Zimmerman - Content Coordinator; Nikki Amdur – Editor; George Robertson, Scott Shepard, June Yoshimura - Renderings **Client:** The Chemical Heritage Foundation

1

2

3

1 Creative Firm: Mattel, Inc. - El Segundo, CA **Client:** Mattel, Inc. **2 Creative Firm:** Beth Singer Design - Arlington, VA **Creative Team:** Beth Singer – Art Director; Howard Smith – Art Director; Barbara Bose – Designer; Carla Aguiar – Production Artist **Client:** American Israel Public Affairs Committee (AIPAC) **3 Creative Firm:** Primary Design, Inc. - Haverhill, MA **Creative Team:** Stephanie Byers – Graphic Designer; Jules Epstein – Creative Director **Client:** Avalon Bowery Place

PLATINUM

Creative Firm: Hornall Anderson Design Works - Seattle, WA

Creative Team: Ashley Arhart – Creative Director; Andrew Wicklund – Creative Director; Jamie Monberg – Interactive Director; Jay Hilburn – Designer; Chris Monberg – Interactive Producer; Paula Cox – Production Designer

Client: Willis Tower (formerly known as Sears Tower)

URL: www.hornallanderson.com

Hornall Anderson Aims High

When lining up for a trip to the top of the tallest building in North America for the first time, it takes a little acclimation to fully grasp the magnitude of the Willis Tower (formerly known as the Sears Tower). Seeking to bridge its iconic legacy with its state-of-the-art vision of the future, Skydeck Chicago enlisted Seattle's Hornall Anderson to create an end-to-end immersive Skydeck queuing experience to celebrate this world-renowned tourist destination and demonstrate real connections to the legacy and future of the Tower, while achieving key business goals of increasing visitor traffic and driving additional revenue per guest. Hornall Anderson created three major experiences that blend environmental graphics, digital interaction and sculptural elements designed to engage visitors and

encourage visual and tactile interaction. The Tower Room, the Iconic Chicago Room and Skyscrapers—the latter filled with "fun with height" comparisons, which, for example, informs visitors that the Tower is the height of 262 Michael Jordans.

"The scope of the overall project includes the Skydeck identity redesign, visitor queuing experience, movie and elevator ride, with plans to grow the experience design to a more holistic extension," says the agency. "The experience emphasizes creating memories the visitor will never forget, whether virtually looking down from 103 stories high, to learning various factoids about the Tower and the city's cultural life through a mix of digital touch screens, wall graphics and a movie compilation of the Tower's history."

1

2

3

4

1 Creative Firm: Beth Singer Design - Arlington, VA **Creative Team:** Beth Singer – Art Director; Howard Smith – Designer **Client:** American Israel Public Affairs Committee (AIPAC) **2 Creative Firm:** Kimak Design - Orangeburg, NY **Creative Team:** James Kimak – Designer/Artist/Photographer; Thomas Hemming – Project Manager; Gayle Irwin – Gallery Director **Client:** Children's Hospital of Pittsburgh **3 Creative Firm:** Hornall Anderson Design Works - Seattle, WA **Creative Team:** Ashley Arhart – Creative Director; Jamie Monberg – Interactive Director; Debbie Glasband – Strategist; John Rousseau – Designer; Chris Monberg – Interactive Producer; Sam Stubblefield – Experience Designer **Client:** Madison Square Garden **URL:** www.hornallanderson.com **4 Creative Firm:** Hornall Anderson Design Works - Seattle, WA **Creative Team:** Larry Anderson – Art Director; David Phillips – Designer; Chang-Ling Wu – Designer; Ethan Keller – Designer; Ricki Pasinelli – Account Director; Lara Swimmer – Photographer **Client:** Microsoft

1

2

3

4

1 Creative Firm: Hornall Anderson Design Works - Seattle, WA **Creative Team:** Mark Popich – Creative Director; Sunita Richardson – Strategy Director; Danial Crookston – Interactive Producer; Andrew Well – Designer; Tony DeVincenzi – Designer; Nathan Young – Interactive Designer **Client:** Microsoft **URL:** www.hornallanderson.com
2 Creative Firm: Grain Creative Consultants - Surry Hills, Australia **Creative Team:** Jure Leko – Creative Director; Jeremy Tombs – Senior Designer **Client:** Jacob's Creek Wines **3 Creative Firm:** Grain Creative Consultants - Surry Hills, Australia **Creative Team:** Jure Leko – Creative Director **Client:** Richmond Grove Wines **4 Creative Firm:** Karen Skunta & Company - Cleveland, OH **Creative Team:** Karen Skunta – Creative Director; Jamie Spencer Sr. – Graphic Designer/Exhibits; Felix Lee Sr. – Graphic Designer/Interactive; Jen Maxwell – Graphic Designer; Kristal Ernst – Graphic Designer; Blue Robot – Interactive Development **Client:** CSU Nance College of Business

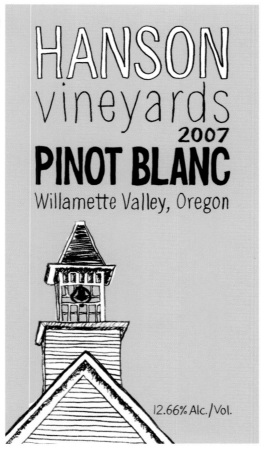

1 Creative Firm: Greenfield/Belser Ltd. - Washington, D.C. **Creative Team:** Lindsay Mead - Account Executive; Margo Howard - Designer; Burkey Belser - Creative Director; Mark Ledgerwood – Art Director **Client:** Hanson Vineyards

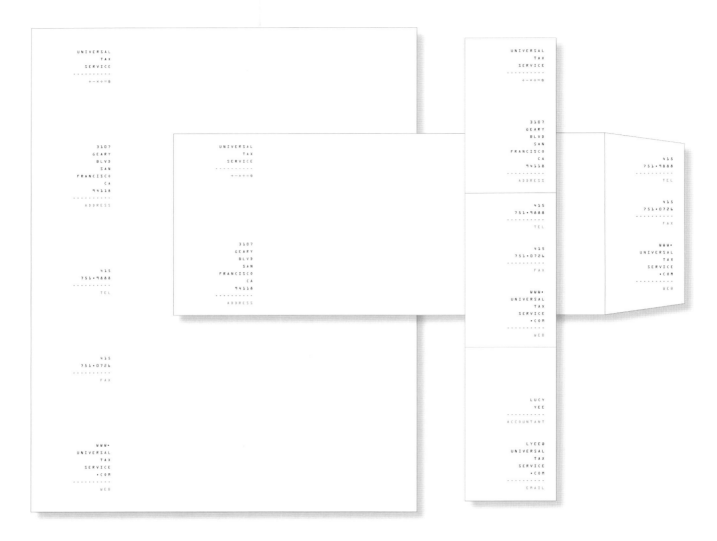

PLATINUM

Creative Firm: Gee + Chung Design - San Francisco, CA
Creative Team: Earl Gee - Creative Director/Designer/Illustrator
Client: Universal Tax Service

Idea + Execution = Great Design

Accounting is serious business, and Universal Tax Service in San Francisco wanted to convey their no-nonsense approach through its stationery. " Whenever [the client] sat down with us to do our taxes, we were always amazed at how facile she was with her adding machine," says Gee + Chung Design, also in San Francisco. "We felt the adding machine printout would be an ideal solution to effectively convey the firm's dedication to organization, precision and accuracy. Our biggest challenge was to not over-design, but to allow the simplicity of the typography and layout to come forward."

Gee + Chung used the adding machine conceit to make Universal's letterhead and envelope sets; the stationery's typography, flush right layout and three-panel business card design, indeed, suggest an adding machine printout, complete with familiar arithmetic symbols. Additionally, "throughout each stationery component, the address, telephone and fax numbers, Web site, title and e-mail fields are highlighted in red, creating a typographic system in which each group of information is defined by a sum total." The client recognized the inspiration right away. "She immediately got it, and we hoped her clients would have the same reaction," says the agency. It did—Universal Tax Service says that the stationery's clear, concise and conceptual design helped attract a significant number of new clients. Gee + Chung couldn't be happier: "Our goal was to 'make it count,' and it appears we were successful."

1

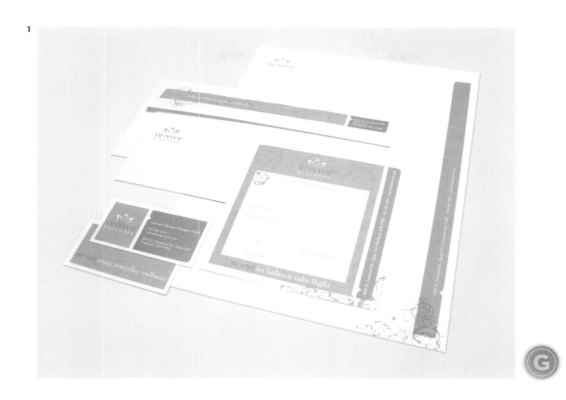

2

1 Creative Firm: UNIT design collective - San Francisco, CA **Creative Team:** Ann Jordan - Creative Director/Designer; Shardul Kiri - Creative Director **Client:** Re:Vive Bodywork **2 Creative Firm:** Idea2 Designers - Groningen, Netherlands **Creative Team:** Henk de Graaf - Graphic Designer; Erwin Zinger – Graphic Designer **Client:** het Zonneleen

 **PLATINUM**

Creative Firm: MOCK, the agency - Atlanta, GA
Creative Team: Donald Mock - Creative Director/Art Director/Designer; Rob Broadfoot - Creative Director
Client: City of Richmond, California

A Fresh Spin On The Familiar

Libraries have changed significantly in the last couple of decades, but their place in the community remains as necessary as ever. Atlanta design agency MOCK sought to rebrand the Richmond County Public Library with a mark that would hover in the space between familiarity and freshness: "The simple, dimensional logo speaks literally to what we all connote with libraries—books—as well as tipping its hat to the multimedia information resource that the Richmond County Public Library has become."

The selection of green suggests a sense of the new, and the library's tagline, "Find Everything," invites patrons to explore all the library has to offer and consider it a familiar place to think of in a whole new light.

1 Creative Firm: Hornall Anderson Design Works - Seattle, WA **Creative Team:** John Rousseau - Art Director; Leo Raymundo - Designer; Chang-Ling Wu - Designer ;Yuri Shvets - Designer; Nathan Braceros – Designer **Client:** PDS **2 Creative Firm:** Crabtree + Company - Falls Church, VA **Creative Team:** Susan Angrisani - Creative Director; Rodrigo Vera - Art Director; Rob Harlow - Designer; William Weinheimer - Production Artist; Lisa Suchy – Production Manager **Client:** Worm Law Firm **3 Creative Firm:** Hornall Anderson Design Works - Seattle, WA **Creative Team:** Andrew Wicklund - Art Director; Peter Anderson - Designer; Jay Hilburn - Designer; Kathleen Kennelly Ullman - Designer; Jessica Lennard – Designer **Client:** Coffee Bean & Tea Leaf **4 Creative Firm:** Mel Lim Design - San Diego, CA **Creative Team:** Mel Lim – Designer **Client:** Tiny Ginger LLC **5 Creative Firm:** Zeeland Oy - Helsinki, Finland **Creative Team:** Nina Rintala - Graphic Designer; Ulla Jämä – Project Manager **Client:** Porin Seudun Kehittämiskeskus Oy

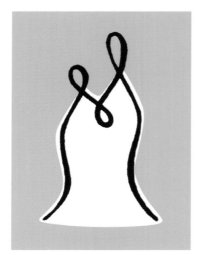

1 Creative Firm: Zero Gravity - San Marcos, TX **Creative Team:** Ivanete Blanco – Principal Designer **Client:** Maria Videtta **2 Creative Firm:** formul8 Pte. Ltd. - Singapore **Creative Team:** Fiona Bartholomeusz - Managing Director; Kok Hoe Wong - Account Director; Sylvia Sin - Design Director; Eran Husni Amir Husni - Art Director/Designer **Client:** formul8 Pte. Ltd. **URL:** www.formul8.com **3 Creative Firm:** Hornall Anderson Design Works - Seattle, WA **Creative Team:** Jack Anderson - Creative Director; David Bates - Art Director; Javas Lehn - Designer; Laura Jakobsen - Strategy Director; Julie Lock – Typography **Client:** Mammoth Mountain Ski Area **4 Creative Firm:** Hornall Anderson Design Works - Seattle, WA **Creative Team:** Andrew Wicklund - Creative Director; Jay Hilburn - Designer; Javas Lehn - Designer; David Bates - Designer ;Joseph King - Designer; Peter Anderson – Designer **Client:** Willis Tower **5 Creative Firm:** UNIT design collective - San Francisco, CA **Creative Team:** Ann Jordan - Creative Director/Designer; Shardul Kiri - Creative Director **Client:** Presh

1

 2

 3

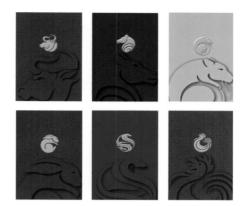 4

 5

 6

1 Creative Firm: Van Vechten Creative - San Diego, CA **Creative Team:** Charles Van Vechten - Creative Director; Kristen Lucci - Designer; Kathy McGraw – Senior Designer **Client:** Terranea Resort **2 Creative Firm:** Studio J - North Highlands, CA **Creative Team:** Angela Jackson – Graphic Designer **Client:** Angela Jackson **URL:** http//:www.88avenue.com **3 Creative Firm:** UNIT design collective - San Francisco, CA **Creative Team:** Ann Jordan - Creative Director; Shardul Kiri - Creative Director; Ryne Schillinger – Designer **Client:** Re:Vive Bodywork **4 Creative Firm:** Object 9 - Baton Rouge, LA **Client:** Digital FX **5 Creative Firm:** Hornall Anderson Design Works - Seattle, WA **Creative Team:** Andrew Wicklund - Creative Director; Jay Hilburn - Designer; Javas Lehn - Designer; David Bates - Designer; Joseph King - Designer; Peter Anderson – Designer **Client:** Willis Tower **6 Creative Firm:** komp|rehensive design - King of Prussia, PA **Creative Team:** Jeanne Komp - Creative Director **Client:** Pink Rhino Kids

1

 2

 3

 4

 5

 6

1 Creative Firm: SIGNI - Mexico **Creative Team:** Daniel Castelao - President **Client:** Blue Label Mexico **2 Creative Firm:** Baily Brand Consulting - Plymouth Meeting, PA **Creative Team:** Steve Perry - Creative Director; David Kusiak – Designer **Client:** Gary Kimball **3 Creative Firm:** Suka - New York, NY **Creative Team:** Brian Wong - Creative Director; Matthew Carl - Designer; Dave Caputo – Designer **Client:** The GO Project **4 Creative Firm:** IE Design + Communications - Hermosa Beach, CA **Creative Team:** Marcie Carson - Creative Director; Jane Lee - Art Director; Nicole Bednarz - Senior Designer; Christine Kenney – Designer **Client:** Aspiriant **5 Creative Firm:** Mendes Publicidade - Sao Paulo, Brazil **Creative Team:** Oswaldo Mendes - Creativity Director; Natali Ikikame – Art Director **Client:** Ótica Britânica **6 Creative Firm:** createTWO - Auburn, AL **Creative Team:** Kevin Smith – Designer **Client:** Auburn University **URL:** www.createtwo.com

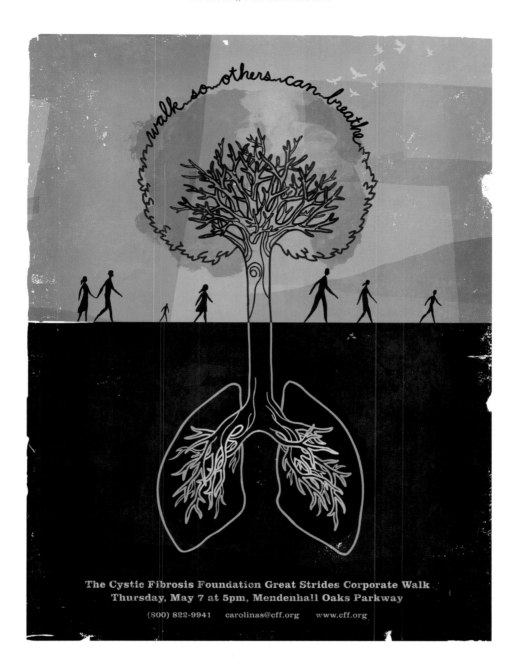

 **PLATINUM**

A Walk In The Park

Creative Firm: Thompson Creative - Greensboro, NC
Creative Team: Gary Thompson - Art Director; Kyle Webster – Illustrator
Client: Cystic Fibrosis Foundation

Cystic Fibrosis (CF) is a rare genetic disease that primarily attacks the respiratory system, and longtime supporters Thompson Creative in Greensboro, North Carolina created this poster to promote the Cystic Fibrosis Foundation's annual Great Strides Corporate Walk. In order to meet the dual goal of raising public awareness about the disorder and recruiting participants, Thompson Creative developed a simple visual concept juxtaposing oxygen-giving trees with lungs. The legend, "Walk so others can breathe," and the connection of the scenic park setting of the walk with the respiratory nature of the disease, says agency president and creative director Gary Thompson, fulfilled a challenge: "With so many worthy causes competing for donation dollars, the challenge is to communicate quickly with your audience while still connecting on an emotional level."

1

G

2

3

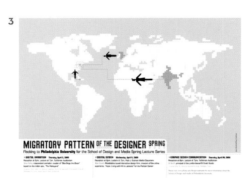

5

S

4

1 Creative Firm: Thompson Creative - Greensboro, NC **Creative Team:** McKenzie Stevenson - Designer; Gary Thompson – Creative Director **Client:** Big Wheel Productions
2 Creative Firm: richard zeid design - Evanston, IL **Creative Team:** Richard Zeid – Designer **Client:** Chinese American Friendship Association **3 Creative Firm:** Kradel Design
- Philadelphia, PA **Creative Team:** Maribeth Kradel-Weitzel – Principal **Client:** Philadelphia University **4 Creative Firm:** New York Institute of Technology - Manama, Bahrain
Creative Team: Zeeshan Shah – Assistant Professor **Client:** Bahrain Youth Health Association **5 Creative Firm:** STUDIO SONDA - Porec, Croatia **Creative Team:** Kristina
Poropat - Creative Director; Jelena Simunovic - Art Director; Sean Poropat - Art Director; Ana Bursic - Designer; Tina Erman - Designer; Aleksandar Živanov - Designer
Client: BOOKtiga 2009

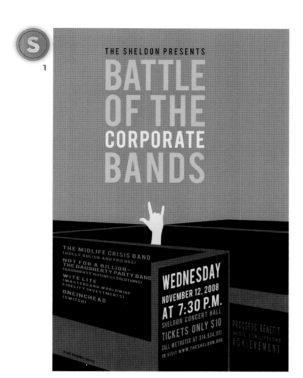

1 **Creative Firm:** Paradowski Creative - St. Louis. MO **Creative Team:** Maggie Middeke - Account Manager; Scott Tripp – Designer **Client:** The Sheldon Concert Hall
2 **Creative Firm:** STUDIO SONDA - Porec, Croatia **Creative Team:** Kristina Poropat - Creative Director; Jelena Simunovic - Art Director; Sean Poropat - Art Director; Ana Bursic - Designer; Tina Erman - Designer; Aleksandar Živanov - Designer **Client:** Bravarija Art Remont/Porec 3 **Creative Firm:** Paradowski Creative - St. Louis, MO **Creative Team:** Maggie Middeke - Account Manager; Joy Marcus – Designer **Client:** The Sheldon Concert Hall 4 **Creative Firm:** Paradowski Creative - St. Louis, MO **Creative Team:** Maggie Middeke - Account Manager; Jenny Anderson – Designer **Client:** The Sheldon Concert Hall

1

G

2

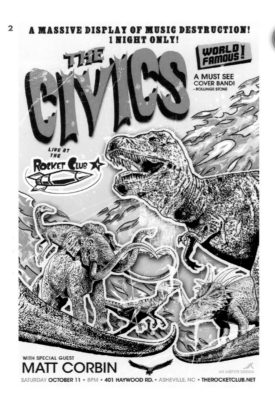

S

3

1 Creative Firm: Zuan Club - Tokyo, Japan **Creative Team:** Akihiko Tsukamoto - Design/Art Direction; Harumi Kimura - Illustration **Client:** Toraya Co., Ltd.
2 Creative Firm: Airtype Studio - Winston-Salem, NC **Creative Team:** Bryan Ledbetter – Creative Director/Designer **Client:** The Civics **3 Creative Firm:** Airtype Studio - Winston-Salem, NC **Creative Team:** Bryan Ledbetter – Creative Director/ Designer **Client:** Piedmont Distillers

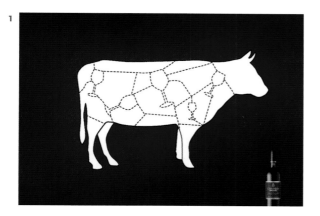

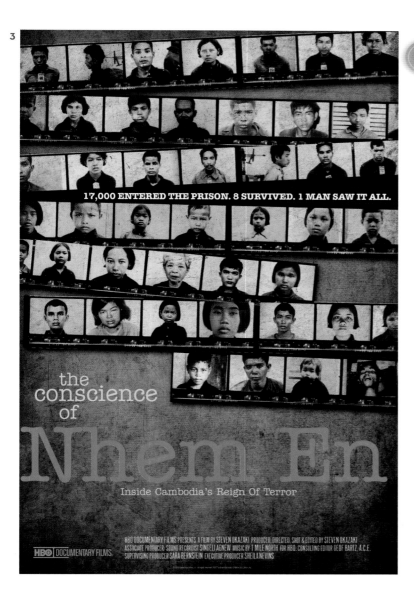

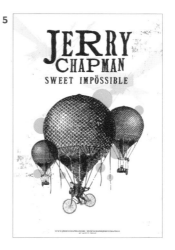

1 Creative Firm: TBWA\Central Asia - Almaty, Kazakhstan **Creative Team:** Juan Pablo Valencia - Creative Director/Copywriter/Art Director **Client:** CARMEN / SANTA RITA
2 Creative Firm: HBO Off-Air Creative Services - New York, NY **Creative Team:** Venus Dennison - Creative Director; Ana Racelis - Design Manager; Jose Mendez - Art Director; Seth Lutsky - Designer; Andrew Kanzer – Copywriter **Client:** HBO Sports **3 Creative Firm:** HBO Off-Air Creative Services - New York, NY **Creative Team:** Venus Dennison - Creative Director; Christian Martillo – Design Manager/Designer; Jen McDearman – Copywriter **Client:** HBO Documentary Films **4 Creative Firm:** Zuan Club - Tokyo, Japan **Creative Team:** Akihiko Tsukamoto Design/Art Direction; Radical Suzuki - Illustration **Client:** Condmania Tokyo **5 Creative Firm:** Airtype Studio - Winston-Salem, NC **Creative Team:** Bryan Ledbetter – Creative Director/Designer **Client:** Jerry Chapman

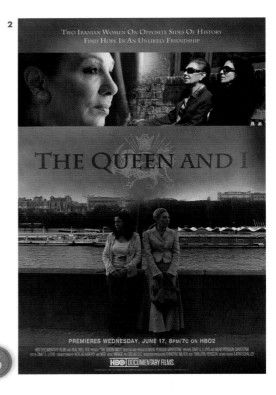

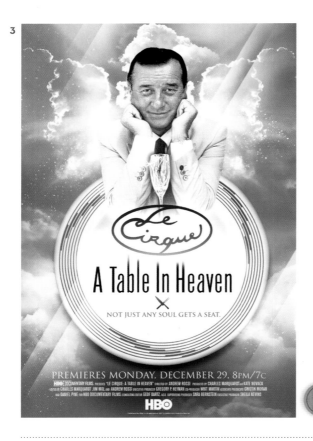

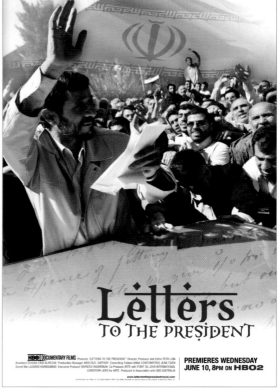

1 Creative Firm: Stake Creative Design - Chester Springs, PA **Creative Team:** David Copestakes – Art Director **Client:** AIGA Philadelphia **2 Creative Firm:** HBO Off-Air Creative Services - New York, NY **Creative Team:** Venus Dennison - Creative Director; Ana Racelis - Design Manager; Anthony Viola - Art Director; Jen McDearman – Copywriter **Client:** HBO Documentary Films **3 Creative Firm:** HBO Off-Air Creative Services - New York, NY **Creative Team:** Venus Dennison - Creative Director; Ana Racelis - Design Manager; Gary St. Clare - Designer; Jen McDearman – Copywriter **Client:** HBO Documentary Films **4 Creative Firm:** HBO Off-Air Creative Services - New York, NY **Creative Team:** Venus Dennison - Creative Director; Ana Racelis - Design Manager; Ron Acquavita - Art Director; Jen McDearman – Copywriter **Client:** HBO Documentary Films

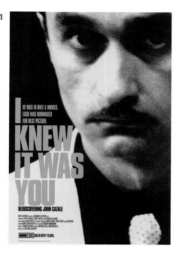

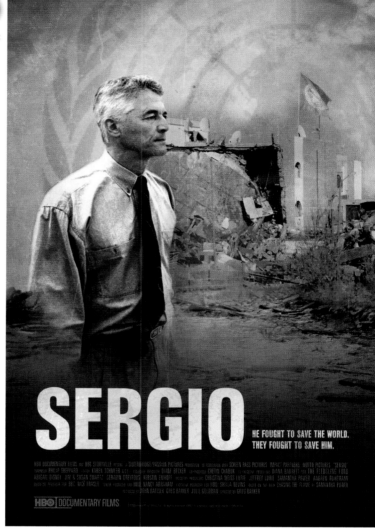

1 **Creative Firm:** HBO Off-Air Creative Services - New York, NY **Creative Team:** Venus Dennison - Creative Director; Ana Racelis - Design Manager; Carlos Tejeda - Art Director; Jen McDearman – Copywriter **Client:** HBO Documentary Films **2 Creative Firm:** HBO - New York, NY **Creative Team:** Venus Dennison - Creative Director; Christian Martillo - Design Manager; Chihiro Nishihara - Designer; Andrew Kanzer – Copywriter **Client:** HBO Documentary Films **3 Creative Firm:** HBO Off-Air Creative Services - New York, NY **Creative Team:** Venus Dennison - Creative Director; Christian Martillo - Design Manager/Designer; Jen McDearman – Copywriter **Client:** HBO Documentary Films **4 Creative Firm:** HBO Off-Air Creative Services - New York, NY **Creative Team:** Venus Dennison - Creative Director; Christian Martillo – Design Manager/Designer; Jen McDearman – Copywriter **Client:** HBO Documentary Films

1

A FILM BY ALEXANDRA PELOSI

RIGHT AMERICA: FEELING WRONGED

SOME VOICES FROM THE CAMPAIGN TRAIL

Snapshots From The Divided States Of America

HBO DOCUMENTARY FILMS PRESENTS "RIGHT AMERICA: FEELING WRONGED—SOME VOICES FROM THE CAMPAIGN TRAIL"
DIRECTED, PRODUCED AND FILMED BY ALEXANDRA PELOSI PRODUCED AND FILMED BY MICHAEL VBS
EDITED BY SARI GILMAN MICHAEL LEVINE PAX WASSERMAN VICTORIA FORD
FOR HBO: PRODUCER EXECUTIVE SUSAN BENAROYA SUPERVISING PRODUCER LISA HELLER EXECUTIVE PRODUCER SHEILA NEVINS

PREMIERES ON PRESIDENT'S DAY ★ MONDAY, FEB. 16 AT 8PM/7C ON HBO

HBO DOCUMENTARY FILMS.

2
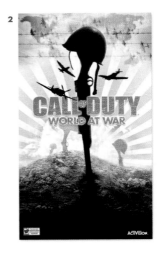

3

4

1 Creative Firm: HBO Off-Air Creative Services - New York, NY **Creative Team:** Venus Dennison - Creative Director; Anthony Viola - Art Director; Allan Wai - Design Manager; Andrew Kanzer – Copywriter **Client:** HBO Documentary Films **2 Creative Firm:** UNIT design collective - San Francisco, CA **Creative Team:** Shardul Kiri - Creative Director; Ann Jordan - Creative Director; Eric Lindsey – Designer **Client:** Activision | Blizzard **3 Creative Firm:** O'Leary and Partners - Newport Beach, CA **Creative Team:** Eric Spiegler - Executive Creative Director; Deidre McQuaide - Executive Creative Director; Rob Pettis - Creative Director; Josh Zipper - Graphic Designer; Matt McNelis - Senior Copywriter; Chris Macabitas – Associate Creative Director **Client:** Kawasaki **4 Creative Firm:** Optima Soulsight - Highland Park, IL **Creative Team:** Adam Ferguson – Creative Director **Client:** Lake Geneva Wine Festival

1

2
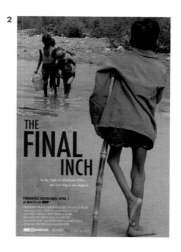

3
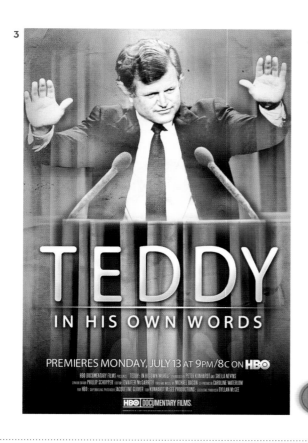

4

1 Creative Firm: Draftfcb - Chicago, IL **Creative Team:** Rob Sherlock - EVP/Chief Creative Officer; Suzanna Bierwirth - VP/Creative Director; Stu Thompson - Senior Copywriter; Gordon Sang - Art Director; Jonathan Petersen - Designer/Typographer; Anthony Arciero – Photographer **Client:** Brown Forman - el Jimador **2 Creative Firm:** HBO Off-Air Creative Services - New York, NY **Creative Team:** Venus Dennison - Creative Director; Christian Martillo - Design Manager; Anthony Viola - Art Director; Andrew Kanzer – Copywriter **Client:** HBO Documentary Films **3 Creative Firm:** HBO Off-Air Creative Services - New York, NY **Creative Team:** Venus Dennison - Creative Director; Allan Wai - Design Manager; Gary St. Clare - Designer; Andrew Kanzer – Copywriter **Client:** HBO Documentary Films **4 Creative Firm:** Zeeland Oy - Helsinki, Finland **Creative Team:** Mikko Vaija - Art Director; Migu Snäll - Creative Director; Anna Korpi-Kyyny - Copywriter; Riitta Bergman – Account Manager **Client:** Oy Kopparberg Finland Ab

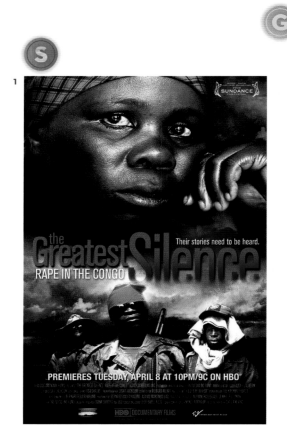

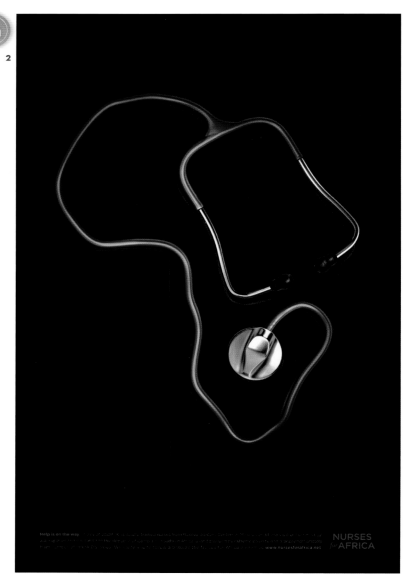

1 Creative Firm: HBO Off-Air Creative Services - New York, NY **Creative Team:** Venus Dennison - Creative Director; Ana Racelis - Design Manager; Jose Mendez - Art Director; Katerina Tsioros - Designer; Andrew Kanzer – Copywriter **Client:** HBO Documentary Films **2 Creative Firm:** MOCK, the agency - Atlanta, GA **Creative Team:** Donald Mock - Creative Director/Art Director/Designer; Rob Broadfoot - Creative Director/Copywriter; Michael Feher - Photographer; Chris Bodie - Illustration/Retouching **Client:** Rosewood Care Centers **URL:** www.nursesforafrica.net **3 Creative Firm:** HBO Off-Air Creative Services - New York, NY **Creative Team:** Venus Dennison - Creative Director; Allan Wai - Design Manager; Gary St. Clare - Designer; Jen McDearman – Copywriter **Client:** HBO Documentary Films **4 Creative Firm:** Marshfield Clinic - Marshfield, WI **Creative Team:** Erik Borreson - Senior Graphic Design Specialist; Nate Piekos – Typographer **Client:** Marshfield Clinic **URL:** www.marshfieldclinic.org

1

2

3

4

5

1 Creative Firm: Paradowski Creative - St. Louis, MO **Creative Team:** Paula Crews - Account Director; Maggie Middeke – Designer **Client:** The Sheldon Concert Hall
2 Creative Firm: Stake Creative Design - Chester Springs, PA **Creative Team:** David Copestakes – Art Director **Client:** AIGA Philadelphia **3 Creative Firm:** createTWO - Auburn, AL **Creative Team:** Kevin Smith – Designer **Client:** Auburn University **URL:** www.createtwo.com **4 Creative Firm:** Rule29 - Geneva, IL **Creative Team:** Justin Ahrens - Principal/Creative Director; Kerri Liu Senior – Designer **Client:** So Cal Fire Project **5 Creative Firm:** Rule29 - Geneva, IL **Creative Team:** Justin Ahrens - Designer; Donovan Berry - Designer; Steve Hartman - Designer; Christine Taylor - Designer; Nate Voss – Designer **Client:** Life In Abundance (LIA) International

1

3

2

1 Creative Firm: Bridgepoint Education - San Diego, CA **Creative Team:** Marc Riesenberg - Creative Director; David Dickey – Sr. Graphic Designer **Client:** Ashford University **2 Creative Firm:** Dunn&Co. - Tampa, FL **Creative Team:** Troy Dunn - Chief Creative Officer; Dan Stevenson - Creative Director; Alex Nieto – Art Director **Client:** ALS Association of Florida **3 Creative Firm:** Thielen Designs - Albuquerque, NM **Creative Team:** Tony Thielen - Creative Director/Art Director; Jacqui Garcia - Copywriter; Cel Jarvis - Photographer; Tony Thielen – Photo Retoucher/Montage **Client:** Kinesio

134

1

2

Q: WHAT IS SMALL, RED AND WHISPERS?

A: A HOARSE RADISH

Q: WHY WAS THE MUSHROOM INVITED TO LOTS OF PARTIES?

A: BECAUSE HE WAS A FUNGI TO BE WITH!

Q: WHY DID THE GRAPE STOP IN THE MIDDLE OF THE ROAD?

A: BECAUSE HE RAN OUT OF JUICE

Q: WHY DID THE BANANA GO TO THE DOCTOR?

A: BECAUSE IT WASN'T PEELING WELL

1 Creative Firm: Hornall Anderson Design Works - Seattle, WA **Creative Team:** Jack Anderson - Creative Director; David Bates - Creative Director; Javas Lehn – Designer **Client:** Mammoth Mountain Ski Area **2 Creative Firm:** American Specialty Health - San Diego, CA **Client:** American Specialty Health

1

2

3

1 **Creative Firm:** Kantorwassink - Grand Rapids, MI **Creative Team:** Dave Kantor; Wendy Wassink; Jason Murray; Tim Calkins **Client:** Nutrilite/Amway **2 Creative Firm:** Martin Williams - Minneapolis, MN **Creative Team:** Tom Moudry - Chief Creative Officer; Jim Henderson - Group Creative Director; Lyle Wedemeyer - Group Creative Director; Toby Balai - Art Director; Chris Gault - Copywriter; R. Jerome Ferraro – Photographer **Client:** Not For Sale **3 Creative Firm:** Copia Creative, Inc. - Santa Monica, CA **Client:** Cappuccine

Creative Firm: Mel Lim - San Diego, CA
Creative Team: Mel Lim - Artist; Cary Ocon - Curator; Bill Berkuta - Master Pressman; Brooks Ocon – Print and Color Master
Client: Aardvark Letterpress

A Tale Of Two Bunnies

Loteria, a Mexican game of chance, provided the inspiration for Aardvark Letterpress' Los Angeles Loteria Series I collection. Aardvark commissioned a variety of artists with strong ties to Los Angeles to create the first group (18 in a series of 54) of original, limited edition letterpress prints. San Diego designer Mel Lim pays homage to both bunnies by recreating their lives in her piece, "BUNNYZILLA! La Lucha de dos Monstruos (The Fight of Two Monsters)." In this particular piece, Lim tells the story of Lila, a bunny who journeys from the east to the City of Angels—"where buildings are big, land is big, food portions are big, and most of all, anyone can dream big and be big," says Lim—where she meets Biga, another bunny, with whom she clashes daily over cultural mores.

Keeping with the Loteria tradition, each card reinterprets a Mexican icon through the lens of the Los Angeles experience, with each artist invited to infuse his or her own style, number and title against the traditional format of the deck. "The singular vision depicted on the Aardvark Loteria cards reflects the diversity of Los Angeles and Angelinos," says Lim. "From drive-in-movie dreams to drive-by wakeup calls, they represent the spectacularly unique highs and lows of living in and loving Los Angeles." Lim says that the set, taken on the vintage Vandercook press, brings out the intensity of both bunny lives with every impression.

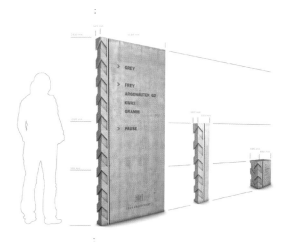

PLATINUM

Creative Firm: KW43 BRANDDESIGN - Dusseldorf, Germany

Creative Team: Christian Vöttiner - Creative Director; Astrid Schröder - Art Director; Marc Schäde – Art Director

Client: Grey Group

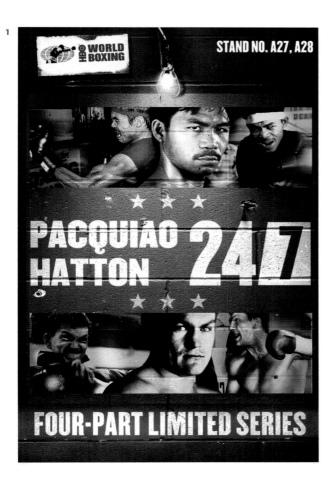

1 **Creative Firm:** HBO Off-Air Creative Services - New York, NY **Creative Team:** Venus Dennison - Creative Director; Christian Martillo - Art Director/Designer; Allan Wai - Design Manager **Client:** HBO Enterprises 2 **Creative Firm:** Launch Creative Marketing - Chicago, IL **Creative Team:** Sarah Wielusz – Associate Art Director **Client:** Sara Lee Corporation

1 Creative Firm: Mendes Publicidade - Sao Paulo, Brazil **Creative Team:** Oswaldo Mendes - Creativity Director; Maria Alice Penna – Art Director **Client:** Governo do Pará

 **PLATINUM**

Creative Firm: EP&M International - Albany, NY

Creative Team: Tiffeny Cantu - Project Manager; Lily Wei – Lead Designer

Client: GE Energy

General Electric Goes Green

Wind power is hot, and the annual Wind-power Conference & Exhibition has quickly grown into the premier international event for every facet of the wind industry. GE Energy required an exhibit design that not only showcased its wind turbine technology, but also extended its commitment to its ecomagination initiative, aimed at helping solve the world's biggest environmental challenges through research and development. With high conference traffic in mind, Albany's Exhibit Planning & Management International (EP&M) designed an open environment with a combination of seating arrangements, and installed several kiosks with plasma screens to provide visitors with interesting project and product

content. Most notably, EP&M created a demo area adapted an actual wind turbine nacelle to illustrate the integration of GE engineering and its initiatives. To bring the focus back to the environment, colored lighting washed throughout the booth, along with graphics featuring flowers swaying in the wind.

Says EP&M project coordinator Deb Flack: "It's important that the design choices we make lead to deeper conversations and a greater understanding of GE Energy's products, technical expertise and commitment to smarter and more efficient use of the world's energy resources."

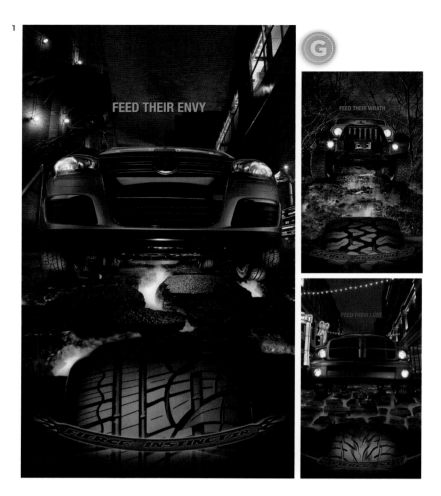

FEED THEIR ENVY

FEED THEIR WRATH

FEED THEIR LUST

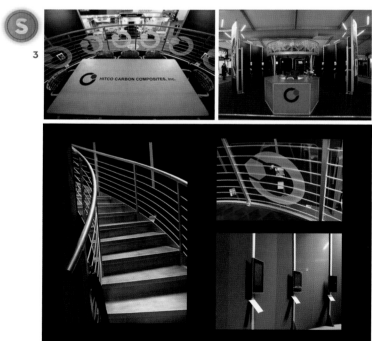

1 Creative Firm: Hitchcock Fleming & Associates Inc. - Akron, OH **Creative Team:** Nick Betro - Executive Creative Director; Patrick Ginnetti - Art Director; Tony Fanizzi - Writer; Mike Campana - Account Executive; Ted Paynter – Account Executive **Client:** Kelly Tires **2 Creative Firm:** EP&M International - Albany, NY **Creative Team:** Gene Lindman - Project Manager; Lily Wei – Lead Designer **Client:** GE Energy **3 Creative Firm:** Advanced Exhibit Methods - Irvine, CA **Client:** Hitco Carbon Composites, Inc. **URL:** www.advancedexhibitmethods.com

1 **Creative Firm:** Advanced Exhibit Methods - Irvine, CA **Client:** Tamalli 2 **Creative Firm:** LUON - Overijse, Belgium **Creative Team:** Onno Hesselink - Creative Director; Chris Dexters - Copywriter; Koen De Vos - Co-Creative Director; Sophie De Smedt - Account; Marjan Kegels – Account **Client:** Eurostation 3 **Creative Firm:** EP&M International - Albany, NY **Creative Team:** Tiffeny Cantu - Project Manager; Lily Wei – Lead Designer **Client:** GE Energy

1

2

3

1 Creative Firm: Goble & Associates - Chicago, IL **Creative Team:** Amy Gavlik - VP/Account Supervisor; Jamie Goade - Account Supervisor; Tony DiOrio - Creative Director; Patrick Tucker - Creative Director/Copy; Theresa Spatt - Senior Account Manager; Dave Raube – EVP/Creative Director **Client:** Phadia **2 Creative Firm:** Copia Creative, Inc. - Santa Monica, CA **Creative Team:** Artisan Cocoa, Inc. **3 Creative Firm:** EP&M International - Albany, NY **Creative Team:** Gene Lindman - Designer; Linda O'Connor – Project Manager **Client:** Angio Dynamics

144

We have simulated McDrive on bus windows.

 **PLATINUM**

Creative Firm: Futura DDB d.o.o. - Ljubljana, Slovenia

Creative Team: Bostjan Napotnik - Creative Director; Uros Strazisar - Graphic Designer/ Art Director; Jure Korenc – Photographer

Client: McDonalds Slovenia

1 Creative Firm: Mani & Company - New York, NY **Creative Team:** Dino Manaci - Art Director; Chris Bartick – Designer **Client:** Spawoof **2 Creative Firm:** Futura DDB d.o.o. - Ljubljana, Slovenia **Creative Team:** Bostjan Napotnik - Creative Director; Uros Strazisar - Art Director/Graphic Designer **Client:** Ljubljanske mlekarne **3 Creative Firm:** Draftfcb Chicago - Chicago, IL **Creative Team:** Rob Sherlock - EVP/Chief Creative Officer; Mary Knight - SVP/Group Creative Director; Chris Kloet - VP/Associate Creative Director; Rob White - VP/Associate Creative Director; Laurie Rubin - Photographer; Jennifer Rowland – EVP/Group Management Director **Client:** Kraft Foods/Stove Top Stuffing
4 Creative Firm: Hitchcock Fleming & Associates Inc. - Akron, OH **Creative Team:** Nick Betro - Executive Creative Director; Patrick Ginnetti - Art Director; Mark Collins - Creative Director; Tony Fanizzi - Writer; Jeff Stager - Computer Graphics Specialist/Artist; Jason Nicolacakis – Account Executive **Client:** Icynene **5 Creative Firm:** Draftfcb Chicago - Chicago, IL **Creative Team:** Rob Sherlock - EVP/Chief Creative Officer; Chuck Rudnick - EVP/Group Creative Director; Tony Sharpe - SVP/Creative Director; Greg Auer – VP/Associate Creative Director **Client:** SCJ/Windex

1

2

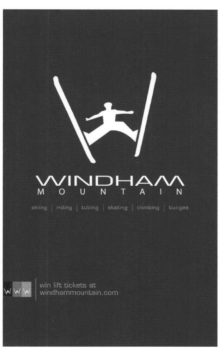

1 Creative Firm: Creative Alliance - Louisville, KY **Creative Team:** Mark Rosenthal - AD/CD; Scott Boswell – Copywriter/CD **Client:** Kentucky Humane Society
2 Creative Firm: Wanderlust **Creative Team:** Mark Shipley - President/Chief Strategic Officer; Sara Tack - EVP Image & Identity; Alan Beberwyck - Copywriter; Patrick Reilly - EVP Planning & Research; Lynn White - Production Manager; Chris Havens – Graphic Artist **Client:** Windham Mountain

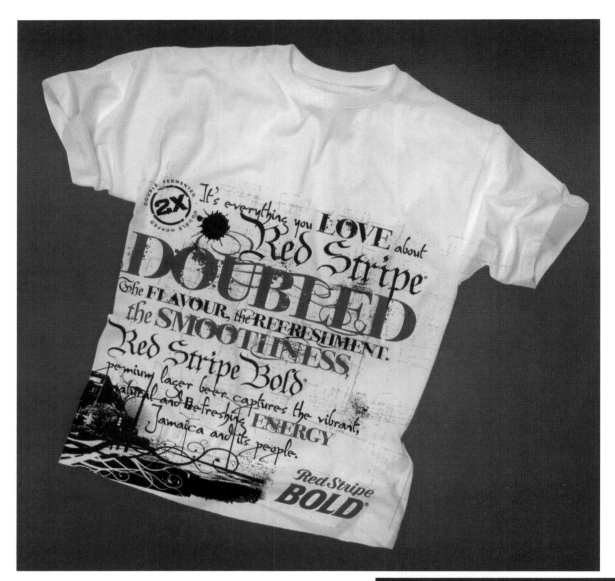

 **PLATINUM**

Creative Firm: Object 9 - Baton Rouge, LA
Client: Diageo

1 **Creative Firm:** Creative Alliance - Louisville, KY **Creative Team:** Mark Rosenthal - AD/CD; Trace Conn - Senior Copywriter; Andy Vucinich – ECD **Client:** Kentucky Humane Society 2 **Creative Firm:** Creative Alliance - Louisville, KY **Creative Team:** Mark Rosenthal - AD/CD; Trace Conn - Senior Copywriter; Andy Vucinich – ECD **Client:** Kentucky Humane Society 3 **Creative Firm:** Creative Alliance - Louisville, KY **Creative Team:** Mark Rosenthal - AD/CD; Trace Conn - Senior Copywriter; Andy Vucinich – ECD **Client:** Kentucky Humane Society 4 **Creative Firm:** Inglefield, Ogilvy & Mather Caribbean Ltd. - Port of Spain, Trinidad & Tobago **Creative Team:** David Gomez - Executive Creative Director; Paula Obe - Senior Copywriter; Tricia Dukhie - Graphic Artist; Shane Lue Choy - Senior Account Executive **Client:** Caribbean Airlines 5 **Creative Firm:** Airtype Studio - Winston-Salem, NC **Creative Team:** Bryan Ledbetter – Creative Director/Designer **Client:** Sixthman Productions 6 **Creative Firm:** Airtype Studio - Winston-Salem, NC **Creative Team:** Bryan Ledbetter – Creative Director/Designer **Client:** Jr Motorsports

1

1 Creative Firm: Gee + Chung Design - San Francisco, CA **Creative Team:** Earl Gee - Creative Director/Designer/Illustrator **Client:** Off-Site Records Management

packaging

 **PLATINUM**

Creative Firm: Launch Creative Marketing - Chicago, IL

Creative Team: Michelle Morales – Creative Director; Erin Pearson – Associate Creative Director

Client: ConAgra Foods

Sweet Display

The salty snack industry is a competitive $8 billion field, and Alexa Crunchy Snacks wanted to get a bite of it. They hired Chicago's Launch Creative Marketing to help distinguish the brand as a truly original, premium snack unlike anything else on the market. Launch sought to convey four objectives: strong visibility, superior taste and quality, awareness of Alexa's use of real vegetables and brand equities such as its commitment to keeping its products 100% natural.

"There's meaning behind each element of our design," the agency says. "The header emerging from the display was [designed] to instantly attract attention. It is static, yet bursts out at the same time, immediately

setting itself apart from other traditional, 'boxy' displays." The 360-degree shopping experience attracts shoppers with appetizing product visuals against a clean white display that itself mimics a bag of Alexa snacks—and is just as easy to open: "Our biggest challenge was to create a unique design with maximum impact and simple setup," Launch says. "We accomplished this by engineering the header to pop open in a simple motion."

1 Creative Firm: Launch Creative Marketing - Chicago, IL **Creative Team:** Michelle Morales – Creative Director **Client:** ConAgra Foods **2 Creative Firm:** Object 9 - Baton Rouge, LA **Client:** Winebow **3 Creative Firm:** Hitchcock Fleming & Associates Inc. - Akron, OH **Creative Team:** Nick Betro – Executive Creative Director; Todd Moser – Art Director; Tony Fanizzi – Writer **Client:** Goodyear Tire & Rubber Co. **4 Creative Firm:** Baily Brand Consulting - Plymouth Meeting, PA **Creative Team:** Dave Fiedler – Creative Director; Gary LaCroix – Group Design Director **Client:** Welch's **5 Creative Firm:** Grain Creative Consultants - Surry Hills, Australia **Creative Team:** Rikki Avenaim – Designer; Jure Leko – Creative Director **Client:** Mighty Soft

PLATINUM

Creative Firm: Wallace Church, Inc. - New York, NY

Creative Team: Stan Church - Creative Director; Marjorie Wood-Guthrie – Art Director (for Dell); Tom Davidson – Design Director (for Wallace Church)/Designer

Client: Dell

Dell's Experience Design Group partnered with Wallace Church to launch its greenest consumer desktop PC—the Dell Studio Hybrid.

Just like the actual product itself, Dell designed the Studio Hybrid packaging from scratch with the goals of sustainability, simplicity, and the complete customer experience in mind.

In its entirety, Dell's designers created Studio Hybrid's packaging to be curbside recyclable and made from 95% recyclable materials. The cushions, which are traditionally made from polystyrene, were replaced with HDPE cushions made from 100% recycled consumer plastic containers. To provide the best customer experience the packaging also includes logically organized contents as well as a convenient easy-to-open and carry handle.

To further reinforce Studio Hybrid's green story, Wallace Church created an organic, free-flowing graphic that

interacts with the product photo to emphasize both the product's stylish and environmental benefits. The lower case "Studio Hybrid" logotype also reinforces the trendy, youthful aspects of the product.

Working with Dell's "Think, Choose, Change" messaging, Wallace Church developed eye-catching icons that help to inspire and influence the consumer's mindset.

Together, Dell and Wallace Church created the perfect package – a fresh structural and graphic design that reinforces Studio Hybrid's environmentally friendly message, has strong shelf impact and engages consumers on many levels.

1

1 Creative Firm: Brand Engine - Sausalito, CA **Creative Team:** Will Burke – Art Director; Bob Hullinger – Designer; Meegan Peery – Designer; Meghan Zodrow – Designer; Bill Kerr – Designer **Client:** Hewlett-Packard

 **PLATINUM**

Creative Firm: Hornall Anderson Design Works - Seattle, WA

Creative Team: Jack Anderson – Creative Director; Andrew Wicklund – Art Director; Jay Hilburn – Designer; Peter Anderson – Designer; Kathleen Kennelly Ullman – Designer; Pamela Farrington – Designer

Client: Coffee Bean & Tea Leaf

Reheating This Cup O' Joe

How do you rebrand a popular coffee and tea retailer that's had a loyal customer following since 1963? This was the challenge Hornall Anderson faced when approached by The Coffee Bean & Tea Leaf to breathe new life into their existing brand and retail experience. The company wanted a rebranding which would in turn steer their business objective to fundamentally drive more sales, enlist an easier rollout package to the new stores and assist with streamlining new store development.

To this end, the Seattle agency "sought to establish clearer way-finding and visual hierarchy within the prototype store"—including simplifying menu boards, leveraging the major point of differentiation and building a brand experience to match the product. The agency worked with architects to optimize the function of the shopping experience, and the design process focused on how to bring the identity to life, exemplified by design and the creation of flavor indicators among the lines of coffee and tea packaging. "Through blending the concept of 'mixing of flavors' with 'handcrafted,' we created a design resolution that incorporates an 'aha!' factor through the discovered view of gazing down into a coffee cup and seeing the steam pattern forming a C and a T," the agency explains. "By focusing on flavor and the art of the beverage, rather than the commodity of the leaf and bean, we successfully elevated the client's brand to reflect 'the good life'—something its customers continue to experience with each visit."

 **PLATINUM**

Creative Firm: Hornall Anderson Design Works - Seattle, WA

Creative Team: Jack Anderson - Creative Director; David Bates - Designer Director; Javas Lehn - Designer; Kathleen Kennelly Ullman - Designer; David Phillips - Designer; Laura Jakobsen – Strategy Director

Client: Starbucks

Via - A Venti Success

Starbucks' signature line, "Never be without great coffee," took on a new meaning when the coffee giant launched VIA, their innovative and category-breaking ready-brew product. Seattle agency Hornall Anderson, which had worked with Starbucks in the past, once again partnered with them to differentiate VIA from the "instant coffee" category with a solid brand strategy, product identity and package design.

Starting with the design, Hornall Anderson sought to immerse consumers in an international-inspired experience. "Since this ready-brew coffee promises to be rich in flavor with a bold Italian and medium Colombian roast, we wanted the packaging colors and imagery (suggesting ideal places to enjoy your brew) to reflect the same evocative flavor of the warm, regional colors of Italy and Colombia," the agency reports. They also offered a variety of "discovered elements," from the mini-manifesto conveying the VIA story tucked inside the packaging, to the personal message from Howard Schultz on the package's inside flap expressing his mission to ensure consumers will "never be without great coffee."

PLATINUM

Creative Firm: Optima Soulsight - Highland Park, IL
Creative Team: Carol Grabowski-Davis – Designer
Client: Lake Champlain Chocolates

Establishing a Premium Organic Visual Language

Inspired by the steady growth of the organic food market, Lake Champlain Chocolates embarked on another exciting project—the introduction of Organic Chocolate Bars & Squares. There was a huge opportunity to strengthen and refresh its organic image to better highlight the award-winning, delectable, delicious product offerings. Tantalizing the senses with a diverse blend of exotic flavors and chocolates, each chocolate is crafted from the purest ingredients grown with the strictest organic standards—ideal for both adventure seekers and those pursuing organic alternatives with no loss of flavor or experience. The Organic line needed to clearly express the company's spirit and passion for premium, small batch, and all-natural chocolates.

To consumers, Vermont represents a more natural, 'organic' region, presenting Lake Champlain Organics with a distinct advantage and positive consumer perception. To highlight Organic's natural, pure personality, Soulsight designed a look that was clean and minimal. A color palette evocative of the rest of the Lake Champlain family gave the Organic line a unified look. The visual identity was based on simple, graphic illustrations and a hand-crafted brandmark. Knowing that Organic's "adventurous connoisseur" target would appreciate any and all ingredient information, Soulsight highlighted the flavors and cocoa content in bold color.

Soulsight sourced earth-friendly packaging, including organic recycled paper from a supplier using 100% renewable energy.

1 **Creative Firm:** Haugaard Creative Group - Chicago, IL **Creative Team:** Robert Pearson – Senior Designer; Edward Griffin – Illustrator **Client:** Chicago Custom Foods 2 **Creative Firm:** Haugaard Creative Group - Chicago, IL **Creative Team:** Robert Pearson – Senior Designer; Edward Griffin – Illustrator **Client:** Quaker Oats 3 **Creative Firm:** Miya Graphix - Tokyo, Japan **Creative Team:** Manabu Miya – Art Direction & Design **Client:** LOTTE Co., Ltd. 4 **Creative Firm:** Hornall Anderson Design Works - Seattle, WA **Creative Team:** Elmer dela Cruz - Design Director; Yuri Shvets - Designer; Jay Hilburn - Illustrator; Lorna Harrington – Account Manager **Client:** Widmer Brothers

1

2

3

1 Creative Firm: Hornall Anderson Design Works - Seattle, WA **Creative Team:** Mary Hermes – Creative Director; Yuri Shevts – Designer; Kathleen Kennelly Ullman – Designer; Jin Kwon – Designer; Holly Craven – Designer; Judy Dixon – Production Director **Client:** Frito–Lay **2 Creative Firm:** Surveillance - Rushcutter's Bay, Australia **Creative Team:** James Armstrong – Creative Director **Client:** A Bottle Of **3 Creative Firm:** Hornall Anderson Design Works - Seattle, WA **Creative Team:** Jack Anderson – Art Director; Bruce Stigler - Art Director; Bruce Branson Myer - Designer; Elmer dela Cruz - Designer; Vu Nguyen – Designer; Julie Valdez – Production Designer **Client:** Redhook Brewery

1

2

3

---

1 Creative Firm: Hornall Anderson Design Works - Seattle, WA **Creative Team:** Mary Hermes - Creative Director; Belinda Bowling - Designer; Elmer dela Cruz - Designer; Tiffany Place - Designer; Beckon Wyld - Production Designer; Laura Jakobsen – Strategy Director **Client:** Millennium Products **2 Creative Firm:** Design Resource Center - Naperville, IL **Creative Team:** Don Dzielinski - Creative Director; John Norman - Art Director; Traci Milner – Designer **Client:** Sol Elixirs LLC **3 Creative Firm:** Hornall Anderson Design Works - Seattle, WA **Creative Team:** Bruce Stigler - Creative Director; Bruce Branson Meyer - Creative Director; Andrew Well - Designer; Peg Johnson - Production Designer; Jonas Land – Production Designer **Client:** Redhook

1 **Creative Firm:** Flowdesign Inc. - Northville, MI **Creative Team:** Dan Matauch - Creative Director; Dennis Nalezyty – Graphic Designer **Client:** Stubb's Legendary Kitchen
2 **Creative Firm:** biz-R - Totnes, United Kingdom **Creative Team:** Blair Thomson - Art Director/Designer; Clive Tagg - Photography; Tish England - Copywriter; Paul Warren – Copywriter **Client:** Langage Farm 3 **Creative Firm:** Flowdesign Inc. - Northville, MI **Creative Team:** Dan Matauch - Creative Director; Allison Graw – Graphic Designer **Client:** Synaura International 4 **Creative Firm:** Little Big Brands - Nyack, NY **Creative Team:** John Nunziato - Creative Director; Little Big Design Team; Phil Foster - Illustrator **Client:** The Lion Brewery

1 **Creative Firm:** Cornerstone Strategic Branding - New York, NY **Client:** Nestle USA, Inc. **2 Creative Firm:** Cornerstone Strategic Branding - New York, NY **Client:** Coca-Cola North America **3 Creative Firm:** Cornerstone Strategic Branding - New York, NY **Client:** International Food Company **4 Creative Firm:** Cornerstone Strategic Branding - New York, NY **Client:** Cerveceria Cuauhtemoc Moctezuma **5 Creative Firm:** CBX - New York, NY **Client:** Swedish Match **URL:** www.cbx.com

1

3

2

4

5

1 **Creative Firm:** Cornerstone Strategic Branding - New York, NY **Client:** Nestle Waters North America 2 **Creative Firm:** Cornerstone Strategic Branding - New York, NY **Client:** Nestle USA, Inc. 3 **Creative Firm:** Cornerstone Strategic Branding - New York, NY **Client:** Coca-Cola North America 4 **Creative Firm:** Zunda Group, LLC - South Norwalk, CT **Creative Team:** Charles Zunda – Creative Director/Principal **Client:** Atticus Bakery 5 **Creative Firm:** Zunda Group, LLC - South Norwalk, CT **Creative Team:** Charles Zunda – Creative Director/Principal **Client:** Chabaso Bakery

1

2

3

1 **Creative Firm:** Cornerstone Strategic Branding - New York, NY **Client:** Cerveceria Cuauhtemoc Moctezuma 2 **Creative Firm:** Zeeland Oy - Helsinki, Finland
Creative Team: Roy Gonzalez - Art Director; Totti Toiskallio - Copywriter; Riina Pyöttiö - Project Manager; Juuso Enala - Planner **Client:** River Café Oy
3 **Creative Firm:** Brand Engine - Sausalito, CA **Creative Team:** Bob Hullinger - Art Director; Meghan Zodrow - Designer; Kenn Lewis – Designer **Client:** Plum Organics

1

2

3

1 Creative Firm: Brand Engine - Sausalito, CA **Creative Team:** Bob Hullinger - Art Director; Meegan Peery - Designer; Bill Kerr - Designer; Geoff Nilsen – Photographer **Client:** Little Bug **2 Creative Firm:** Object 9 - Baton Rouge, LA **Client:** Reily Foods **3 Creative Firm:** Optima Soulsight - Highland Park, IL **Creative Team:** Adam Ferguson - Creative Director; Justin Berglund - Designer; Erin Paul – Account Director **Client:** MillerCoors

1

The specific features of labels for Jezeršek alcoholic beverages are photos of food which best suit the drinks.

2

3

4

1 Creative Firm: Futura DDB d.o.o. - Ljubljana, Slovenia **Creative Team:** Zare Kerin - Creative Director; Andraz Filac - Art Director; Ana Por – Account Manager **Client:** Jezersek **2 Creative Firm:** Optima Soulsight/Sponge - Highland Park, IL **Creative Team:** James Pietruszynski – Creative Director **Client:** Cracker Barrel Old Country Store **3 Creative Firm:** Baily Brand Consulting - Plymouth Meeting, PA **Creative Team:** Dave Fiedler - Creative Director; Gary LaCroix – Group Design Director; Christian Williamson – Senior Designer **Client:** Twinings USA **4 Creative Firm:** CBX - New York, NY **Client:** Del Monte **URL:** www.cbx.com

1

2

3

4

5

1 Creative Firm: Launch Creative Marketing - Chicago, IL **Creative Team:** Liz Schwartz – Associate Creative Director **Client:** Sara Lee Corporation **2 Creative Firm:** Launch Creative Marketing - Chicago, IL **Creative Team:** David Lind - Creative Director; Romina Kuppe – Senior Art Director **Client:** Sara Lee Corporation **3 Creative Firm:** Copia Creative, Inc. - Santa Monica, CA **Client:** Artisan Cocoa, Inc. **4 Creative Firm:** CBX - New York, NY **Client:** Dr. Pepper Snapple Group **URL:** www.cbx.com **5 Creative Firm:** Shikatani Lacroix Design - Toronto, ON, Canada **Creative Team:** Kim Yokota - Art Director/Designer; Mark Willard - Photographer; Susan Jennings – Senior Production Artist **Client:** Tetley Canada

PLATINUM

Creative Firm: Acosta Design Inc. - New York, NY
Creative Team: Mauricio Acosta – Art Director;
Katarina Sjoholm – Creative Director;
John Dionaldo – Designer
Client: Jurlique

Earth Friendly Product & Packaging

The gift market is tough, but never as competitive as it is during the holiday gift-giving season. Skincare products brand Jurlique asked New York's Acosta Design to create a colorful holiday line as a departure from its traditional white packaging and also to reflect the "organic life force" of its plant-based products while also adhering to strict environmental requirements. Inspired by Jurlique's lavender, rose and tangerine ingredients sourced from a biodynamic farm in southern Australia, "we incorporated images and textures of the plant-based ingredients to create a rich, deeply colored painting-like effect, with each box set having its own vibrant color," the agency says. The producers then worked with a sustainable printing company to ensure the packaging was made according to certified sustainable forestry methods, with all recycled and recyclable materials, soy ink and 100% wind power. Acosta's elegant design and Jurlique's good scents combined to create, in the end, an effective and environmentally friendly gift.

1

2

4

3

1 Creative Firm: Wallace Church, Inc. - New York, NY **Creative Team:** Stan Church - Creative Director; Becca Reiter – Designer/Director of Photography **Client:** Alberto Culver **2 Creative Firm:** Design Resource Center - Naperville, IL **Creative Team:** Don Dzielinski - Creative Director; John Norman - Art Director; Traci Milner – Designer **Client:** Wahl Clipper Corporation **3 Creative Firm:** Little Big Brands - Nyack, NY **Creative Team:** John Nunziato - Creative Director; Little Big Design Team; Stephen Shirak - Illustrator **Client:** Lornamead, Inc. **4 Creative Firm:** Zunda Group, LLC - South Norwalk, CT **Creative Team:** Charles Zunda - Principal/Creative Director; Dan Price – Senior Designer **Client:** Unilever Home and Personal Care

1 Creative Firm: Storm Corporate Design - Auckland, New Zealand **Creative Team:** Rehan Saiyed - Designer/Design Director/Typographer/Art Director/Illustrator; Evan Matthews – Creative Director **Client:** Horleys, Auckland, New Zealand **2 Creative Firm:** CBX - New York, NY **Client:** Schering Plough **URL:** www.cbx.com **3 Creative Firm:** Shikatani Lacroix Design - Toronto, ON, Canada **Creative Team:** Christopher Woo - Graphic Designer; Mark Willard – Photographer **Client:** Purity Life **4 Creative Firm:** Shikatani Lacroix Design - Toronto, ON, Canada **Creative Team:** Kim Yokota - Creative Director/Designer; Mark Willard – Photographer **Client:** Purity Life

 **PLATINUM**

Creative Firm: Brand Engine - Sausalito, CA
Creative Team: Bob Hullinger - Art Director; Meegan Peery - Designer; Bob Hullinger – Designer
Client: Clorox

Clean Design

In the era of swine flu and personal products for fighting germs, disinfecting wipes have emerged from under the counter to the top of everyone's office desk and kitchen counter. Clorox—a name synonymous with bleach and cleanliness—asked Sausalito branding firm Brand Engine to design the exterior for their new oval format disinfecting wipes dispenser. As the first visual translation of Brand Engine's renewed brand strategy for Clorox, "The goal was to create beautiful designs that stayed true to the Clorox brand while resonating with Clorox's predominantly female consumer and encouraging them to leave the

Clorox Disinfecting Wipes out on their countertops, increasing wipes usage," says Brand Engine. By taking a successful product and elevating its presentation to appeal to growing consumer demand for off-the-shelf style, Brand Engine managed to preserve the integrity of the original product—all while bringing forth an attractive and up-to-date look to the traditional blue-and-white Clorox brand.

1

2

3

1 Creative Firm: Rosslyn Snitrak Design - Seattle, WA **Creative Team:** Rosslyn Snitrak – Graphic Designer **Client:** Rosy Rings **2 Creative Firm:** Rosslyn Snitrak Design - Seattle, WA **Creative Team:** Rosslyn Snitrak – Graphic Designer **Client:** Rosy Rings **3 Creative Firm:** Rosslyn Snitrak Design - Seattle, WA **Creative Team:** Rosslyn Snitrak – Graphic Designer **Client:** Rosy Rings

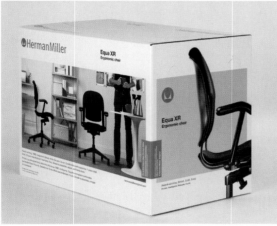

1 Creative Firm: People Design Inc - Grand Rapids, MI **Creative Team:** Michele Brautnick - Design Director; Yang Kim - Creative Director; Kevin Budelmann - Creative Director; Adam Rice - Designer; Curt Wozniak – Writer **Client:** Herman Miller **2 Creative Firm:** Grain Creative Consultants - Surry Hills, Australia **Creative Team:** Jure Leko - Creative Director; Jane Skamp - Senior Designer; Jeremy Tombs – Senior Designer/Illustrator **Client:** Ambi Pur Australia

1

the ROLLERS

SOUTHERN SOUL
Head south with Cabo Wabo Blanco
Tequila, Cointreau Orange Liqueur,
Monin Habañero Lime, Finest Call
Lime Sour and fresh lime

FLIRTARITA
Sauza Conmemorativo Tequila is
shaken with fresh strawberries,
blueberries and raspberries and
Monin Blood Orange to create a
decadent margarita

S&M MARGARITA
This rita combines Hornitos Plata
Tequila, Midori Melon Liqueur and
guava nectar to tease your palate

the ROCKERS

BLACK MAGIC WOMAN
She'll put a spell on you with Effen
Black Cherry Vodka over muddled
fresh basil, thyme, lime, brown sugar,
raspberries and blueberries topped
with soda

THE CZAR
Our upgraded Bloody Mary combines
SKYY Vodka, Garlic Tabasco Sauce,
beet horseradish, Clamato, cucumber
and fresh lemon

MUSICAL MOJO
Deliciously rhythmic, BACARDI Limon
Rum mixes with muddled fresh lime,
mint and brown sugar and topped
with soda

the FRUIT

STRAWBERRY SOUL
Let it speak to you ...
Leblon Cachaca mixed with fresh
muddled strawberries, basil, lime
and brown sugar

**LYCHEE
GRAPEFRUIT MARTINI**
East meets west with our blend of
Ketel One Citroen Vodka, Svedka
Vodka, Soho Lychee Liqueur, Ruby
Red grapefruit juice and ginger ale

STRAWBERRY COSMO
A new twist, Grey Goose Vodka
and Cointreau Orange Liqueur
over muddled fresh strawberries
and brown sugar topped with
cranberry juice

PLATINUM

Creative Firm: Patrick Henry Creative Promotions, Inc.
- Stafford, TX

Creative Team: Holly McAllister - Art Director; Smith
Photography – Photographer

Client: House of Blues

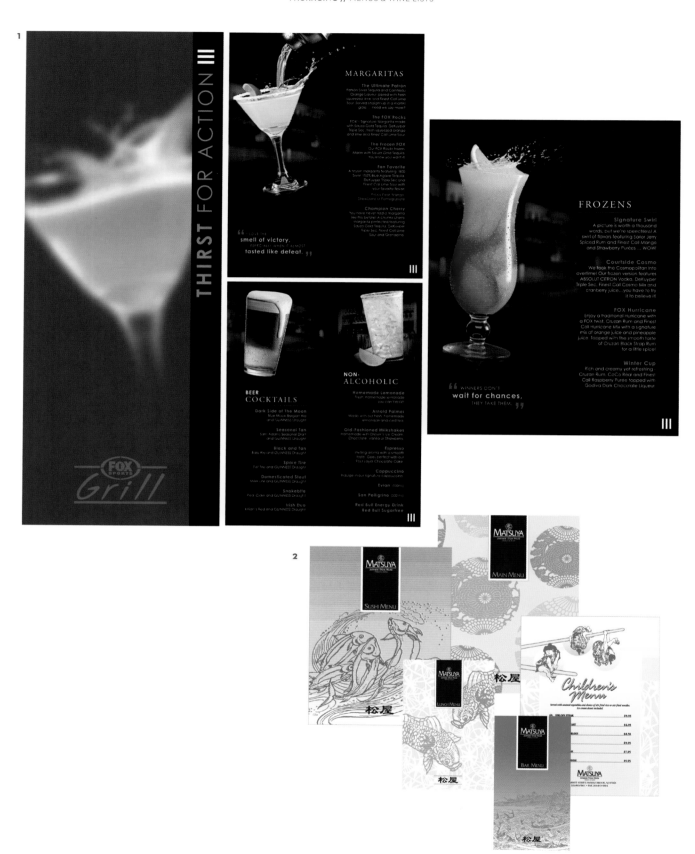

1 Creative Firm: Patrick Henry Creative Promotions, Inc. - Stafford, TX **Creative Team:** Kaye Breaux - Account Executive; Holly McAllister - Art Director; Smith Photography – Photography **Client:** FOX Sports Grill **2 Creative Firm:** Stephen Longo Design Associates - West Orange, NJ **Creative Team:** Stephen Longo - Art Director **Client:** Matsuya Restaurant

 **PLATINUM**

Creative Firm: Signature Ltd - Hong Kong
Creative Team: Joseph Lui – Creative Director
Client: Levi's

The Original 501

In 2008, Levi Strauss & Co. launched the global release of its iconic Levi's Original 501® jean with a campaign as evocative as the brand's storied history with the theme, "Live Unbuttoned"—defined by Hong Kong design firm Signature Ltd. as "to be completely yourself, unrestrained and unembarrassed... It's about freedom and expressing yourself."

To achieve maximum impact for the launch, Signature integrated the "unbuttoned" image with the die-cut shape for a limited edition outer box. "The use of a wooden box as inner packaging [was] kept traditional to preserve the rich heritage and authenticity of the 501® jean," the agency says. "We had to project the brand's commitment to quality and authenticity."

1 **Creative Firm:** yellobee studio - Atlanta, GA **Creative Team:** Alison Scheel - Creative Director; Jeff Walton – Graphic Designer **Client:** Timberland Investment Resources 2 **Creative Firm:** Grain Creative Consultants - Surry Hills, Australia **Creative Team:** Jure Leko - Creative Director; Steven Popovic – Designer/Photoshop rendering **Client:** Wyndham Estate 3 **Creative Firm:** MediaConcepts Corporation - Assonet, MA **Creative Team:** Greg Dobos - Creative Director/Art Director; Mary Kate Marchard - Illustrator **Client:** Ocean Spray 4 **Creative Firm:** MediaConcepts Corporation - Assonet, MA **Creative Team:** Greg Dobos - Creative Director/Art Director; Chuck Medeiros - Illustrator **Client:** Ocean Spray

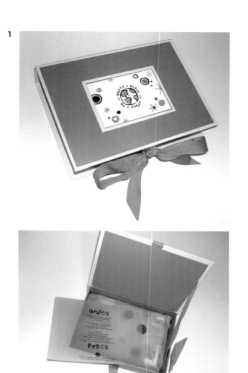

1 **Creative Firm:** Design Nut - Kensington, MD **Creative Team:** Brent Almond – Designer/Illustrator **Client:** Design Nut 2 **Creative Firm:** NBC Universal Global Networks Italia SRL - Rome, Italy **Creative Team:** Maria Theresia Braun – Marketing Director **Client:** NBC Universal Global Networks Italia 3 **Creative Firm:** MediaConcepts Corporation - Assonet, MA **Creative Team:** Greg Dobos - Creative Director/Art Director; Chuck Medeiros – Illustrator **Client:** Ocean Spray 4 **Creative Firm:** TypographicSpell - Istanbul, Turkey **Creative Team:** Didem Carikci Wong - Graphic Designer/Art Director **Client:** Didem Carikci

1 Creative Firm: Finished Art Inc. - Atlanta, GA **Creative Team:** Li Kim Goh - Art Director/Designer; MJ Hasek Hasek - Illustrator **Client:** Finished Art Inc. **2 Creative Firm:** Wallace Church, Inc. - New York, NY **Creative Team:** Stan Church - Creative Director; Kevin Sams - Art Director; Chris Cook - Designer; Tiphaine Guillemet - Designer; Rich Rickaby – Project Manager **Client:** Wallace Church, Inc **3 Creative Firm:** Finished Art Inc. - Atlanta, GA **Creative Team:** Donna Johnston - Creative Director; Dave Lawson - Designer **Client:** Finished Art Inc.

1

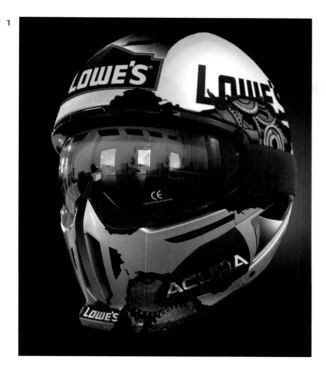

2

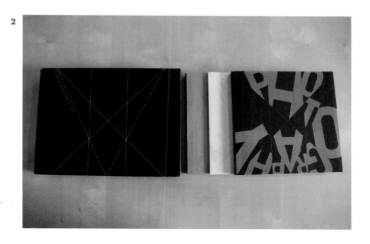

3

1 **Creative Firm:** SiMPLE DESIGN INC. - Kenosha, WI **Creative Team:** Robert Mitchell – Designer **Client:** Fernandez Racing LLC. 2 **Creative Firm:** Bernstein & Andriulli - New York, NY **Creative Team:** Groundwave Design - Designer; Pamela Esposito - Production Manager; Louisa St. Pierre; Glen Serbin **Client:** Bernstein & Andriulli **URL:** www.ba-reps.com 3 **Creative Firm:** Use creative communication - Hendrik Ido Ambacht, Netherlands **Creative Team:** Dennis Bodmer - Art Director; Henriëtte Bodmer – Designer **Client:** Moton Suspension Technology

P PLATINUM

Creative Firm: Optima Soulsight - Highland Park, IL
Creative Team: James Pietruszynski - Creative Director; Stephanie Crair – Designer
Client: FTD

Reinventing an Icon

Nearly 100 years after the company originated as the first drop ship floral company, FTD faced growing competition from new online retailers, losing its long-held leadership position. In order to again capture the imagination of consumers, FTD knew it needed to elevate its brand and create an ownable identity to reflect their "class for the masses" brand promise. In part, they needed a distinctive line of floral box packaging—their most emotional and visible touchpoint.

Soulsight created a brand identity and package design system centered around their globally recognized brand icon, the fleet-footed Mercury Man. We removed him from the constraints of the FTD logo and gave him a life of his own, making him bolder and more dynamic.

Drawing from FTD's strong black and gold equity, we put the emphasis on black—an unusual choice for a flower company—and created a striking backdrop for FTD's colorful floral arrangements.

Rather than using a traditional corrugated brown cardboard box to house the flowers, the beautiful shipper became an eye-catching advertisement— the ideal place to bring the brand icon to life. A proprietary floral pattern printed in metallic gold was incorporated on the inside of the box and the bouquet wrap. The box was lined with gold organza, and the Mercury Man made another appearance on the delicate gift cards and floral care booklet, creating a holistic premium experience.

1 Creative Firm: Aniden Interactive - Houston, TX **Creative Team:** Serena Lin Bush - Designer; Jeremy Shelton – Designer **Client:** Hewlett-Packard **2 Creative Firm:** Launch Creative Marketing - Chicago, IL **Creative Team:** David Lind - Creative Director; Liz Schwartz - Associate Creative Director; Romina Kuppe – Senior Art Director **Client:** Sanford Corporation

1 **Creative Firm:** The UXB - Beverly Hills, CA **Creative Team:** Glenn Sakamoto - Creative Director; NancyJane Goldston - Creative Director; Brittan Cortney – Creative Coordinator **Client:** Cleatskins **URL:** www.cleatskins.com 2 **Creative Firm:** Launch Creative Marketing - Chicago, IL **Creative Team:** David Lind - Creative Director; Monika Banaszak – Art Director **Client:** Sanford Corporation

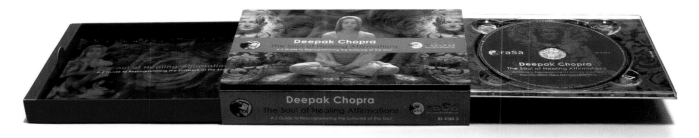

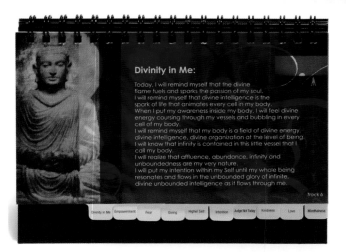

PLATINUM

Creative Firm: Leon Montana Graphic Design - Brooklyn, NY

Client: RASA music

187

1

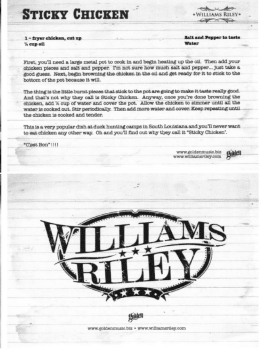

2

3

1 Creative Firm: Airtype Studio - Winston-Salem, NC **Creative Team:** Bryan Ledbetter – Creative Director/Designer **Client:** Golden Music **2 Creative Firm:** Intelligent Fish Studio - Woodbuy, MN **Creative Team:** Brian Danaher - Art Director/Designer/Illustrator **Client:** Clutter Bear Records **URL:** www.briandanaher.com **Creative Team:** Bryan Ledbetter – Creative Director/Designer **Client:** Golden Music **3 Creative Firm:** Higgins Design - Shoreline, WA **Creative Team:** Jane Higgins - Designer; Tim Foley – Illustrator **Client:** Raspberry Records/Paul Lippert

alternative
media

9

 **PLATINUM**

Creative Firm: Sapient Interactive - Palmetto Bay, FL
Creative Team: Anthony Yell – Vice President Creative; Casey Sheehan – Associate Creative Director; Jeremy Conescu – Manager Interactive Development; Mike Hansen – Senior Art Director; Graham Engebretsen – Manager Program Management; Michael Leonard – Director Program Management
Client: The Coca-Cola Company

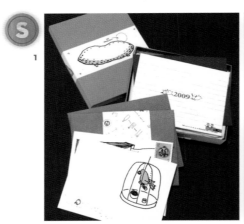

1 Creative Firm: FINE Design Group - San Francisco, CA **Creative Team:** Melissa Chan - Web Designer; Clare Barnes - Print Designer; Bon Kijkrailas - Print Designer; Kenn Fine - Art Director **Client:** FINE Design Group **URL:** www.finedesigngroup.com/share **2 Creative Firm:** Futura DDB d.o.o. - Ljubljana, Slovenia **Creative Team:** Petra Trontelj – Account Manager; Zoran Gabrijan – Creative Director; Saso Petek – Copywriter; Miha Grobler – Art Director; Blaž Topolinjak – Graphic Designer **Client:** Droga Kolinska

PLATINUM

Creative Firm: Dunn&Co. - Tampa, FL

Creative Team: Troy Dunn – Chief Creative Officer; Dan Stevenson – Creative Director; Alex Nieto – Art Director

Client: ALS Association of Florida

To Educate And Commemorate

Most people know that Lou Gehrig suffered from a disease subsequently named for him, but the actual process by which ALS robs its victims of their mobility and, ultimately, their lives is not as well known. Tampa-based advertising agency Dunn&Co. created a unique campaign for the Florida chapter of the ALS Association in order to create greater awareness and increase donations to the organization.

Speaking to ALS sufferers and their families about how the disease took the toll on the body—from gradual loss of mobility to complete paralysis and death—inspired creative director Dan Stevenson's team's resulting campaign, "Piece by Piece." "Our creative interpretation for the campaign, including ambient media element, utilized the metaphor of mannequin torsos without heads, legs or arms to show the dreaded effect ALS has on its victims," says Stevenson. "Mannequins were deemed creatively close enough to spark a real emotional connection, but distant enough from reality as not to portray another 'victim-of-that' type of campaign." The haunting and poignant memorial, which toured the state, featured hundreds of mannequin torsos, each shrouded in a T-shirt with an actual ALS victim's epitaph, name and birth and death dates. To further commemorate and memorialize a particular person, higher figure donors could purchase a shirt in honor of a loved one and his or her battle with ALS.

 **PLATINUM**

Creative Firm: Euro RSCG Chicago - Chicago, IL
Creative Team: Steffan Postaer - Chairman/Chief
Creative Officer; Blake Ebel - Executive Creative
Director; Amanda Butts/Elyse Maguire - Creative
Directors; Puja Shah/Ecole Weinstein - Art Director/
Copywriter; Julia Cunningham - Art Buyer;
Monica Wilkins - Agency Producer
Client: Valspar Paint

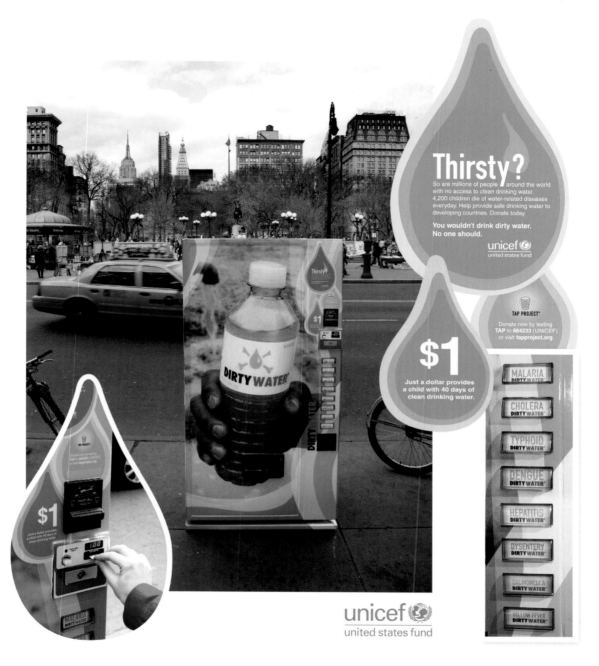

Thirsty?

So are millions of people around the world with no access to clean drinking water. 4,200 children die of water-related diseases everyday. Help provide safe drinking water to developing countries. Donate today.

You wouldn't drink dirty water. No one should.

unicef
united states fund

TAP PROJECT
Donate now by texting **TAP** to **864233** (UNICEF) or visit tapproject.org

$1
Just a dollar provides a child with 40 days of clean drinking water.

MALARIA DIRTY WATER
CHOLERA DIRTY WATER
TYPHOID DIRTY WATER
DENGUE DIRTY WATER
HEPATITIS DIRTY WATER
DYSENTERY DIRTY WATER
SALMONELLA DIRTY WATER
YELLOW FEVER DIRTY WATER

unicef
united states fund

PLATINUM

Creative Firm: Casanova Pendrill - New York, NY
Creative Team: Elias Weinstock - VP/Executive Creative Director; Alejandro Ortiz - Creative Director; Gil Arevalo - Copywriter/Art Director; Dámaso Crespo - Art Director/Copywriter; James Long – Editor; Keith Olwell – Post-production Supervisor
Client: UNICEF
URL: www.dirtywaterinfo.com

Can I Get You A Drink?

Clean water is something most everyone takes for granted and assumes is practically free. That's half true for much of the world, and in its campaign for UNICEF, New York agency Casanova Pendrill tried to find an interesting, groundbreaking way of making the desensitized New Yorker aware of the global water issue and motivate them to donate to bring clean water to children in need—all without a budget. "The client wanted us to convey that just $1 provides a child with 40 days of safe drinking water," the agency reports. With its skull-and-crossbones-inspired logo, the mock product of bottled "dirty water," the agency says, was an easy and direct way to brand this new lethal kind of bottled water, with varieties drawn from the commercial bottled water industry: "The names of each flavor/illness were selected from the most common and lethal waterborne diseases found in the developing countries lacking clean water."

1

We placed stickers with scratches on expensive cars in large cities and filmed reactions of car owners with a hidden camera. Then, we placed the video on YouTube and sent a link to marketing weblogs

We used guerrilla marketing tactics to build brand awareness for VrijVerzekerd, a Dutch online insurance company. We placed stickers with scratches on expensive cars. Stickers could be easily removed, because they were printed on Static Paper. This paper has no glue on it and sticks because it's charged with static electricity

The article on our guerrilla campaign was published by about 20 blogs, news sites an online communities in the Netherlands and Belgium, and drew attention of above 42.000 people. The daily traffic on the site tripled, and the time spent on the site increased by 20%. The campaign budget stayed under 1.000 euros

We invited blog readers to test the stickers on their friends (to share the fun and because we love co-creation). This is an example of co-creation: the sticker is placed on a Vespa scooter parked on the Amsterdam's main shopping street (Vespas are very popular in Amsterdam)

When you get closer to the car, you can read the sticker text:
"We repair your damages as easily as you remove this sticker.
Insure your car on VrijVerzekerd.nl and get a discount of 10-49%"

The video got above 7.000 views in the first 3 weeks and achieved #29 in the YouTube ranking for the Most viewed humor videos in Holland (7.000 means a lot of views for such a small country as Holland:-)

1 Creative Firm: Novocortex/Red Graphic - Woerden, Netherlands **Creative Team:** Serge Fenenko - Creative Director; Nadia Zelenkova - Creative Director; Ilya Andreyev - Copywriter; Irina Znosok – Art Director **Client:** VrijVerzekerd Insurances **URL:** novocortex.com/guerrilla_marketing/

1

SCI FI - ALIEN CRASH

Sci Fi is the unknown that surround us, the space dedicated to the imagination, where anything is possible. Superheroes, paranormal phenomena, trips into the future and the past, through programmes containing a mixture of mystery and adventure ranging from first showings of big series to cult classics.

To promote the Sci Fi branded block on Steel, we created a Guerrilla operation: a parked car crashed by an UFO engine.
In the meanwhile, actors wearing a sterile containment suit gave away flyers similar to the car accident report. The message was: Don't be afraid of alien collision! On Sci Fi, Close Encounters of the Third Kind are "insured".

1 **Creative Firm:** Endeavour Digital Marketing - Roncaglia **Creative Team:** Arnaldo Funaro - Creative Director/Copy; Ariberto Anastasi - Art Director **Client:** NBC Universal Global Networks Italia

1

1 Creative Firm: Draftfcb Chicago - Chicago, IL **Creative Team:** Rob Sherlock - EVP/Chief Creative Officer; Jon Flannery - SVP/Group Creative Director; Doug Behm - SVP/Group Creative Director; Kayu Tai - Junior Art Director; Brad Simpson - Interactive Associate/Creative Director; Kevin Willard – Copywriter **Client:** KFC National Council & Advertising Cooperative **URL:** itunes.apple.com/WebObjects/MZStore.woa/wa/viewSoftware?id=312591922&mt=8

CREATIVE CATEGORY

publications

9

 **PLATINUM**

Creative Firm: Futura DDB d.o.o. - Ljubljana, Slovenia

Creative Team: Zare Kerin – Creative Director; Barbara Ogric Markez – Graphic Designer; Tina Tomazevic – Account Manager

Client: Golden Drum Festival

1

2

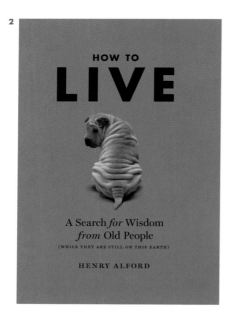

3

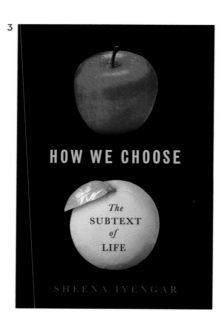

4

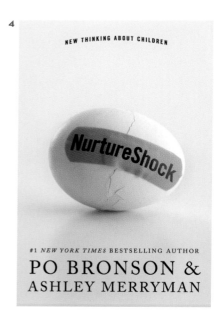

1 Creative Firm: Splash Productions Pte Ltd - Singapore **Creative Team:** Stanley Yap – Art Director; Brice Li – Art Director; Terry Lee – Copywriter **Client:** Singapore Civil Defence Force **URL:** www.scdf.gov.sg **2 Creative Firm:** Hachette Book Group - New York, NY **Creative Team:** Anne Twomey – Creative Director; Eric Baker – Design **Client:** Hachette Book Group/Twelve **3 Creative Firm:** Hachette Book Group - New York, NY **Creative Team:** Anne Twomey – Creative Director **Client:** Hachette Book Group/Twelve **4 Creative Firm:** Hachette Book Group - New York, NY **Creative Team:** Anne Twomey – Creative Director; Henry Sene Yee – Design; Veer, Inc – Cover Photo **Client:** Hachette Book Group

1

2

3
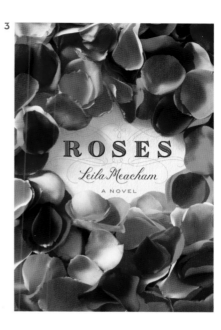

4

1 **Creative Firm:** Hachette Book Group - New York, NY **Creative Team:** Anne Twomey – Creative Director; Evan Gaffney – Design; Danny Clinch – Cover Photo; Jo Lopez – Back Cover Photo **Client:** Hachette Book Group 2 **Creative Firm:** Hachette Book Group - New York, NY **Creative Team:** Henry Sene Yee – Designer; Anne Twomey – Creative Director; Flag Tonuzi – Art Director; Steve Peterson/Zuma – Photographer **Client:** Hachette Book Group/Twelve 3 **Creative Firm:** Hachette Book Group - New York, NY **Creative Team:** Anne Twomey – Creative Director/Design; Elizabeth Watt – Cover Photo **Client:** Hachette Book Group 4 **Creative Firm:** Hachette Book Group - New York, NY **Creative Team:** Diane Luger – Creative Director; DesignWorks – Design **Client:** Hachette Book Group

1

2

3

1 Creative Firm: Crescent Hill Books and HV Anderson Design - Louisville, KY **Creative Team:** Hans Anderson – Principal **Client:** Rockport Publishers
2 Creative Firm: Dreamedia Studios - Little Rock, AR **Creative Team:** Kyle Holmes – Designer/Creative Director; Jack Melton – Photographer; Steven Walenta – Photographer **Client:** Gary Hendershott Museum Consultants **3 Creative Firm:** TF marketing d.o.o. - Zagreb, Croatia **Creative Team:** Suzana Kulas – Creative Director; Antica Arsov – Art Director; Ivana Strukelj – Copywriter **Client:** HPB

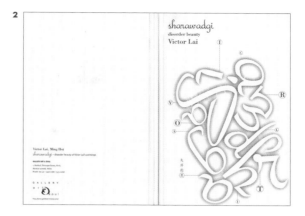

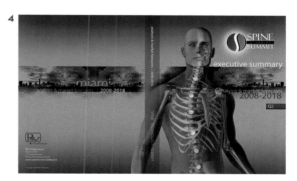

1 Creative Firm: Anderson Design Group - Nashville, TN **Creative Team:** Joel Anderson – Principal; Edward Patton; Kristi Smith; Darren Welch **Client:** Crescent Hill Books and Collins Design **2 Creative Firm:** Twice Graphics - Kowloon, Hong Kong **Creative Team:** Steve Lau – Design Director; Clement So – Graphic Designer **Client:** Mr. Victor Lai **3 Creative Firm:** Creative Alliance - Louisville, KY **Creative Team:** Greg Nehring – Senior Designer; Andy Vucinich, ECD Welch Printing – Printer; Maureen St. Vrain – Print Production; Margaret Lane – Editor **Client:** Kentucky Community & Technical College System **4 Creative Firm:** Dreamedia Studios - Little Rock, AR **Creative Team:** Kyle Holmes – Designer/Creative Director **Client:** RRY Publications **5 Creative Firm:** Zero Gravity - San Marcos, TX **Creative Team:** Ivanete Blanco – Principal Designer **Client:** Roger Jones **6 Creative Firm:** Graphicat Ltd. - Wanchai, Hong Kong **Creative Team:** Colin Tillyer – Creative Director; Ada Ng – Graphic Designer **Client:** FormAsia

PLATINUM

Creative Firm: Rule29 - Geneva, IL
Creative Team: Justin Ahrens – Principal & Creative Director; Kerri Liu – Senior Designer; Kara Merrick – Designer; Craig Clark – Designer
Client: Life In Abundance (LIA) International

Life in Abundance

Issues associated with healthcare, economic empowerment, HIV/AIDS education and community development in the most impoverished areas of the world are difficult to describe to someone who has never seen it close up. According to Rule29 Creative in Geneva, Illinois, charitable organization Life in Abundance (LIA) wanted to "capture the beauty of the people they serve while at the same time show the need and the various factors that they deal with in their world." Rule29 created LIA's Urban & Rural Hope Book, a publication designed to help tell the story of the reality in sub-Saharan Africa and raise money for the organization. Imbued with classically pan-African colors and textures communicating some of the "ever-present grit" in the urban and rural slums, the book's pictures tell most of the story: The agency found it difficult to edit down the abundance of photographs showing people who have so little abundance of their own.

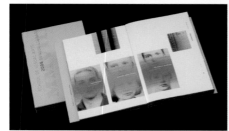

 **PLATINUM**

Creative Firm: Poulin + Morris - New York, NY

Creative Team: Richard Poulin – Designer;
Richard Wilde – Chair/Advertising/Graphic Design
Department SVA

Client: School of Visual Arts

207

1

2

1 Creative Firm: Splash Productions Pte Ltd - Singapore **Creative Team:** Stanley Yap – Art Director; Brice Li – Art Director; Terry Lee – Copywriter **Client:** Singapore Civil Defence Force **URL:** www.scdf.gov.sg **2 Creative Firm:** Creative Alliance - Louisville, KY **Creative Team:** Greg Nehring – Senior Designer; Andy Vucinich, ECD Welch Printing – Printer; Maureen St. Vrain – Print Production; Margaret Lane – Editor **Client:** Kentucky Community & Technical College System

1

3

The Golden drum book was published for the 15th anniversary of Golden drum advertising festival.

2

1 Creative Firm: Anderson Design Group - Nashville, TN **Creative Team:** Joel Anderson – Principal; Darren Welch; Edward Patton; Kristi Smith **Client:** Crescent Hill Books and Collins Design **2 Creative Firm:** Scott Adams Design Associates - Minneapolis, MN **Creative Team:** Scott Adams – Designer; David Lamb – Photographer; Shawn Presley – Project Manager **Client:** Kenyon College **3 Creative Firm:** Futura DDB d.o.o. - Ljubljana, Slovenia **Creative Team:** Zare Kerin – Creative Director; Barbara Ogric Markez – Graphic Designer; Tina Tomazevic – Account Manager **Client:** Golden Drum Festival

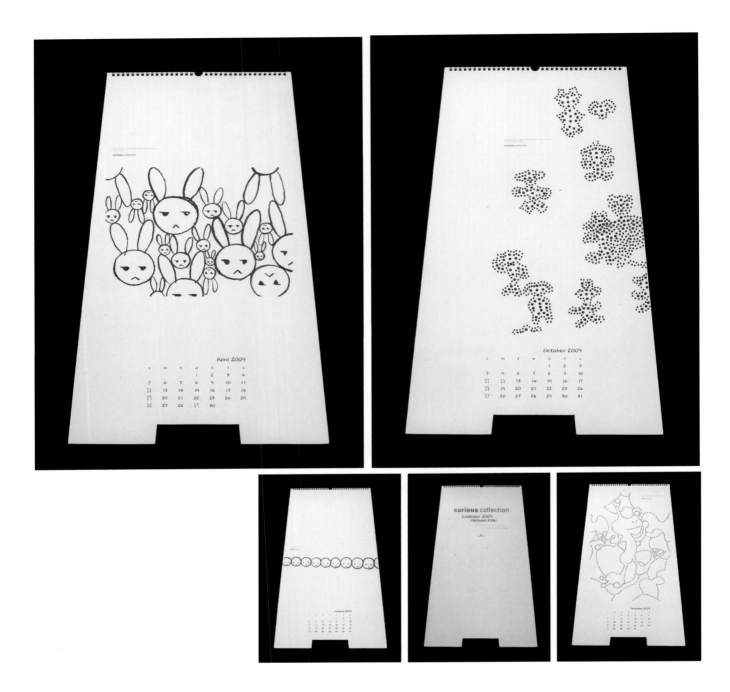

 **PLATINUM**

Creative Firm: Zuan Club - Tokyo, Japan
Creative Team: Akihiko Tsukamoto – Design/
Art Direction; Masami Ouchi – Creative Direction;
Nobuya Hoki – Art
Client: ARJOWIGGINS K.K.

A Year of Fun

Everyone is at least a little curious about what the future will bring, and Tokyo design firm Zuan Club seized upon this when creating a playful calendar for paper company Arjowiggins. The illustrations, including scowling bunnies to a connect-the-dots frog, are decidedly not corporate in feel—but from the A shape of the paper to the tactile sensations of textured and metallic paper (including Arjowiggins' new gold stock on the cover), the calendar is designed to remind Arjowiggins' customers of its origins every day. Says the designer: "[Illustrator] Nobuya Hoki's works are filled with ideas and I created the cheerful calendar to make everyone's heart light."

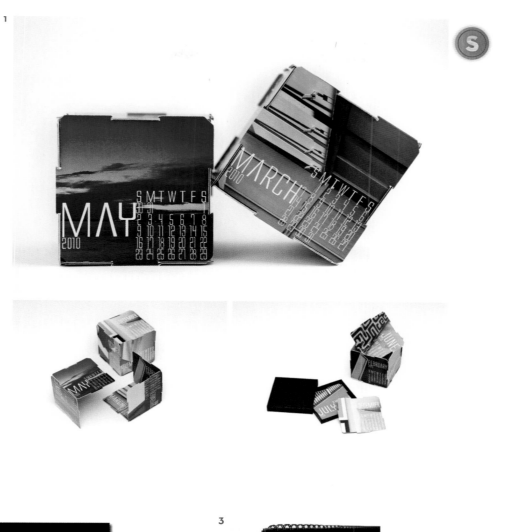

1 Creative Firm: Eye.Ris Concepts - Granville, Australia **Creative Team:** Lillian Martinez – Designer/Digital Retoucher **Client:** Eye.Ris Concepts **2 Creative Firm:** Creative Services - Baker Hughes, Inc. - Houston, TX **Creative Team:** Courtney Loving – Graphic Artist; Melissa Pastrano – Marketing Communications Manager; Bill Poplin – Art Director **Client:** Baker Hughes, Inc. **3 Creative Firm:** INC Design - New York, NY **Creative Team:** Alejandro Medina – Senior Art Director; Martine Chepigin – Managing Partner; William Ferguson – Managing Partner **Client:** International Securities Exchange

PLATINUM

Creative Firm: INK Publishing - Brooklyn, NY

Creative Team: Shane Luitjens – Art Director;
Tim Vienckowski – Graphic Designer;
Elsie Aldahondo – Graphic Designer

Client: AirTran Airways

Not Your Typical Office

The American office—not to mention the American Office—is familiar to millions, and Brooklyn's INK Publishing wanted to channel the mindset that makes the NBC program resonate with so many when creating a photograph to accompany an article on The Office star Jenna Fischer for AirTran's in-flight magazine, Go. INK's designers scoured stock photography collections for classic office images, and knew that they'd struck gold when they found the water cooler shot: "Add the classic time clock and the 8-bit elements, and we all get the in-joke of how such a rigid system can't restrain individual personalities."

By adding to the mix antiquated (but still familiar) Windows interfaces, INK found a fun way to present a story, as well as pay homage to its interactive predecessors. INK still had its own set of office hijinks to deal with in designing the piece, explains one designer. "When working with stock photography, there are limitations as to how to bring it to someplace different than its original usage, while also keeping to the brand's signature elements. I like to use Go's celebrity feature to add a little humor and place it between articles on restaurants and travel trends. The challenge is bringing it all to cohesion."

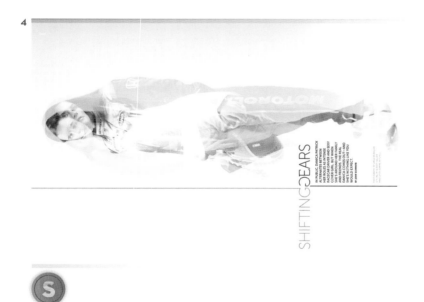

1 **Creative Firm:** INK Publishing - Brooklyn, NY **Creative Team:** Shane Luitjens – Art Director; Tim Vienckowski – Graphic Designer **Client:** Midwest Airlines 2 **Creative Firm:** Emphasis Media Limited - North Point, Hong Kong **Creative Team:** Innes Doig - Editorial Director; Percy Chung – Associate Creative Director; Teresita Khaw – Art Director; Eva Chan – Photo Editor **Client:** SilkAir 3 **Creative Firm:** INK Publishing - Brooklyn, NY **Creative Team:** Shane Luitjens – Art Director; Tim Vienckowski – Graphic Designer; Elsie Aldahondo – Graphic Designer **Client:** AirTran Airways 4 **Creative Firm:** INK Publishing - Brooklyn, NY **Creative Team:** Shane Luitjens – Art Director; Tim Vienckowski – Graphic Designer; Elsie Aldahondo – Graphic Designer **Client:** AirTran Airways

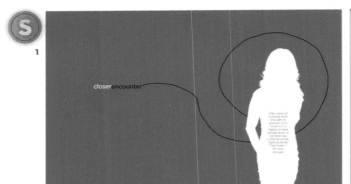

1 **Creative Firm:** INK Publishing - Brooklyn, NY **Creative Team:** Shane Luitjens – Art Director; Tim Vienckowski – Graphic Designer; Elsie Aldahondo – Graphic Designer **Client:** AirTran Airways **2 Creative Firm:** INK Publishing - Brooklyn, NY **Creative Team:** Shane Luitjens – Art Director; Tim Vienckowski – Graphic Designer **Client:** Midwest Airlines **3 Creative Firm:** Emphasis Media Limited - North Point, Hong Kong **Creative Team:** Innes Doig – Editorial Director; Percy Chung – Associate Creative Director; Eva Chan – Photo Editor **Client:** Hongkong Land **4 Creative Firm:** Emphasis Media Limited - North Point, Hong Kong **Creative Team:** Innes Doig – Editorial Director; Percy Chung – Associate Creative Director; Eva Chan – Photo Editor **Client:** Hongkong Land **5 Creative Firm:** Emphasis Media Limited - North Point, Hong Kong **Creative Team:** Innes Doig – Editorial Director; Percy Chung – Associate Creative Director; Eva Chan – Photo Editor **Client:** Hongkong Land **6 Creative Firm:** Emphasis Media Limited - North Point, Hong Kong **Creative Team:** Innes Doig – Editorial Director; Percy Chung – Associate Creative Director; Eva Chan – Photo Editor **Client:** Hongkong Land

The road is an unknown world.

 **PLATINUM**

Security To Start Your Day

Creative Firm: Dieste - Dallas, TX

Creative Team: Aldo Quevedo - Chief Creative Officer; Carlos Tourne - Executive Creative Director; Gabriel Puerto - Creative Director/Copywriter; Alex Arellano - Art Director; Walter Barraza – Art Director

Client: Nationwide Insurance

Despite what the calendar says, each day is a mystery. We get up, the sun is shining or it's raining, we get dressed, have breakfast, get ready to go out and start our lives. "But the adventure begins when the garage opens, we start the car and we go forth to a world where anything can happen," says Dieste, a Dallas firm speaking of their magazine ads for Nationwide Insurance. The ads depict what lies beyond the garage door as vast and mysterious as the sea or a distant galaxy. "It sometimes it can seem like a nice place, but more often it's an uncontrollable world, full of unexpected events," Dieste says. "That's why there's Nationwide, to be on your side and give you a feeling of security, along with the guarantee that no matter what happens, everything will be OK."

To express this idea in a simple way that reflects our day-to-day lives, Dieste's creative team literally interpreted the highway as "that chaotic, unknown world... like outer space, like underground caves or the bottom of the sea." So buckle your seatbelt—as the tagline says, "The road is an unknown world."

The road is an unknown world.

PLATINUM

Creative Firm: Dieste - Dallas, TX

Creative Team: Aldo Quevedo - Chief Creative
Officer; Carlos Tourne - Executive Creative Director;
Gabriel Puerto - Creative Director/Copywriter;
Alex Arellano - Art Director;
Walter Barraza – Art Director

Client: Nationwide Insurance

Security To Start Your Day

Despite what the calendar says, each day is a mystery. We get up, the sun is shining or it's raining, we get dressed, have breakfast, get ready to go out and start our lives. "But the adventure begins when the garage opens, we start the car and we go forth to a world where anything can happen," says Dieste, a Dallas firm speaking of their magazine ads for Nationwide Insurance. The ads depict what lies beyond the garage door as vast and mysterious as the sea or a distant galaxy. "It sometimes it can seem like a nice place, but more often it's an uncontrollable world, full of unexpected events," Dieste says. "That's why there's Nationwide, to be on your side and give you a feeling of security, along with the guarantee that no matter what happens, everything will be OK."

To express this idea in a simple way that reflects our day-to-day lives, Dieste's creative team literally interpreted the highway as "that chaotic, unknown world... like outer space, like underground caves or the bottom of the sea." So buckle your seatbelt—as the tagline says, "The road is an unknown world."

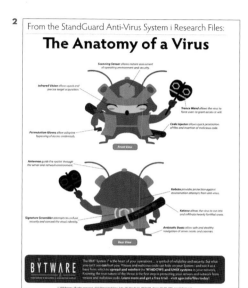

1 Creative Firm: Dieste - Dallas, TX **Creative Team:** Aldo Quevedo - Chief Creative Officer; Carlos Tourne - Executive Creative Director; Gabriel Puerto - Creative Director/Copywriter; Alex Arellano - Art Director; Walter Barraza – Art Director **Client:** Nationwide Insurance **2 Creative Firm:** Stellar Debris - Hadano-shi, Japan **Creative Team:** Christopher Jones - Creative Director/Designer/Writer; Isaac Zamora - Illustrator **Client:** Bytware **3 Creative Firm:** Futura DDB d.o.o. - Ljubljana, Slovenia **Creative Team:** Ana Por - Account Manager; Zare Kerin - Creative Director; Jure Korenc - Copywriter; Janez Vizjak – Graphic Designer **Client:** Samaritan Magazine

experience **passion**

You may expect BKD CPAs and advisors to be cool, calm and collected but what you may not realize is how passionate we are about our communities. As one of the Top 10 U.S. CPA and advisory firms, we contribute our time, money and experience to the places we live and work. Our support of the annual Lincoln Day Dinner is one example of a civic commitment that never cools.

experience **responsiveness**

experience **support**

experience **attention**

Creative Firm: Greenfield/Belser Ltd. - Washington, D.C.

Creative Team: Lindsay Mead - Account Executive;
Tae Jeong - Senior Designer;
Burkey Belser - Creative Director;
Joe Walsh - Creative Director;
Mark Ledgerwood - Art Director;
Gene Shaffer – Production Artist

Client: BKD

Double Entendre

An ideal marketing campaign emphasizes the experience of the client in its field while creating an experience by which the reader can identify with the service or product marketed. Greenfield/Belser, a Washington, D.C. marketing firm, combined the two in a series of ads for BKD, a national CPA and advisory company with 30 offices across 12 states. "Our goal was to position BKD as a national firm with all the resources and talent of a Big Four firm, combined with the personal touch the Big Four notoriously lack," the agency says.

The campaign centers on the double meaning of the word "experience"—the type of relationship one encounters and the type of expertise one receives—and interesting images used to visually speak to each word: "Experience support" illustrated by a house figure made of stones, for example. Greenfield/Belser added to the mix copy that calls to attention facts that seek to "drive home the idea that they BKD is not your local accounting firm, but a firm that has breadth and depth needed to succeed in a wide variety of states and industries."

1

2

3

1 Creative Firm: People Design Inc - Grand Rapids, MI **Creative Team:** Brian Hauch - Design Director; Kevin Budelmann – Creative Director **Client:** Cumberland Furniture
2 Creative Firm: STEELE+ - Alpharetta, GA **Creative Team:** Chris Steele - CEO; Tim Smith - Creative Director; Chris Breen - Creative Director; Scott Coleman - President; Chris Stanford – Photographer **Client:** Georgia-Pacific Wood Products **3 Creative Firm:** Goble & Associates - Chicago, IL **Creative Team:** Nancy Finigan - EVP/Account Group Director; Chad Smith - Account Supervisor; Terry Lawrence - Senior Art Director; Denis O'Keefe - Copy Supervisor; Dave Raube - EVP/Creative Director; Austin Kirksey – Account Manager **Client:** Hospira

1

2

3

1 Creative Firm: Cline Davis and Mann LLC - New York, NY **Creative Team:** Mark Friedman - Managing Partner/Creative Director; Glenn Batkin - Associate Creative Director; Ben Ingersoll - Managing Partner/Creative Director; Adam Siers - Associate Creative Director; Armando Saja - Art Supervisor; Alyssa Farquhar - Group Copy Supervisor **Client:** Genentech **2 Creative Firm:** Foodmix - Westmont, IL **Creative Team:** Foodmix Creative/Production Team **Client:** Coca-Cola Foodservice **3 Creative Firm:** Thielen Designs - Albuquerque, NM **Creative Team:** Tony Thielen - Creative Director/Art Director; Chris Sadlier - Copywriter; Cel Jarvis - Photographer; Alice Blue – Photo Retoucher/Montage **Client:** Kinesio

1 Creative Firm: REVOLUCION - New York, NY **Creative Team:** Alberto Rodriguez - Creative Director; Henry Alvarez – Art Director **Client:** Palm Bay International
2 Creative Firm: The UXB - Beverly Hills, CA **Creative Team:** Glenn Sakamoto - Creative Director; NancyJane Goldston - Creative Director; Brittan Cortney – Creative Coordinator **Client:** Cleatskins **URL:** www.cleatskins.com **3 Creative Firm:** State Farm Insurance - Bloomington, IL **Creative Team:** Patty Dirker - Marketing Analyst; Mariana Rutledge - Marketing Analyst; Tim Thomas - Marketing Analyst; Jim Stahly - Marketing Analyst; Shelia Law - Marketing Analyst; Greg Sutter – Marketing Manager **Client:** State Farm

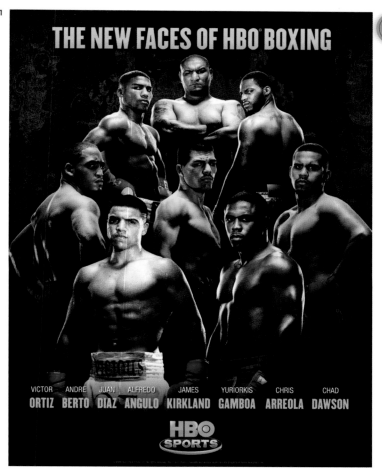

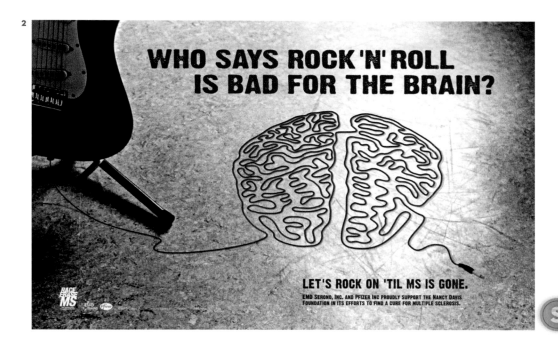

1 Creative Firm: HBO Off-Air Creative Services - New York, NY **Creative Team:** Venus Dennison - Creative Director; Christian Martillo - Art Director; Allan Wai - Design; Manager Monte Isom – Photography **Client:** HBO Sports **2 Creative Firm:** Cline Davis and Mann LLC - New York, NY **Creative Team:** Mark Friedman - Managing Partner/ Creative Director; Don Matera - Group Creative Director; Ben Ingersoll - Managing Partner/Creative Director; Carolyn O'Neill - Group Creative Director; Jamie Nusbaum - Art Director; Elisa Wright – Copy Supervisor **Client:** EMD Serono **3 Creative Firm:** Alcone Marketing - Irvine, CA **Creative Team:** Shivonne Miller - Sr. Art Director; Carlos Musquez - Creative Director; Luis Camano – VP/Creative Director **Client:** Seeds of Change

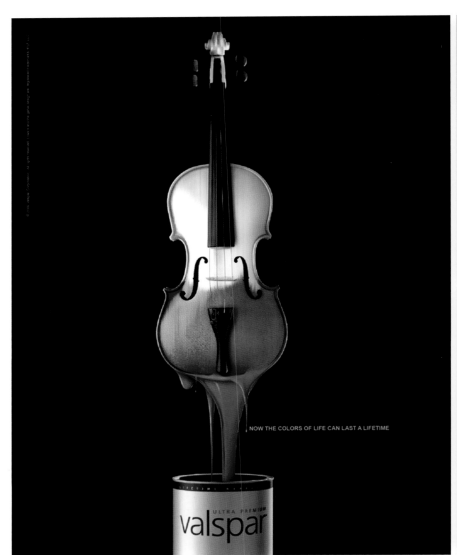

NOW THE COLORS OF LIFE CAN LAST A LIFETIME

 **PLATINUM**

Creative Firm: Euro RSCG Chicago - Chicago, IL

Creative Team: Steffan Postaer - Chairman & Chief Creative Officer; Blake Ebel - Executive Creative Director; Amanda Butts - Creative Director; Elyse Maguire - Creative Director; Ecole Weinstein - Copywriter; Puja Shah – Art Director

Client: Valspar Paint

1

2

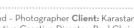

1 Creative Firm: Mani & Company - New York, NY **Creative Team:** Dino Maniaci - Art Director; Chris Bartick - Designer; Cory Radlund – Photographer **Client:** Karastan
2 Creative Firm: O'Leary and Partners - Newport Beach, CA **Creative Team:** Matt McNelis - Senior Copywriter; Eric Spiegler - Executive Creative Director; Paul Christensen - Senior Art Director; Carol Knaeps – Director of Print Production **Client:** Mothers Car Polishes

225

1

2

1 Creative Firm: State Farm Insurance - Bloomington, IL **Creative Team:** Patty Dirker - Marketing Analyst; Shelia Law - Marketing Analyst; Jim Stahly - Marketing Analyst; Tim Thomas - Marketing Analyst; Mariana Rutledge - Marketing Analyst; Greg Sutter – Marketing Manager **Client:** State Farm Insurance **2 Creative Firm:** Saatchi & Saatchi Italy - Rome, Italy **Creative Team:** Agostino Toscana - Creative Director; Luca Pannese - Art; Luca Lorenzini - Copy; Michael Koelsch – Illustrator **Client:** NBC Universal Global Networks Italia

1

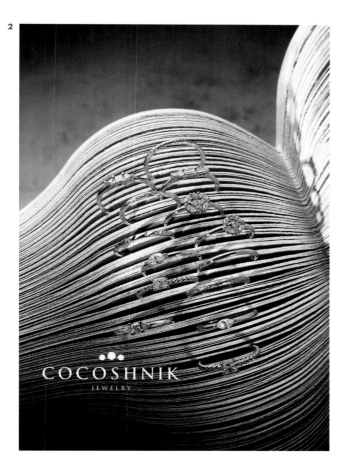

2

1 **Creative Firm:** Kantorwassink - Grand Rapids, MI **Creative Team:** Dave Kantor; Wendy Wassink; Tim Calkins; John Ferin **Client:** Nutrilite/Amway **2 Creative Firm:** omdr co., ltd. - Tokyo, Japan **Creative Team:** Osamu Misawa - Creative Director/Art Director; Mamoru Takeuchi - Designer; Toshitaka Niwa – Photographer **Client:** WORLD CO., LTD

1

2

1 **Creative Firm:** HBO Off-Air Creative Services - New York, NY **Creative Team:** Venus Dennison - Creative Director; Christian Martillo - Design Manager; Maria Eugenia Marcial - Designer; Jen McDearman - Copywriter **Client:** HBO 2 **Creative Firm:** Sherman Advertising/Mermaid, Inc. - New York, NY **Creative Team:** Sharon McLaughlin - Creative Director; Stephen Morse – Retoucher **Client:** Carnegie Hall Tower

1 Creative Firm: Sherman Advertising/Mermaid, Inc. - New York, NY **Creative Team:** Sharon McLaughlin - Creative Director **Client:** Stillman Development International

HELP JUVENILE PROTECTIVE ASSOCIATION STOP ALL CHILD ABUSE. WWW.JUVENILE.ORG

HELP JUVENILE PROTECTIVE ASSOCIATION STOP ALL CHILD ABUSE. WWW.JUVENILE.ORG

HELP JUVENILE PROTECTIVE ASSOCIATION STOP ALL CHILD ABUSE. WWW.JUVENILE.ORG

PLATINUM

Creative Firm: Euro RSCG Chicago - Chicago, IL

Creative Team: Steffan Postaer - Chairman & Chief Creative Officer; Blake Ebel - Executive Creative Director; Eugene Fuller - Copywriter; Puja Shah - Art Director; Scott Giannini - Retouching; Julia Cunningham – Art Buyer

Client: Juvenile Protective Association

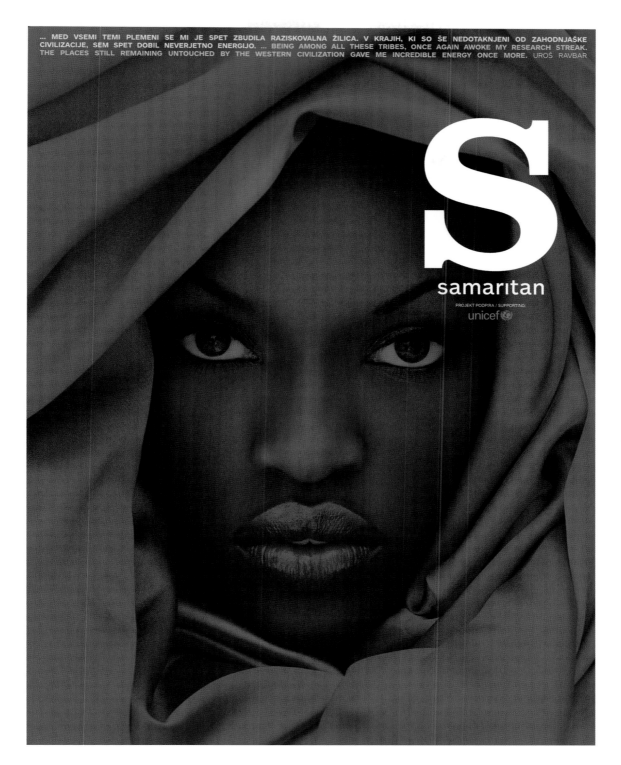

... MED VSEMI TEMI PLEMENI SE MI JE SPET ZBUDILA RAZISKOVALNA ŽILICA. V KRAJIH, KI SO ŠE NEDOTAKNJENI OD ZAHODNJAŠKE CIVILIZACIJE, SEM SPET DOBIL NEVERJETNO ENERGIJO. ... BEING AMONG ALL THESE TRIBES, ONCE AGAIN AWOKE MY RESEARCH STREAK. THE PLACES STILL REMAINING UNTOUCHED BY THE WESTERN CIVILIZATION GAVE ME INCREDIBLE ENERGY ONCE MORE. UROŠ RAVBAR

S
samaritan
PROJEKT PODPIRA / SUPPORTING:
unicef

PLATINUM

Creative Firm: Futura DDB d.o.o. - Ljubljana, Slovenia

Creative Team: Zare Kerin - Creative Director;
Matjaz Luzar - Graphic Designer;
Ana Por – Account Manager

Client: Samaritan Foundation

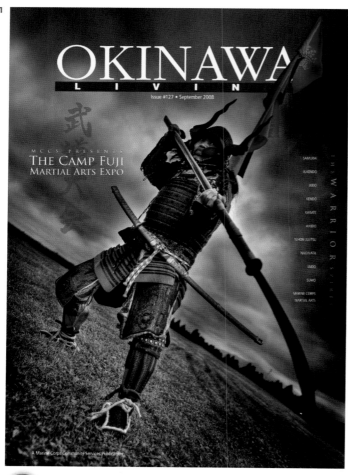

 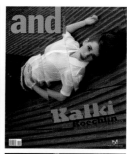

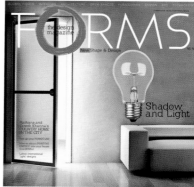

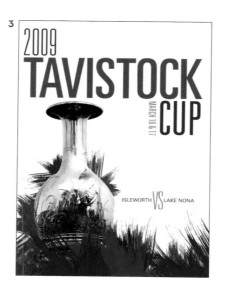

1 **Creative Firm:** Marine Corps Community Services Marketing Branch - FPO, CA **Creative Team:** John R. Burgreen III – Art Director/Photographer **Client:** Marine Corps Community Services 2 **Creative Firm:** MaXposure Media Group - New Delhi, India **Creative Team:** Himanshu - Art Director; Dolly Jain - Assistant Art Director; Prasenjit Chowdhury – Graphic Designer **Client:** MaXposure Media Group 3 **Creative Firm:** Tavistock Group - Orlando, FL **Creative Team:** Kelly Lafferman - Vice President of Marketing; Karl Dinkler - Graphic Designer; Tina Holmes – Graphic Designer **Client:** Tavistock Cup

Creative Firm: housemouse - Melbourne, Australia
Client: housemouse

By Designers For Designers

Melbourne magazine Fluoro is a designer's design magazine, and local design firm housemouse made sure that its "pride and joy" inspired people like they themselves had been. "[It is] design inspiration for anyone and everyone who would gain inspiration from a magazine like Fluoro by pushing the boundaries of print and design," the agency says.

With the pilot issue, Fluoro5, housemouse made it a priority to make the publication "inspire, push boundaries and deliver an experience like no other," a task achieved by pushing its creators' own boundaries to make a magazine they as designers would enjoy as well. Details such as foiling and fine detail on the front cover, then carried through to the very last page, took design elements and presented them as a collective personality.

Distributed with 9,000 copies of Design Quarterly magazine throughout Australia and around the world, Fluoro5 invited readers to "enter the unique world of Fluoro and show off the design caliber that comes out of Australia." The sourcing, too, had its own local stamp, reports housemouse: "Fluoro5 is based around the city of Melbourne and is reflective of the expressive elements that the [design] team love about their city." housemouse says that the designers kept in mind the long-term effect of their work when designing the physical magazine itself. "In the mind of the designers, when paper stocks and inks were selected and features were designed, the importance of environmentally sustainable practices within a variety of design industries had to be highlighted."

1

2

3

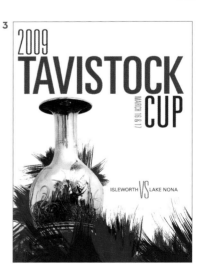

1 Creative Firm: Simon & Goetz Design GmbH & Co. KG - Frankfurt, Germany **Creative Team:** Dörte Fischer - Art Direction; Gerrit Hinkelbein - Art Direction; Christina Schirm – Art Direction **Client:** Sal. Oppenheim jr. & Cie. **2 Creative Firm:** Arnold. Inhalt und Form AG - Staefa, Switzerland **Client:** Credit Suisse **3 Creative Firm:** Tavistock Group - Orlando, FL **Creative Team:** Kelly Lafferman - Vice President of Marketing; Karl Dinkler - Graphic Designer; Tina Holmes – Graphic Designer **Client:** Tavistock Cup

1

2

3

1 **Creative Firm:** Arnold. Inhalt und Form AG - Staefa, Switzerland **Client:** Credit Suisse 2 **Creative Firm:** Marine Corps Community Services Marketing Branch - FPO, CA **Creative Team:** Rachel Veit - Art Director; Richenda Sandlin-Tymitz - Managing Editor; Cindy Ramos - Managing Editor; John R. Burgreen III - Director of Photography; Mina Furusho - Contributing Photographer; Henry Ortega MCCS – Art Director **Client:** Marine Corps Community Services 3 **Creative Firm:** Futura DDB d.o.o. - Ljubljana, Slovenia **Creative Team:** Zare Kerin - Creative Director; Matjaz Luzar - Graphic Designer; Ana Por – Account Manager **Client:** Samaritan Foundation

Horizons

Horizon
where the sky
meets the earth

THE QUARTERLY NEWSLETTER OF QANTAS GROUP AIRPORTS

02
FEB 2008

A380

A380 test week a big success

Airport staff from Ramp Services, Product Delivery, Learning and Development and Fleet Presentation were all directly involved in the A380 trials held in Sydney 3–7 December 2007.

The week's activities were only successful thanks to the participation and efforts of many Airport staff not only during the week, but also in the weeks leading up to the trials. Staff overcame disruption from electrical storms each day, a medical emergency and last minute schedule movements.

The feedback from Airbus was that they were very happy to work with Qantas, because when things did not go to plan, Qantas staff remained professional and sought out the solution—not something found in all their carrier experiences.

Well done Airport Services team!

See page 18 for more details.

1 Creative Firm: Surveillance - Rushcutters Bay, Australia **Creative Team:** James Armstrong - Creative Director; Nina Duric – Designer **Client:** Qantas Airport Services

1

1 Creative Firm: Missouri Botanical Garden - Brentwood, MO **Creative Team:** Ellen Flesch - Senior Graphic Designer; Jeff Ricker – Graphic Designer **Client:** Missouri Botanical Garden

1

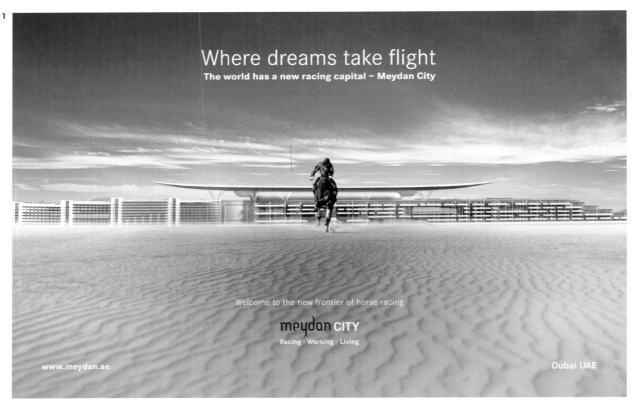

2

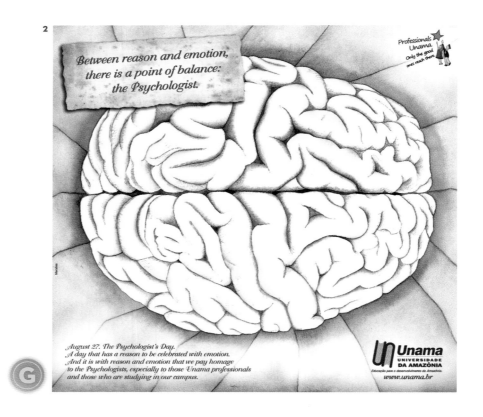

1 Creative Firm: formul8 Pte. Ltd. - Singapore **Creative Team:** Fiona Bartholomeusz - Managing Director; Kok Hoe Wong - Account Director; Derrick Kuah - Art Director; Eran Husni Amir Husni - Art Director; Chloe Huang - Senior Account Executive; Jennifer Lee – Copywriter **Client:** Meydan Group LLC **URL:** www.meydan.ae
2 Creative Firm: Mendes Publicidade - Belém, Brazil **Creative Team:** Oswaldo Mendes - Creativity Director; Márcia Miranda - Copywriter; Marcelo Amorim – Art Director **Client:** Unama.

1

TWO NOBEL LAUREATES AND A GENIUS WALK INTO A BAR... AT LEAST THEY DO AT OUR HOLIDAY PARTY.

At Chicago GSB, we have always believed that our faculty has the passion, intellect, and talent to change the world. And the Nobel selection committee tends to agree. With Nobel Laureates and a MacArthur "genius" award winner among our faculty, we think you might agree as well. Chicago GSB. It isn't just a business school, it's a business *force.*

CHICAGO BOOTH
The University of Chicago Booth School of Business
CHICAGO LONDON SINGAPORE CHICAGOBOOTH.EDU

THE SMARTEST GUY IN THE ROOM HAS MADE QUITE A NAME FOR HERSELF.

CHICAGO BOOTH
The University of Chicago Booth School of Business

WE'RE BIG IN SWEDEN.

CHICAGO BOOTH
The University of Chicago Booth School of Business

WE'RE BIG IN SWEDEN portion

YOU ARE READING OUR ALUMNI NEWSLETTER.

CHICAGO BOOTH
The University of Chicago Booth School of Business

2

missing

Imagine a World Without Bees.
Honey bees pollinate around 1/3 of all natural foods. In fact, nearly half of our all-natural Häagen-Dazs® ice cream flavors rely on them. But they're dying at an alarming rate.

Help Bees Get Busy. Buy Häagen-Dazs, Plant a Flower.

1 Creative Firm: Kantorwassink - Grand Rapids, MI **Creative Team:** Dave Kantor; Wendy Wassink; John Ferin **Client:** The University of Chicago Booth School of Business
2 Creative Firm: Alcone Marketing - Irvine, CA **Creative Team:** Chad Lasota - Digital Designer; Renata Carroll - Art Director; Carlos Musquez - Creative Director; Kevin Kleber - Creative Director; Alan Josey - Copywriter; Luis Camano – VP/Creative Director **Client:** Haagen-Dazs

मैं रोज अपने पापा के साथ सिगरेट पीता हूँ

पैसिव स्मोकिंग उतना ही खतरनाक है जितना एक्टिव स्मोकिंग... अपने प्रियजनों को सिगरेट के दुष्प्रभावों की भयंकर सौगात न दीजिए. सिगरेट छोड़िए, अपने परिवार के लिए, खुद अपने लिए. इस कार्य में हम आपकी मदद करेंगे... पढ़ते रहिए, दैनिक भास्कर.

दैनिक भास्कर

 **PLATINUM**

Creative Firm: Purple Focus Pvt. Ltd. - Indore, India
Creative Team: Aarish Nandedkar - Copywriter; Vipin Rathore - Designer
Client: Dainik Bhaskar

No Translation Needed

Whether you can read Hindi or don't even recognize the type as your own, the image requires no translation: a fresh-faced, long-lashed baby is smoking, or at least is suggesting the motion of it. Purple Focus Pvt. Ltd. in Indore, India created a powerful public service ad released on the occasion of the WHO's World No Tobacco Day with an aim to educate people about the harmful effects of smoking on family members, especially children. "It is an insight that an average smoker realizes in his heart that smoking is not good for the health of his loved ones, but is too caught up by the habit to quit," Purple

Focus says. "Considering this fact, we decided to create an in-the-face type of advertisement where we used a cute infant, delivering a shocking statement that he smokes with his father every day." The minimalist, stark treatment underscores the seriousness of the message while emotionally and emphatically appealing to the heart of a smoker who shares his or her home with small children who are impressionable in more ways than one.

1 **Creative Firm:** Mendes Publicidade - Belém, Brazil **Creative Team:** Oswaldo Mendes - Creativity Director; Márcia Miranda - Copywriter; Marcelo Amorim – Art Director **Client:** Unimed Belm. 2 **Creative Firm:** Inca Tanvir Advertising - Sharjah, UAE **Creative Team:** Tanvir Kanji - Creative Director; Max D'Lima - Art Director; Sunil Anand; Ernest Desai; Rhea Dixit **Client:** Khaleej Times

1 Creative Firm: The EGC Group - New York, NY **Creative Team:** Jeff Bockman - Copywriter; Richard DeSimone - Art Director; Bob Costible – Creative Director **Client:** Rainforest Alliance **2 Creative Firm:** Planet Ads and Design P/L - Singapore **Creative Team:** Hal Suzuki - Creative Director; Suzanne Lauridssen - Senior Copywriter; Edwin Enero – Art Director **Client:** Singapore Armed Forces Reservists Assoc (SAFRA)

CREATIVE CATEGORY
film + video

1 **Creative Firm:** Luminus Creative - Zagreb, Croatia **Creative Team:** Renato Grgic – Creative Director/Script; Kristijan Petrovic – Director; Tonci Klaric – Script; Hrvoje Boljkovac – Production; Davor Bobic – Sound; Zeljko Grgic – Graphics **Client:** City of Varazdin

 **PLATINUM**

Creative Firm: link technologies llc - Hillside, NJ

Creative Team: Brandon Jameson – Producer/
Director; Sewra Kidane – Editor; Jose Rios,
Chris Edwards – DP

Client: P&G Petcare

It's A Dog's Life

Proctor & Gamble's pet division, P&G
Petcare, enlisted link technologies llc in
Hillside, New Jersey to create the Eu-
kanuba Profiles in Performance series.
Art director Brandon Jameson's produced three videos to introduce viewers
to three sets of dog owners—a teen with
cerebral palsy, dog breeders and police
officers—who employ their Eukanuba-fed
dogs in their daily lives in the capacities
of, respectively, companion animal, show
dogs and K-9 police support. Jameson
says, "Through the kindheartedness,
courage and commitment of our cast,
they have given the world the gift of
transformation, love and inspiration."

1

2

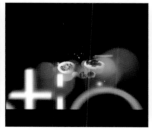

1 Creative Firm: Rosebud Inc. - Vienna, Austria **Creative Team:** Ralf Herms – Creative Director; Michael Balgavy – Director; Christof Dertschei – Animator **Client:** Wien Tourismus **2 Creative Firm:** tara del mar productions inc - New York, NY **Creative Team:** Terry Dagrosa – Executive Producer/Creative Director; Scott Mushinskie – Cameraman/Editor, Gueststar Motion Graphics & Design; Stefan Konowalskyj – Field Producer; Eric D Morrison – Music **Client:** Seduction Meals **URL:** www.seductionmeals.com

1 Creative Firm: EURO RSCG C&O - Suresnes, France **Creative Team:** Olivier Moulierac – Creative Director; Jerome Galinha – Creative Director; Alain Picard – Copywriter; Ricolas Harlamoff – Art Director; Catherine Jamaux – Agency Producer; Adam Berg – Director **Client:** EDF **2 Creative Firm:** Gotham Inc. - New York, NY **Creative Team:** Marty Orzio – Chief Creative Officer; Carl Ceo – CD/Art Director; Dan Sheehan – CD/Copywriter; Neal Bergman – Producer **Client:** 46664/The Nelson Mandela Foundation **URL:** www.mandeladay.com

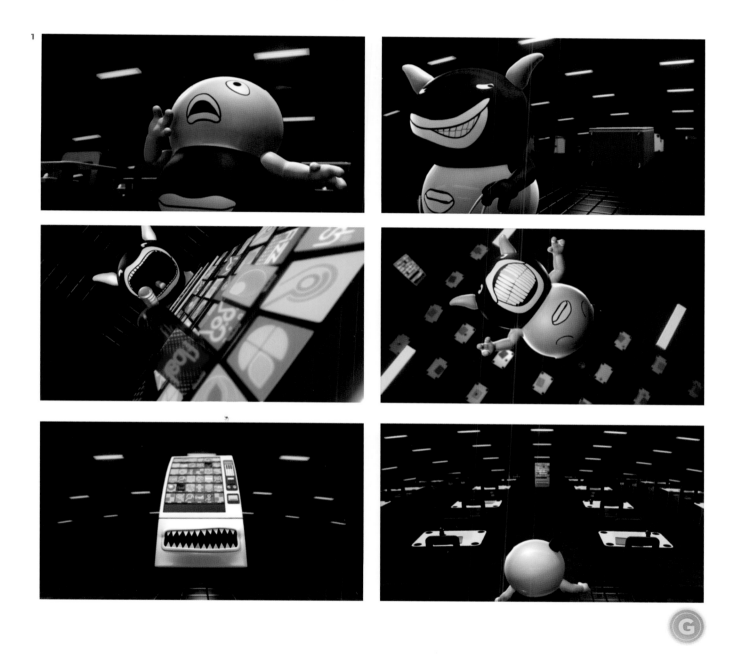

1 Creative Firm: Sticky Pictures - Brooklyn, NY **Creative Team:** Michael Darmanin – Director; Nol Kittiampon – Lead Animator; Matt Choi – Designer **Client:** Sticky Pictures

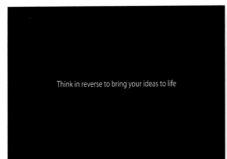

PLATINUM

A to Z

Creative Firm: Aniden Interactive - Houston, TX

Creative Team: James Taylor – Creative Director, HP; Deepa Kumar – Video Producer, HP; Mark Pulda – Executive Producer; Bret Stout – Creative Director; Brandon White – Producer; Kristin Monzingo – Motion Graphic Artist

Client: Hewlett-Packard

Ever wonder where products get their names? Aniden Interactive in Houston wanted to know exactly that when they set out to promote Hewlett-Packard's new Z Workstation. Absent of a reason, Aniden felt that their first task was to develop a concept giving the "Z "a purpose. "In crafting our story, it was important to focus on one vertical, animation and one key product message, innovation," the agency says. "So, how do we tie 'innovation' with 'Z'? Here lies our challenge."

Aniden created a story to describe how the workstation received its name, while focusing on its innovative design. By asking, "Where does innovation begin," Aniden re-alized that as the last letter of the alphabet, the workstation's innovation began with the end in mind, and that's where they started their dynamic, animation-rich, illustrated story. The story "was a big idea explaining where big ideas come from. Innovation begins with the end in mind... innovation begins with Z."

1 **Creative Firm:** Aniden Interactive - Houston, TX **Creative Team:** June Sugg – Art Director; Bret Jones – Designer; Darren Edge – Designer; Jeremy Shelton – Designer; Jody Cochran – Designer; Kristin Monzingo – Designer **Client:** Hewlett-Packard

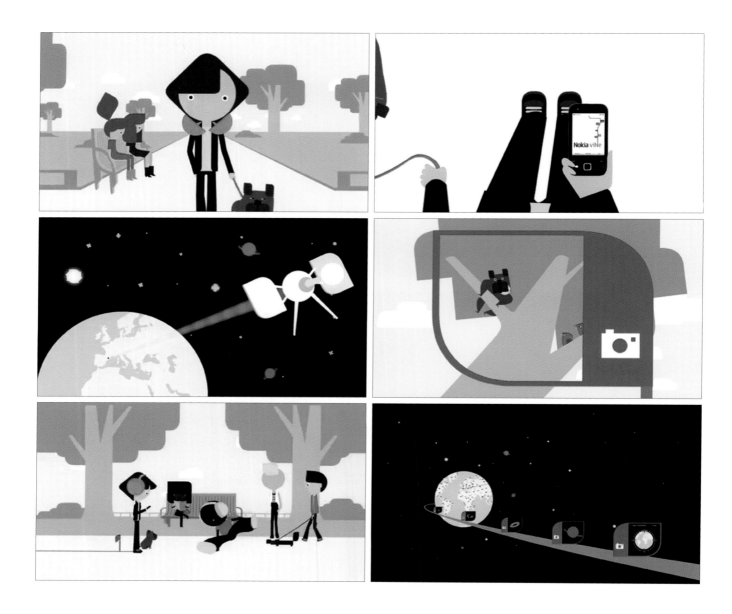

 **PLATINUM**

Creative Firm: Airside - London, UK
Client: RG/A

Heard It Through viNe

With rapid advances in mobile phone technology and applications—along with a fiercely competitive market—London design studio Airside had its work cut out for it when Nokia hired them to sell its latest app. To showcase viNe, a new application for the Nseries mobile phone line that enables users to tag and share music played and photos taken to a specific geographic location using GPS tracking, Airside created an engaging short film. By using bright colors and hip, lively anima-

tion to explain the concept to a nontechnical audience, the film breezily explains how the lay user can use the technology in day-to-day life.

 252

FIAT ECO:DRIVE
Category: Film & Video – Infomercials

Fiat's new eco:Drive technology is the world's first
in-car device that allows drivers to monitor how
much CO2 their driving creates. Airside were asked
to create film to introduce the eco:Drive technology
and to demonstrate how it can be used to reduce a
journey's emissions.
We created two characters Franco and Merv to
explain the technology.

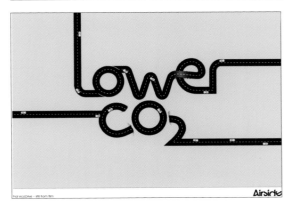

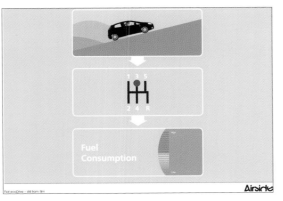

1 Creative Firm: Airside - London, United Kingdom **Client:** AKQA

What if we bottled the dirty water that millions in developing countries drink every day...

. . . and offered it on the streets of New York?

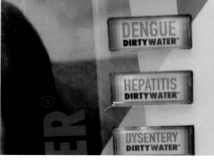

DENGUE
DIRTY WATER®

HEPATITIS
DIRTY WATER®

DYSENTERY
DIRTY WATER®

Nobody drank any Dirty Water, but many donated.

$1

DIRTY WATER®
is not an actual product but a
real problem for millions of
children around the world.
TAP PROJECT.ORG

PLATINUM

Creative Firm: Casanova Pendrill - New York, NY

Creative Team: Elias Weinstock - VP/ Executive Creative Director; Alejandro Ortiz - Creative Director; Gil Arevalo - Copywriter/Art Director; Dámaso Crespo - Art Director/Copywriter; James Long - Editor; Keith Olwell – Post-production Supervisor

Client: UNICEF

URL: www.dirtywaterinfo.com

Can I Get You A Drink?

Clean water is something most everyone takes for granted and assumes is practically free. That's half true for much of the world, and in its campaign for UNICEF, New York agency Casanova Pendrill tried to find an interesting, groundbreaking way of making the desensitized New Yorker aware of the global water issue and motivate them to donate to bring clean water to children in need—all without a budget. "The client wanted us to convey that just $1 provides a child with 40 days of safe drinking water," the agency reports. With its skull-and-cross-bones-inspired logo, the mock product of bottled "dirty water," the agency says, was an easy and direct way to brand this new lethal kind of bottled water, with varieties drawn from the (presumably clean) commercial bottled water industry: "The names of each flavor/illness were selected from the most common and lethal waterborne diseases found in the developing countries lacking clean water."

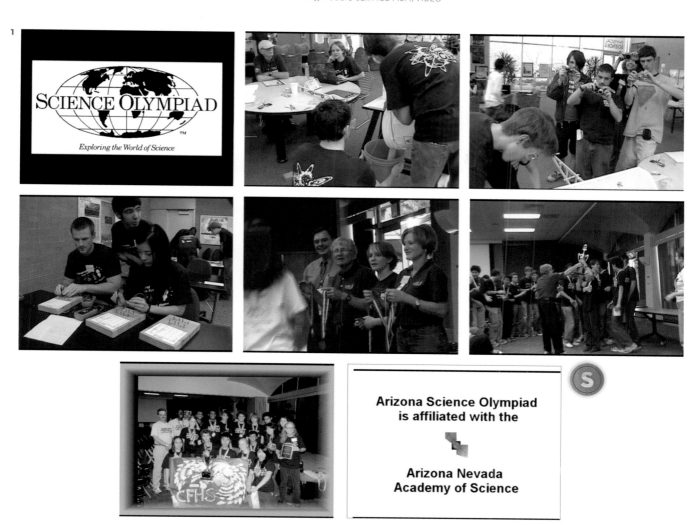

1 Creative Firm: CouryGraph Productions - Glendale, AZ **Creative Team:** Ed Sharpe – Director/Photographer; Bette Sharpe - Photographer; Karen Conzelman - Scriptwriter; Tamara McDaniel - Voiceover **Client:** AZ Science Olympiad **url** www.smecc.org **2 Creative Firm:** EURO RSCG C&O - Suresnes, France **Creative Team:** Olivier Moulierac - Creative Director; Jerome Galinha - Creative Director; Capucine Lewalle - Copywriter; Rodolphe Hirsch - Copywriter; Catherine Labro - Art Director; Volker Gehr - Art Director **Client:** INPES

PLATINUM

Creative Firm: FATHOM Communications - Chicago, IL
Creative Team: Brett Morgen - Director; Al Saltiel -
Executive Producer; Mike Cerilli - Executive
Producer; Peter Groome - Chief Creative Officer;
Mark Leger - Managing Director/Producer;
Lori Nelson – Account Director
Client: International Truck

1

A day in the life
with Moblin

2

1 **Creative Firm:** Airside - London, United Kingdom **Client:** Moblin 2 **Creative Firm:** Sapient Interactive - Palmetto Bay, FL **Creative Team:** Gaston Legorburu - Chief Creative Officer; Tomas Siedleczka - Group Creative Director; Jim Houck- Director of Entertainment; Eddie Gomez – ACD/Interactive; Donald Ngai - ACD/Design; Nicole Peraita – Senior Art Director **Client:** Celebrity Cruise Lines

 **PLATINUM**

Creative Firm: Airside - London, United Kingdom

Client: Number One Films

1 **Creative Firm:** Primal Screen - Atlanta, GA **Creative Team:** Doug Grimmett - Creative Director; Donald Emerson - Director; Jeremy Seymour - Art Director; Ciara Cordasco - Designer; Steve Mank – Sound & Music **Client:** PBS KIDS

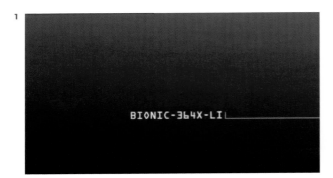

1 Creative Firm: NBC Universal Global Networks Italia - Rome, Italy **Client:** NBC Universal Global Networks Italia **2 Creative Firm:** NBC Universal Global Networks Italia - Rome, Italy **Client:** NBC Universal Global Networks Italia

1 Creative Firm: Primal Screen - Atlanta, GA **Creative Team:** Doug Grimmett - Creative Director; Shane McGee - Director; Rick Newcomb - Art Director; Teresa Cloud - Production Artist; Steve Mank – Sound & Music **Client:** TCM

1 **Creative Firm:** NBC Universal Global Networks Italia - Rome, Italy **Client:** NBC Universal Global Networks Italia 2 **Creative Firm:** Primal Screen - Atlanta, GA **Creative Team:** Doug Grimmett - Creative Director; Rob Shepps - Director; Rob Shetler - 3D Animator; Brennan Isbell - Compositor; Teresa Cloud - Production Coordinator/Production Artist; Steve Mank – Sound & Music **Client:** NickToons

illustration,
photography +
typography

9

1

STUDIO RENDERING   ARTIST INTERPRETATION   MONARCH ROOM   GETTYS

1 Creative Firm: Studio Rendering, Inc. - Chicago, IL **Creative Team:** Sonny Sultani - CEO; Ashfaq Mohammed - Creative Director; Derar Ibrahim – 3D Artist **Client:** Gettys Group

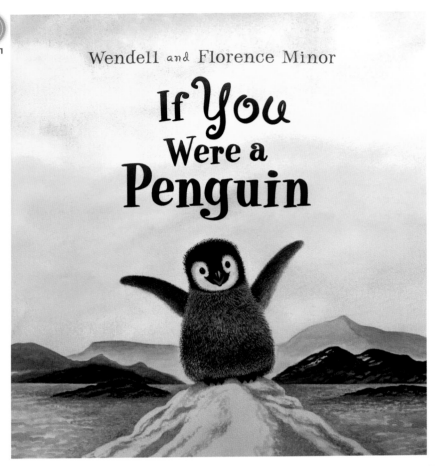

1 Creative Firm: Wendell Minor Design - Washington, CT **Creative Team:** Florence Minor - Author; Wendell Minor – Illustrator; Martha Rago - Art Director; Dana Fritts – Designer **Client:** HarperCollins

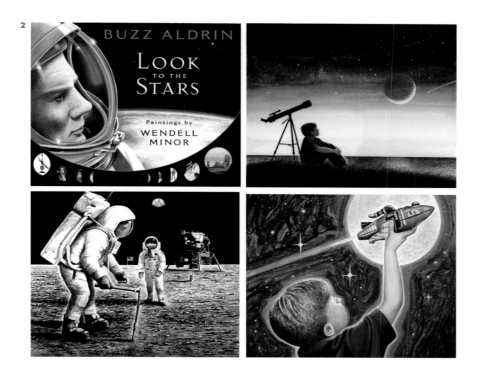

1 Creative Team: Ami Shin - Surbiton, United Kingdom **2 Creative Firm:** Wendell Minor Design **Creative Team:** Buzz Aldrin - Author; Wendell Minor - Illustrator; Martha Rago - Art Director; Dana Fritts – Designer **Client:** G.P. Putnam's Sons

PLATINUM

True To The Original

Creative Firm: United States Postal Service - Arlington, VA

Creative Team: Richard Sheaff - Art Director/ Designer/Typographer; Mark Summers – Artist

Client: United States Postal Service

The bearded image of Abraham Lincoln is a familiar one—on a five dollar bill, a penny and the Lincoln Memorial, to name a few places where millions of Americans see his face every day. Add to that list a set of postage stamps that depicts the sixteenth president during various (clean shaven) phases of his life, from his youth, time as a lawyer and politician and to the White House, along with relevant backgrounds.

"No one individual stamp should be more dominant than the others," say the creators, illustrator Mark Summers and art director Richard Sheaff, who created the four stamps for the United States Postal Service. "This was difficult when one stamp showed a solitary figure in the outdoors and another had three figures indoors. It required playing with shadows and time of day to make sure the balance of tone was

equal." Summers and Sheaff relied on a team of consultants, who looked at the images during their creation and advised the artist of Lincoln's appearance and fashions of the times as Summers drew the portraits on scratchboard, painstakingly re-creating the lines and tone of Lincoln's face. "You don't want these stamps to become valuable because of an inaccuracy, so we spent quite a bit of time tracking down contemporary images and descriptions of such things as Lincoln's clothing and the courtrooms in which he practiced law."

1 Creative Firm: United States Postal Service - Arlington, VA **Creative Team:** Derry Noyes - Art Director/Designer/Typographer; Jeanne Greco – Artist **Client:** United States Postal Service - Arlington, VA **2 Creative Firm:** United States Postal Service **Creative Team:** Carl Herrman - Art Director/Designer/Typographer; Art Fitzpatrick – Artist **Client:** United States Postal Service **3 Creative Firm:** United States Postal Service - Arlington, VA **Creative Team:** Richard Sheaff - Art Director/Designer/Typographer; Michael Deas – Artist **Client:** United States Postal Service

1 **Creative Firm:** United States Postal Service - Arlington, VA **Creative Team:** Carl Herrman - Art Director/Designer/Typographer; Michael Deas – Artist **Client:** United States Postal Service 2 **Creative Firm:** United States Postal Service - Arlington, VA **Creative Team:** Richard Sheaff - Art Director/Designer; Michael Bartolos – Artist/Typographer **Client:** United States Postal Service 3 **Creative Firm:** Diversified Apparel - Sylvania, OH **Creative Team:** Carol Wilerson - Vice President of Sales; James Steward – CEO **Client:** Illustration Promotion for Diversified Apparel 4 **Creative Firm:** United States Postal Service - Arlington, VA **Creative Team:** Carl Herrman - Art Director/Designer/Typographer; Dan Cosgrove – Artist **Client:** United States Postal Service

1
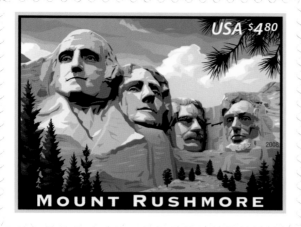

2

3

4

5

6

1 Creative Firm: United States Postal Service - Arlington, VA **Creative Team:** Carl Herrman - Art Director/Designer/Typographer; Dan Cosgrove – Artist **Client:** United States Postal Service **2 Creative Firm:** United States Postal Service - Arlington, VA **Creative Team:** Ethel Kessler - Art Director/Designer; Kam Mak - Artist; Greg Berger – Typographer **Client:** United States Postal Service **3 Creative Firm:** United States Postal Service - Arlington, VA **Creative Team:** Derry Noyes - Art Director/Designer/Typographer **Client:** United States Postal Service **4 Creative Firm:** United States Postal Service - Arlington, VA **Creative Team:** Derry Noyes - Art Director/Designer/Typographer; Gregory Manchess – Artist **Client:** United States Postal Service **5 Creative Firm:** United States Postal Service - Arlington, VA **Creative Team:** Ethel Kessler - Art Director/Designer/Typographer; Matt Mahurin – Artist **Client:** United States Postal Service **6 Creative Firm:** United States Postal Service - Arlington, VA **Creative Team:** Carl Herrman - Art Director/Designer/Typographer; Kadir Nelson – Artist **Client:** United States Postal Service

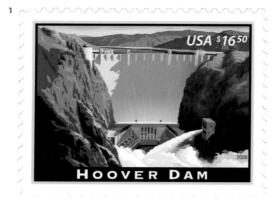

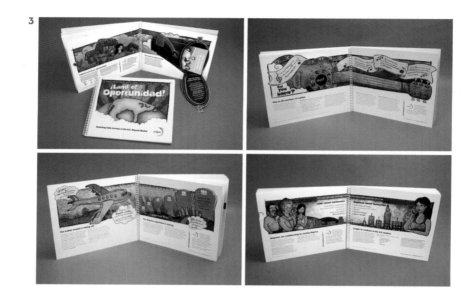

1 Creative Firm: United States Postal Service - Arlington, VA **Creative Team:** Carl Herrman - Art Director/Designer/Typographer; Dan Cosgrove – Artist **Client:** United States Postal Service **2 Creative Firm:** United States Postal Service - Arlington, VA **Creative Team:** Carl Herrman - Art Director/Designer/Typographer; Dan Cosgrove – Artist **Client:** United States Postal Service **3 Creative Firm:** Eclipse Marketing Services, Inc. - Morristown, NJ **Creative Team:** Charles Borgerding - Designer/Illustrator; Barbara Johnston – Creative Director **Client:** Eclipse Marketing Services **4 Creative Team:** Ami Shin - Surbiton, United Kingdom

1 Client: You Magazine **2 Creative Firm:** Incisive Media - New York, NY **Creative Team:** Joan Ferrell - Design Director; David Plunkert – Illustrator **Client:** The American Lawyer **3 Creative Firm:** Sue Todd Illustration - Toronto, ON, Canada **Creative Team:** Sue Todd – Illustrator **Client:** Cricket Magazine **URL:** www.suetodd.com **4 Creative Firm:** Incisive Media - New York, NY **Creative Team:** Joan Ferrell - Design Director; Mick Wiggins – Illustrator **Client:** The American Lawyer

PLATINUM

Creative Firm: Erickson Productions, Inc - Petaluma, CA

Creative Team: Jim Erickson - Director;
Nicki Krinsky - Creative; Channon Cederna - Creative;
Michael O'Neill – First Assistant

Client: Erickson Stock

Creating A Relationship With Clients

Looking at a stock photography Web site is akin to glimpsing infinity, with a seemingly endless collection of images for every possible use. To help bring one of the most popular themes into focus, Erickson Stock in Petaluma, California created a book with relationships front and center. "*The Relationships Book*" was designed with the intent to showcase the wide range of imagery available for sale, while still maintaining the common thread of the 'relationships' theme," says Erickson. "The message behind the book was to exemplify how every person, every thing, and every minute is related." The title supported the theme on every page with photographs painstakingly chosen from Erickson's extensive library and combined in a way to best exemplify what relationships are all about.

1

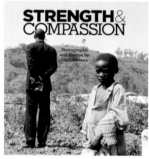

2

3

1 Creative Firm: Beth Singer Design - Arlington, VA **Creative Team:** Beth Singer - Art Director; Howard Smith - Art Director; Deborah Eckbreth - Designer; Eric Greitens - Photographer/ Writer; Rachel Wald – Editor **Client:** Eric Greitens **2 Creative Firm:** Nesnadny + Schwartz - Cleveland, OH **Creative Team:** Mark Schwartz - Creative Director; Michelle Moehler - Designer; Garie Waltzer - Photographer; Geoffrey Gund - Writer; David Abbott - Writer; Deena Epstein - Writer **Client:** The George Gund Foundation **3 Creative Firm:** Nesnadny + Schwartz - Cleveland, OH **Creative Team:** Mark Schwartz - Creative Director; Ricky Salsberry - Designer; Jim Dow - Photographer; Lance Ringel - Writer **Client:** Vassar College

PLATINUM

Creative Firm: Marine Corps Community Services Marketing Branch - FPO, CA
Creative Team: John R. Burgreen III – Art Director/ Photographer
Client: Marine Corps Community Services

Skillful Photography Brightens Marine's Days

The practice of martial arts is popular for exercise and fitness, but at its core it is still martial—a system designed for hand-to-hand combat. The U.S. Marine Corps celebrated its tradition through a martial arts festival at the base of Mt. Fuji, and this photo spread, shot by John R. Burgreen III for *Okinawa Living* magazine, captures the beauty of this most ancient form of fighting. "Marine Corps Community Services (MCCS) is responsible for the morale, welfare and recreation for the Marines stationed at Camp Fuji," says Burgreen. "Since this was a photo essay, the emphasis was on getting strong images that tell a story--in this case, the story of the warriors themselves." Designed with the intention of making the warriors appear as if they'd just walked off a movie set, Burgreen employed strong angles, dynamic poses and clean images.

The weather, however, wasn't as clean as Burgreen and MCCS art director Henry C. Ortega would have liked. Overcast skies, mud and rain ended up making for uncomfortable conditions but a vibrant palette enhanced by Burgreen's seven-shot bracketing, which Ortega then merged in Photoshop to create high dynamic range (HDR) images that span the entire tonal range to dramatic effect. "Having all of the highlight and shadow detail retained made the post production so much easier in the end," he says.

1 **Creative Firm:** Jeff Harris Photography - New York, NY **Creative Team:** Jeff Harris - Photographer; Jon Birdseye - Digital Imaging; Peter Tran – Prop Stylist **Client:** Jeff Harris Photography 2 **Creative Firm:** Andre Mulas - Surabaya, Indonesia **Creative Team:** Andre Eko Prasetyo - Director/Photographer; Siti Fatimah Febrina – Assistant Director

IT'S NOT ACCEPTABLE TO TREAT A WOMAN LIKE ONE.

IT'S NOT ACCEPTABLE TO TREAT A WOMAN LIKE ONE.

 **PLATINUM**

Creative Firm: Michael Indresano Photography - Boston, MA

Creative Team: Michael Indresano - Photographer; Michele Doucette - Producer; Christopher Lee Donovan - Retoucher; Tim Needham - Creative Director; Kevin Acciaioli - Copywriter

Client: Rhode Island Coalition Against Domestic Violence

Taking A Stand Against Domestic Violence

Real men know that women are not punching bags—but to get the point across further, Michael Indressano Photography created a memorable campaign for the Rhode Island Coalition Against Domestic Violence using familiar images from the gym and even "Rocky." "Most domestic violence messages speak directly to women," says Boston-based Indressano, but his creative director Tim Needham and copywriter Kevin Acciaioli took a different approach, aiming to speak to a male audience and tell them that they too could have a positive influence on the issue.

The resulting campaign depicts a punching bag and a slab of meat (contributed by a local butcher for the cause) wearing women's attire and the caption, "It is not acceptable to treat a woman like one"—"one" being the underlying object of aggression. A female colleague modeled the dress for photographs, which were then retouched for the final images. "There were some challenges trying to make the clothing fit the meat and punching bag, but [retoucher] Chris Donovan really took the time to make it look as realistic as possible, as the concept could've fallen flat if it weren't well executed," says Indressano. "In the end, the team had a finished product that could motivate men to take a stand against domestic abuse."

1 **Creative Firm:** Mel Lindstrom Photography - San Francisco, CA **Creative Team:** Mel Lindstrom; Kuumba Dancers 1; Robin Allen - Producer; Adrienne Parker - Art Director **Client:** Kuumba Kinetics 2 **Creative Firm:** Mel Lindstrom Photography - San Francisco, CA **Creative Team:** Mel Lindstrom - Photographer; Robin Allen - Producer; Adrienne Parker – Art Director **Client:** Kuumba Kinetics 3 **Creative Firm:** Trained Eye Graphics - El Sobrante, CA **Creative Team:** Barry Barnes - Graphic Designer/ Photographer **Client:** Trained Eye Print Gallery

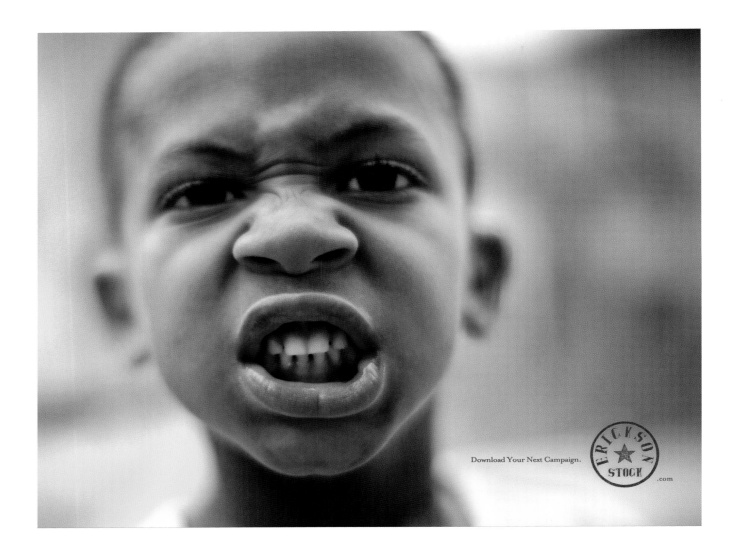

Download Your Next Campaign.

ERICKSON STOCK .com

PLATINUM

Still Life

Creative Firm: Erickson Productions, Inc. - Petaluma, CA

Creative Team: Jim Erickson - Photographer;
Nicki Krinsky – Creative

Client: Erickson Stock

A young boy stares into the camera, teeth clenched, emotion on his face. Is he angry? Determined? Excited? Erickson Stock in Petaluma, California created an image that users could use to illustrate any of these, but the photographer's original impression simply was the exuberance of being a kid. "This image was taken while shooting stock in Texas," Erickson reports. "The image truly captures the essence of the human spirit and the innocence and carefree nature of childhood. The title of 'Purity' was chosen to depict the gift that every child inherently possesses."

1

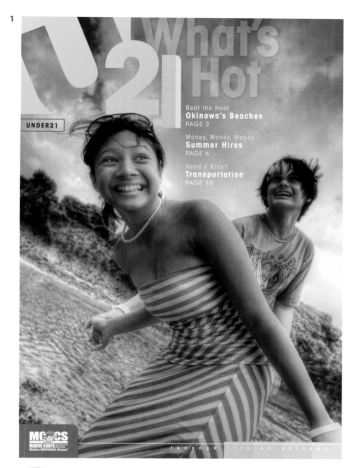

2

1 **Creative Firm:** Marine Corps Community Services Marketing Branch - FPO, CA **Creative Team:** Rachel Veit - Art Director; John R. Burgreen III - Director of Photography; Cindy Ramos - Managing Editor; Richenda Sandlin-Tymitz - Managing Editor; Mina Furusho - Contributing Photographer; Henry Ortega – MCCS Art Director **Client:** Marine Corps Community Services **2 Creative Firm:** Emphasis Media Limited - North Point, Hong Kong **Creative Team:** Dan Hayes - Editor; Mike Wescombe – Art Director **Client:** CNN

1 **Creative Firm:** Emphasis Media Limited - North Point, Hong Kong **Creative Team:** Dan Hayes - Editor; Mike Wescombe – Art Director **Client:** CNN **2 Creative Firm:** Erickson Productions, Inc. - Petaluma, CA **Creative Team:** Jim Erickson - Photographer; Nicki Krinsky – Creative **Client:** Erickson Stock

1

2

3

1 **Creative Firm:** Incisive Media - New York, NY **Creative Team:** Joan Ferrell - Design Director; Morris Stubbs - Art Director; Maggie Soladay - Photo Editor; Max S. Gerber – Photographer **Client:** The American Lawyer 2 **Creative Firm:** Erickson Productions, Inc. - Petaluma, CA **Creative Team:** Jim Erickson - Photographer; Nicki Krinsky – Creative **Client:** Erickson Stock 3 **Creative Firm:** Incisive Media - New York, NY **Creative Team:** Joan Ferrell - Design Director; Elizabeth Williams - Photo Editor; Siddharth Siva – Photographer **Client:** The American Lawyer

 PLATINUM

Putting Smile On Discomfort

Creative Firm: Mel Lindstrom Photography - San Francisco, CA

Creative Team: Mel Lindstrom – Photographer; Bill Rehelander – Art Director

Client: OneMagazine

Intestinal discomfort is no laughing matter, but San Francisco photograph Mel Lindstrom captured some of the best (and most humorous) expressions of it when doing a spec piece for a biomedical client who wanted to show just that. "When working with real people, the biggest challenge is always making them feel comfortable in front of the camera, but in this case it was especially challenging since we had to pull more out of them than just a nice smile," says Lindstrom of the portraits. "We had to

get them to dig down deep and really come up with a great expression."

The shots, the "Before" in a "Before and After" juxtaposition, gave Lindstrom the opportunity to create some fun and unique images for the pitch, and allowed him to work on his "DZone" photographic technique, which emphasizes facial lines and colors. "This technique is a great way to show every facial flaw a person has, but still make a wonderful image," he says.

1

2

3

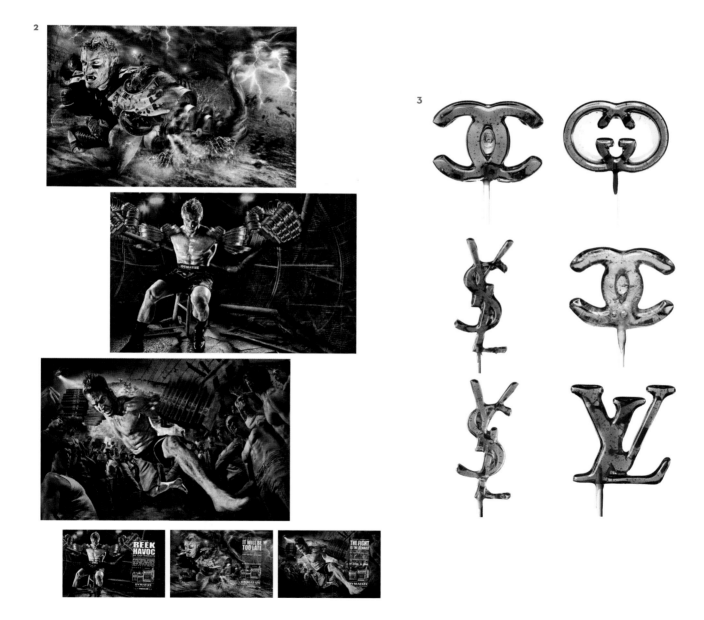

1 Creative Firm: Nelson Schmidt - Milwaukee, WI **Creative Team:** Jane Kramer - Creative Director/Art Director; Chris Wimpey - Photographer **Client:** Automatic Data Processing Inc. (ADP) **2 Creative Firm:** George Kamper Inc. - Fort Lauderdale, FL **Creative Team:** George Kamper - Photographer; Kyle Lane - Illustrator; Scott Crowell – Art Director **Client:** Dymatize **3 Creative Firm:** Massimo Gammacurta Photographer - South Orange, NJ **Creative Team:** Amanda Tsui - AD; Charlie Matz - Props; Andi Kuonath - Retouching; Cat Baker – Styling **Client:** I LOVE U Magazine **URL:** www.gammacurta.com

1 Creative Firm: Fitting Group - Pittsburgh, PA **Creative Team:** Andrew Ellis - Designer; Travis Norris – Creative Director **Client:** Pittsburgh Urban Magnet Project

Love Letters – Wallpaper July issue

Airside

PLATINUM

....

Creative Firm: Airside - London, United Kingdom

....

Client: Wallpaper*

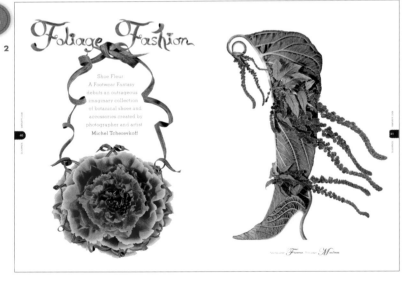

1 Creative Firm: Emphasis Media Limited - North Point, Hong Kong **Creative Team:** Innes Doig - Editorial Director; Percy Chung - Associate Creative Director; Teresita Khaw - Art Director; Eva Chan – Photo Editor **Client:** SilkAir **2 Creative Firm:** Emphasis Media Limited - North Point, Hong Kong **Creative Team:** Innes Doig - Editorial Director; Percy Chung - Associate Creative Director; Teresita Khaw - Art Director; Eva Chan – Photo Editor **Client:** SilkAir **3 Creative Firm:** Emphasis Media Limited - North Point, Hong Kong **Creative Team:** Innes Doig - Editorial Director; Percy Chung - Associate Creative Director; Teresita Khaw - Art Director; Eva Chan – Photo Editor **Client:** SilkAir

9

new media +
web design

PLATINUM

Creative Firm: Robin Horton Design - Old Greenwich, CT

Creative Team: Robin Horton – Principal/Creative Director

Client: Urban Gardens

URL: www.urbangardensweb.com

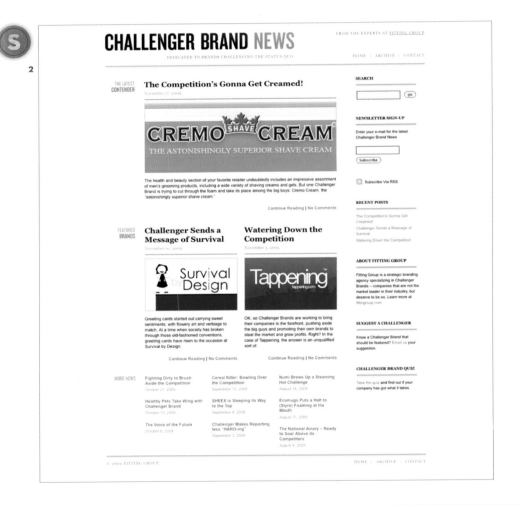

1 **Creative Firm:** W. Lynn Garrett Art Direction + Design - Valley Glen, CA **Creative Team:** W. Lynn Garrett – Founder/Art Director/Designer/Writer **URL:** www.hiddenlosangeles.com 2 **Creative Firm:** Fitting Group - Pittsburgh, PA **Creative Team:** Andrew Ellis – Designer; Travis Norris – Creative Director; Tim Emanuel – Web Developer; Jeff Fitting – Interactive Director; Siri Espy – Writer **Client:** Fitting Group **URL:** www.challengerbrandnews.com/

Wall-E Takes Over

Creative Firm: Deadline Advertising - Los Angeles, CA

Creative Team: Eric Kahn – Creative Director; Matthew Hockman – Producer

Client: Walt Disney Studios Home Entertainment

URL: www.dead-line.com

WALL-E was the number one animated film of the year, and to market the home entertainment release of the movie, Disney/Pixar enlisted Deadline Advertising in Los Angeles to make their big hit even bigger. Says Deadline: "A few things were certain: Amazon.com would build a boutique site dedicated to all WALL-E home entertainment products, and of course the ad running on that page had to knock your socks off."

Deadline created the first-ever takeover banner on the site, featuring fun and interactive animations of the characters WALL-E and M-O, to drive attention to the Amazon.com WALL-E store. Deadline and Amazon.com technical teams worked hand in hand, forgoing the need for any third parties. "The execution had to be something

WALL-E fans would notice, get excited about and share with their friends, thus becoming viral and facilitating additional site traffic," the agency says. The little robot that could delivered: The takeover ad garnered interaction rates which were above and beyond all expectations, with average click-through rates of over 38% and a further interaction rate of 84%.

1 **Creative Firm:** IAC Advertising Solutions - New York, NY **Creative Team:** Michael Calleia – Creative Director; Laurie Satler – Custom Solutions Manager; Alberto Langton – Art Director; Tara Scott – Sr. Designer; Bobby Reif – Designer **Client:** Bacardi 2 **Creative Firm:** IAC Advertising Solutions - New York, NY **Creative Team:** Michael Calleia – Creative Director; Alberto Langton – Art Director; Laurie Satler – Custom Solutions Manager **Client:** Miller Coors 3 **Creative Firm:** Hitchcock Fleming & Associates Inc. - Akron, OH **Creative Team:** Nick Betro – Executive Creative Director; Patrick Ginnetti – Art Director; Tony Fanizzi – Writer; Jason Nicolacakis – Account Executive; Jeff Stager – Computer Graphics Specialist/Artist **Client:** Goodyear Tire & Rubber Co. **URL:** thebuzzwerks.com

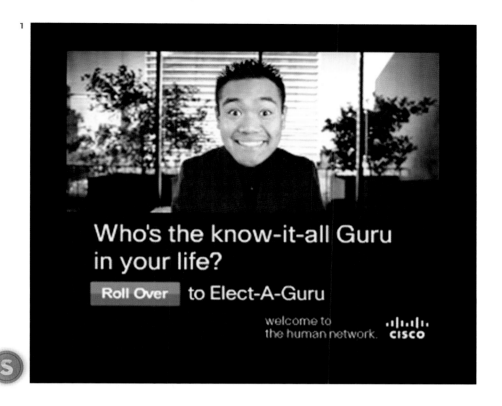

1 Creative Firm: Ogilvy West - Culver City, CA **Creative Team:** Peter Kang - Group Creative Director; Bob Strickland - Group Creative Director; Jeff Compton Group – Creative Director; Johann Conforme – Creative Director; Noel Kouwenhoven – Art Director; Graham Simon – Copywriter **Client:** Cisco Systems, Inc. **URL:** www.ogilvywest.net
2 Creative Firm: Hitchcock Fleming & Associates Inc. - Akron, OH **Creative Team:** Nick Betro – Executive Creative Director; Milissa Shrake – Assoc. Creative Director; Tony Fanizzi – Writer; Rene McCann – Sr. Art Director/Interactive; Jaime Brannan – Account Executive **Client:** Goodyear Tire & Rubber Co. **URL:** thebuzzwerks.com **3 Creative Firm:** Hitchcock Fleming & Associates Inc. - Akron, OH **Creative Team:** Nick Betro – Executive Creative Director; Rene McCann – Sr. Art Director/Interactive; Milissa Shrake – Assoc. Creative Director; Tony Fanizzi – Writer; Chris Stahl – Web Developer; Shelly Morton – Project Manager **Client:** Goodyear Tire & Rubber Co. **URL:** thebuzzwerks.com

1

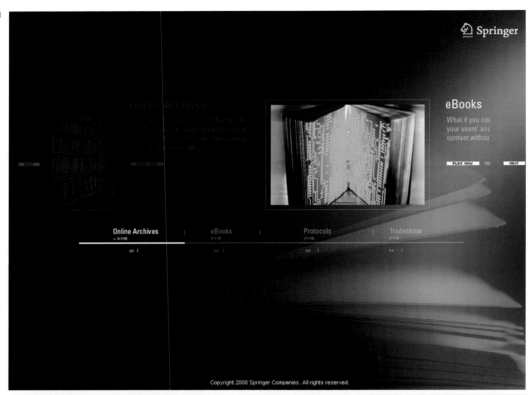

1 Creative Firm: Juno Studio - Jersey City, NJ **Creative Team:** Jun Li – Creative Director/Designer; Matt Weiss – Producer **Client:** Springer US

1

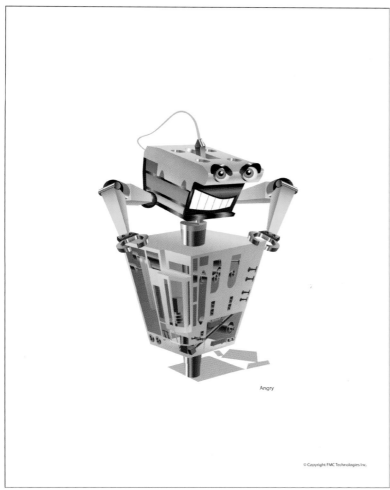

Angry

© Copyright FMC Technologies Inc.

Concerned

© Copyright FMC Technologies Inc.

Smiling

© Copyright FMC Technologies Inc.

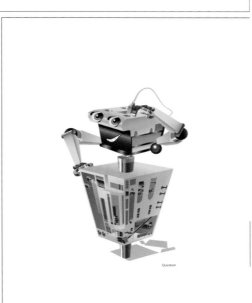

Question

© Copyright FMC Technologies Inc.

1 Creative Firm: Stan Gellman Graphic Design, Inc. - St. Louis, MO **Creative Team:** Barry Tilson – President; Teresa Thompson – Vice President; Bryan Wakeland – Designer **Client:** FMC Technologies, Inc.

No more issues falling through the cracks. TeamSupport's groundbreaking ticket management application keeps everyone in the loop — so you can make customers happier.

Bridging communication gaps and sharing information like never before, your teams in customer service, development, QA and sales will work together better to resolve customer issues. Meanwhile, each team will collect valuable customer feedback, which they can use to improve product quality, capabilities, sales practices and customer satisfaction. Just like that, everyone's happy.

Way better than the alternative, don't you think?

3 USERS FREE

The first 3 company users are free — no risk, no credit card required!

Get free custom data conversion from your existing system and free personalized training when you sign up at least 10 users on a 6-month agreement.

Click here for more information

TeamSupport.com

© 2008 Muroc Systems, Inc.

1 Creative Firm: M/C/C - Dallas, TX **Creative Team:** Todd Brashear – Associate Creative Director; Hillary Boulden – Senior Art Director; Greg Hansen – Vice President/Creative; Amanda Myers – Production Manager; Jim Terry – Vice President/Account Service; Kevin Krekeler – Account Executive **Client:** Team Support **URL:** www.mccstage.com

 **PLATINUM**

No Child Left Behind

Creative Firm: Ember Media - New York, NY

Creative Team: Clayton Banks – Executive Producer; Alexander Grinshpoon – Creative Director; Haldane Henry – Programmer; Jason Freeny – Designer; Alex Britez – Game Programming; Matt Cohen – Project Manager

Client: Scholastic

URL: www.readandrisemag.net

Scholastic, the educational publications company, does more than make mail-order kids' books. The Read & Rise initiative, devised to help build the reading skills of African American children, now has a digital version of its magazine to allow for more aggressive promotion and cost savings on production and distribution of hard copy versions—and its Web site, designed by Ember Media in New York City, aims to engage young readers in a fresh new way.

That doesn't mean kids won't get to enjoy the pleasure of reading from books. "The individual stories and poems of the issue can be set up as miniature versions of interactive books," explains Ember. Each issue's stories feature simple animation based on the original illustrations, the ability to hear the story while words are highlighted and a clickable pronunciation feature that allows readers to hear the right way to say a particular word. To further promote literacy, each e-zine includes age-appropriate interactive activities, delivered regularly to subscribers. Says the agency of the power of digital subscriptions: "This will allow people to subscribe to a digital version of e-zine and will establish a long-term relationship with families. With this highly targeted approach taken, each issue will no longer have to serve the needs of all potential users. Instead, Scholastic will be free to send families the perfect issue."

1 **Creative Firm:** Jacob Tyler Creative Group - San Diego, CA **Creative Team:** Les Kollegian – Creative Director; Gordon Tsuji – Art Director; Adam Roop – Senior Designer; Jessica Recht – Designer; Cole Miller – Junior Designer **Client:** College Magazine **URL:** www.collegemagazine.com 2 **Creative Firm:** Singularity Design - Philadelphia, PA **Creative Team:** Sean Trapani – Creative Director; Owen Linton – Art Director **Client:** Singularity Design

PLATINUM

East Meets West

Creative Firm: Sapient Interactive - Palmetto Bay, FL

Creative Team: Casey Sheehan - Associate Creative Director; Jon Jackson - Associate Creative Director; Mike Hansen - Senior Art Director; Anthony Yell - Vice President Creative; Graham Engebretsen - Manager Program Management; Michael Leonard – Director Program Management

Client: The Coca-Cola Company

URL: preview.sapientem.com/clients/Coke_No_Branding/Multi_Media_Coke_Machine.htm

The 2008 Summer Olympics—which kicked off on the auspicious date of 08-08-08—was the most-watched Olympics in history, with one of the world's most recognized products readily available to those lucky enough to get a ticket to the games. To showcase the WE8 (West East) program coordinated by Sapient Interactive, eight Chinese artists—representing East—received custom eight-ounce aluminum Coca-Cola contour bottles to decorate based on a different Olympic theme. (Eight Western musical artists created a song for each of the same themes.) According to Sapient, the challenge lay in "designing an interface for a well-known device that was not only intuitive but also captured the essence of the Olympic games in Beijing and the themes for each bottle."

The Multi Media Coke Machine Project, revealed at the Olympics, integrated a 46" LCD touch screen into the front of a standard vending machine. By incorporating the official iconographies of the Beijing Olympics and Coca-Cola, the Palmetto Bay, Florida agency developed an experience that brought the graphics to life while celebrating the international spirit of the games.

1

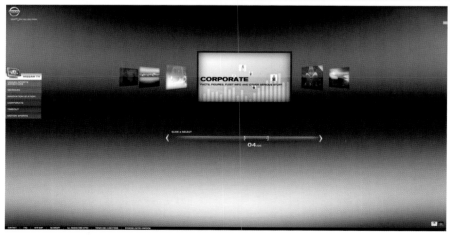

1 Creative Firm: DNA - Neuilly-sur-Seine, France **Creative Team:** Vincent Druguet - Senior Manager; Véronique Beaumont - Senior Manager; Olivier Delas – Creative Director **Client:** Nissan **URL:** www.nissan.co.uk/#nissan-tv

1

2

1 Creative Firm: VSA Partners - Chicago, IL **Creative Team:** Jonathan Sluys - Senior Designer; Christina Brinkerhoff - Account Manager; Thom Wolfe - Associate Partner/ Design Director; Pat Heick – Principal/Creative Director **Client:** McDonald's **2 Creative Firm:** Creative Alliance - Louisville, KY **Creative Team:** Brendan Jackson - Director of Digital Services; Brian Phillips - Executive Creative Director; Zeke Snow – Account Executive **Client:** KFC **URL:** www.surfthecrowds.com/

PLATINUM

Creative Firm: Exopolis - Los Angeles, CA

Creative Team: Garrett Braren - Executive Producer; Magnus Hierta - Director; Casey Hupke - Lead Animator; Danny Duran - Designer/Animator; Ming Hsiung - Designer/Animator; Somatone – Sound Design

Client: Microsoft Xbox

URL: www.exopolis.com/client/overview2/36_xbox/xBox_Final_640_web.mov

 **PLATINUM**

A Porny Celebration

Creative Firm: Caviar - Venice, CA

Creative Team: Keith Schofield - Director; Michael Sagol – Executive Producer

Client: Viral Factory

URL: www.break.com/usercontent/2008/9/Diesel-SFW-XXX-577249.html

Advertising is a sexy business, or at least is perceived as such by the public. That said, fashion company Diesel actually got rather excited about a proposal from the Viral Factory mixing animation and hardcore porn. With a theme of "XXX"—after all, it was Diesel's thirtieth anniversary—creative director Keith Schofield of Caviar in Venice, California, put together a hilarious and jaw-dropping 100-second spoof of 1970s-era adult films, culled from hours of rather raw footage. "You just had to be explicit to describe the scenes," says Schofield of the spot, which promoted Diesel's anniversary bash. "We thought, if [the actors are] humping each other, that might be a good horse riding shot,

and anything in their mouths could be some sort of food item. Then we started looking for types of acts that hadn't been seen yet." Turning, er, classic film acts into actions involving inflating an air mattress and eating corn on the cob was hardly an exercise in subtlety: "It's just porn and cartoons," Schofield says.

The resulting clip was a scandalously funny viral success, garnering 9.2 million hits from its first three weeks online. "Sorting through the massive amount of footage, and then figuring out what shots work best and then what the animation should be was a challenge," says Schofield. "As we went along, we figured it out." Uh-huh.

1

2

1 Creative Firm: Draftfcb Chicago - Chicago, IL **Creative Team:** Joe Gallo - Group Creative Director; Nicole Tomassini - Associate Creative Director; Michele Sloan - Copywriter; Nanako Okubo - Art Director; Greg Lederer - Agency Producer; Jamin Winans - Double Edge Films, Editorial **Client:** Motorola H15 **URL:** creativeawardentries.com/santaswarm/ **2 Creative Firm:** Best Company Ever, Inc. - El Segundo, CA **Creative Team:** BEST* - Director, Best Company Ever, Inc.; Peter Gwinn - Creative Director/AMP Agency; Jennifer Peeples - Producer/AMP Agency; John Genese - Executive Producer/AMP Agency; Diane Castrup - Producer, Best Company Ever, Inc. **Client:** LifeStyles Condoms

1

2

1 Creative Firm: State Farm Insurance - Bloomington, IL **Creative Team:** Patty Dirker - Marketing Analyst; Tim Thomas - Marketing Analyst; Jim Stahly - Marketing Analyst; Mariana Rutledge - Marketing Analyst; Shelia Law - Marketing Analyst; Greg Sutter – Marketing Analyst **Client:** State Farm Insurance **URL:** www.youtube.com/statefarm **2 Creative Firm:** Your Majesty - New York, NY **Creative Team:** Peter Karlsson - Account Director; James Widegren - Creative Director; Heather Reddig - Executive Producer; Dan Johnson - Art Director; Sarah Grant - Developer; Erik Jonsson - Designer **Client:** Campfire/Discovery Channel - Shark Week **URL:** archive.your-majesty.com/frenziedwaters/index2.html

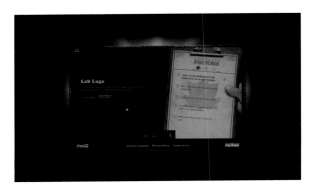

 **PLATINUM**

Creative Firm: Sapient Interactive - Palmetto Bay, FL
Creative Team: Alex Toledo - Flash Developer; Ben Levy - Copywriter; Juan Morales - Creative Director; Mauricio Carrasco - Art Director; Alex Fundora - 3D Animator; Angicel Santos – Project/Account Manager
Client: The Coca-Cola Company
URL: www.sapient.com/Awards/happiness-factory.html

A Visit To Happiness

Coca-Cola has marketed its brand of happiness in a bottle for over a century, and the online extension of that is the 21st Century way. Coke's online experience sought to extend the popularity of its Happiness Factory campaign while focusing on the "physical uplift" found in every bottle of Coke—"that burst of joy, refreshment and energy you get with every sip," describes Sapient Interactive, the Palmetto Bay, Florida firm hired to create a story for the online audience. Sapient created a site that focused on the Factory's average yet indispensable worker responsible for bringing the Coke to the everyday vending machine. With high-definition video content and games

fully rendered in 3D to create a visual experience on par with console games—plus unlockable downloads for virtual (screensavers and ringtones) and (iron-on shirt transfers and worker goggles) rewards—the site offered a look inside the machine and all the way back to the Happiness Factory.

"We wanted to push the limits of what could be done online and make the user experience more immersive, while keeping the site consistent," Sapient says. "The team worked with 3D animators and Psyop models from the original animation for the TV commercials, rather than just pulling clips, to reconstruct the experience online."

1

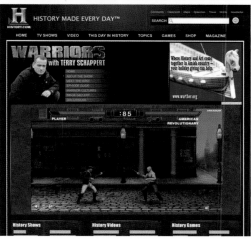

2

1 Creative Firm: Arkadium - New York, NY **Creative Team:** Terrance Peng - Creative Director; Chris Neuman – Game Artist **Client:** A&E History Channel **URL:** www.history.com/warriors-game **2 Creative Firm:** Deadline Advertising - Los Angeles, CA **Creative Team:** Eric Kahn - Creative Director; Chris McCall - Senior Art Director; Phil Hinch – Producer **Client:** Walt Disney Studios Home Entertainment **URL:** adisney.go.com/disneyvideos/animatedfilms/nightmarebeforechristmas/widget/widget-popup.html

1

2

3

1 Creative Firm: Arkadium - New York, NY **Creative Team:** Jeremy Mayes - Director of Game Production; Tom Rassweiler - Manager of Game Development; Chris Walsh – Senior Game Artist **Client:** National Geographic Channel **URL:** channel.nationalgeographic.com/channel/content/expedition-week/game/expedition.html **2 Creative Firm:** Arkadium - New York, NY **Creative Team:** Terrance Peng – Creative Director **Client:** National Geographic Channel **URL:** channel.nationalgeographic.com/channel/hooked-reel-em-in-game **3 Creative Firm:** Agency Republic - London, England **Creative Team:** Alistair Campbell - Creative Director; Nick Horne - Art Director; Rob Ellis - Copywriter; Bertrand Carrera - Designer; Ian Lainchbury - Developer; David Cox – Creative Technologist **Client:** PlayStation **URL:** www.biginteractiveideas.com/caa_killzone

1

2

4

3

1 **Creative Firm:** Sapient Interactive - Palmetto Bay, FL **Creative Team:** Juan Morales - Executive Creative Director; James Allen - Creative Director; Cesar Santos - Sr Art Director; Ben Levy - Copywriter; Alex Toledo - Lead Interactive Developer; Alejandro Villanueva – Interactive Developer **Client:** The Coca-Cola Company **URL:** awards.i4bn.com/burn-alterego 2 **Creative Firm:** Deadline Advertising - Los Angeles, CA **Creative Team:** Eric Kahn - Creative Director; Chris McCall - Senior Art Director; Phil Hinch – Producer **Client:** Walt Disney Studios Home Entertainment **URL:** adisney.go.com/disneyvideos/animatedfilms/nightmarebeforechristmas 3 **Creative Firm:** Deadline Advertising - Los Angeles, CA **Creative Team:** Eric Kahn - Creative Director; Matthew Hockman – Producer **Client:** Walt Disney Studios Home Entertainment **URL:** www.dead-line.com/awards/2009/creativity_annual 4 **Creative Firm:** Exopolis - Los Angeles, CA **Creative Team:** Bridget Sheils - Executive Producer; Shellie Lewis - Producer; Jessica Baker - Associate Producer; Ezra Paulekas - Creative Lead; Danny Duran - Lead Animator; Nathaniel Trienes – Development **Client:** Kirshenbaum Bond + Partners **URL:** luckybuckoff.exopolis.com

1

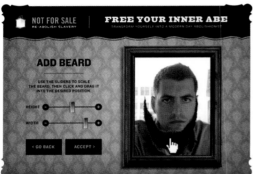

2

3

1 Creative Firm: Martin Williams - Minneapolis, MN **Creative Team:** Tom Moudry - Chief Creative Officer; Jim Henderson - Creative Director; Lyle Wedemeyer - Creative Director; Luke Oeth - Art Director; Shane Mechelke - Interactive Designer; Tyler Knight – Interactive Developer **Client:** Not For Sale **URL:** apps.facebook.com/inner_abe/
2 Creative Firm: Stellar Debris - Hadano-shi, Japan **Creative Team:** Christopher Jones - Creative Director/Writer/Sound Design; Isaac Zamora – Illustration/Flash **Client:** Bytware **URL:** www.moshimoshicorp.com/games/ono_security_quiz.html **3 Creative Firm:** JAK Graphic Design, LLC - Darien, IL **Creative Team:** Jill Kerrigan - Principal/Creative Director; Angelo Rita - Art Director; Marko Masnjak – Web Designer **Client:** World Wildlife Fund **URL:** www.worldwildlife.org/waveforward/fishGame.html

 **PLATINUM**

Creative Firm: Buzz Image Group - Montreal, QC, Canada

Creative Team: Maxime Landreville - Interactive Director; Gabriel Forget - Web Programmer; David St-Amant - 3D Artist; Guillaume Pelletier - 3D Artist; Bruno Blain - 3D Artist; Emmanuelle Couture – 3D Artist (Texture/Shading/Lighting)

Client: Buzz Image Group

URL: www.buzzimage.com

Interactive Studio Creates A "Buzz"

Montreal's Buzz Image Group already had the perfect name but needed an equally evocative interactive portfolio to showcase its work with "integrated media"—live production, live and 3D animation, motion graphics and postproduction. Done in-house, they report that the Web site "had to be a clear demonstration of experience with the expertise gained from typically working in television." In order to stay on track with the company's progressing needs, it was imperative that Buzz exercise a large range of flexibility in terms of the site management and of the content itself. They clearly illustrated this by creating a

platform that would accommodate the different types of communications of the company, including e-mails, demo reels and online presentations, as well as the "sheer uniqueness of the creativity in store," all in a complimentary way.

"The Web site was the first experience of its kind for the company, therefore we needed to learn how to efficiently work the departments together," says Buzz when speaking about the challenge of creating an entirely new experience. "It works well for all across the divisions, but the recipe may change here and there to get there."

1

2

1 Creative Firm: People Design Inc - Grand Rapids, MI **Creative Team:** Kevin Budelmann - Creative Director; Michele Chartier - Design Director; Victor Sirotek - Interaction Designer; Marie-Claire Camp - Interaction Designer; Scott Krieger - Lead Developer; Andy Weber - Developer **Client:** People Design **URL:** www.peopledesign.com **2 Creative Firm:** Ogilvy West - Culver City, CA **Creative Team:** Dan Burrier - Co-President/Chief Creative Officer; Peter Kang - Group Creative Director; Johann Conforme - Creative Director; Henry Kuo - UE Director/Art Director; Meghann Moran - Copywriter; Stephanie Arculli - Art Director **Client:** Cisco Systems, Inc. **URL:** www.ogilvywest.net/awards/w3/cisco/therealm/

1

2

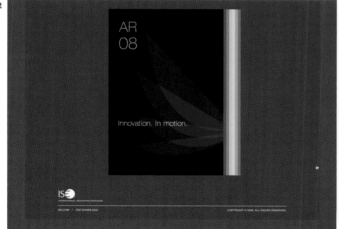

1 Creative Firm: Ogilvy West - Culver City, CA **Creative Team:** Dan Burrier - Co-President/Chief Creative Officer; Peter Kang - Group Creative Director; Johann Conforme - Creative Director; Noel Kouwenhoven - Art Director; Max Bean - Associate Creative Director/Copywriter; Chris Cirak – Information Architect **Client:** Cisco Systems, Inc. **URL:** www.cisco.com/go/getready **2 Creative Firm:** INC Design - New York, NY **Creative Team:** Alejandro Medina - Senior Art Director; Martine Chepigin - Managing Partner; Adam Leder – Web Programmer **Client:** International Securities Exchange **URL:** www.ise.com/Annual_Reports/2008/ISE-2008AR-final-release/index.html

1 Creative Firm: Groove11 - San Rafael, CA **Creative Team:** Mike McGinty - Creative Director/Copywriter; Rainey Straus - Design Director; Bruce Godshall - Lead Designer; Todd Hedgpeth - Designer; Gerardo Perez - Designer; David Creech - Producer **Client:** InfoMotor **URL:** www.infomotor.com **2 Creative Firm:** People Design Inc - Grand Rapids, MI **Creative Team:** Geoffrey Mark - Director of Interaction Design; Marie-Claire Camp - Interaction Designer; Ryan Lee - Interaction Designer; Aaron Vanderzwan - Developer; John Winkelman - Developer; Scott Krieger – Senior Developer **Client:** Whirlpool **3 Creative Firm:** Deadline Advertising - Los Angeles, CA **Creative Team:** Eric Kahn - Creative Director; Chris McCall - Senior Art Director; Stephen Fahlsing – Senior Online Producer **Client:** Walt Disney Studios Home Entertainment **URL:** dep.disney.go.com/

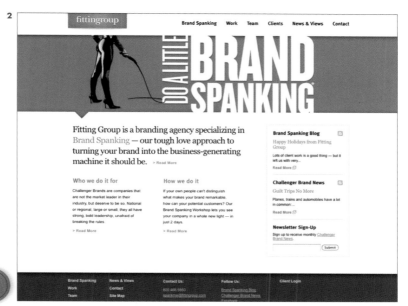

1 Creative Firm: Hitchcock Fleming & Associates Inc. - Akron, OH **Creative Team:** Nick Betro - Executive Creative Director; Greg Pfiffner - Writer; Rene McCann - Sr. Art Director/Interactive; Patrick Ginnetti - Art Director; Jim Kiel - Web Developer; Marie Lepley – Project Manager **Client:** Liquid Nails **URL:** www.liquidnails.com/pro/index. jsp **2 Creative Firm:** Fitting Group - Pittsburgh, PA **Creative Team:** Andrew Ellis - Designer; Travis Norris - Creative Director; Tim Emanuel - Web Developer; Jeff Fitting – Interactive Director **Client:** Fitting Group **URL:** www.fittinggroup.com/ **3 Creative Firm:** Sprokkit - Los Angeles, CA **Client:** Red Mango **URL:** www.RedMangoFranchising. com **4 Creative Firm:** JPL - Harrisburg, PA **Creative Team:** David Haseleu - Project Manager; Mary Pedersen - Creative Director; Jim Mitchell - Art Director; Katy Bastas - Designer; Ryan Pudloski - Flash Developer; Larry Daughenbaugh – Front End Developer **Client:** Harsco **URL:** www.harsco.com

1 Creative Firm: BGT Partners - Miami, FL **Creative Team:** BGT Partners Interactive Team **Client:** ADP **URL:** www.adp.com **2 Creative Firm:** Singularity Design - Philadelphia, PA **Creative Team:** Sean Trapani - Creative Director; Owen Linton - Art Director; Jeff Mills – Sr. Interactive Developer **Client:** DGA-Spych **URL:** www.spychresearch.com **3 Creative Firm: Creative Firm:** RainCastle Communications - Newton, MA **Creative Team:** Paul Regensburg - President/Creative Director; Ji Lee – Senior Designer **Client:** Shawmut Design and Construction **URL:** www.shawmut.com **4 Creative Firm:** Greenfield/Belser Ltd. - Washington D.C. **Creative Team:** Shaun Quigley - Account Director; Nicole Shafer - Account Executive; Burkey Belser - Creative Director; Aaron Thornburgh - Senior Designer; Paul Chang - Web Manager; Dane Harrigan - Web Developer **Client:** Sterne Kessler Goldstein Fox **URL:** skgf.com/home.php

1

1 Creative Firm: JPD Studio - New York, NY **Creative Team:** Jessica Perilla – Creative Director **Client:** DANNIJO **URL:** www.dannijo.com

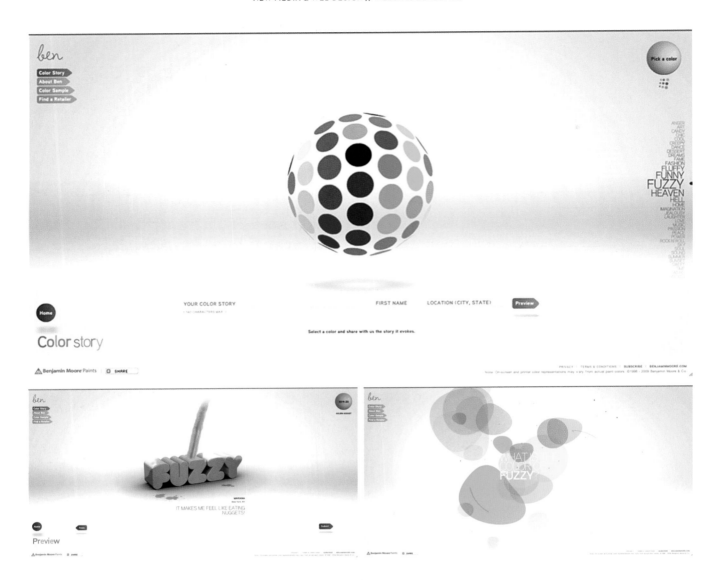

PLATINUM

Ask Ben

Creative Firm: AKQA - New York, NY

Creative Team: Mehera O'Brien - Creative Director; Mariana Bukvic - Senior Art Director; Keith Zang - Copywriter; Kaare Wesnaes - Director of Creative Development; Yi Liu - Senior Creative Developer; Kenny Lin – Creative Developer

Client: Benjamin Moore

URL: work.akqa.com/benjaminmoore/ben/

Marketing paint may seem as exciting as, well, watching it dry. To make buying paint appealing and even fun, Benjamin Moore launched its new paint line, Ben, with the help of New York agency AKQA. The aim was to create an experience that drove brand awareness and consideration among a new audience: young, design-savvy experience seekers. Drawing upon the concept that everyone experiences color differently and across the Benjamin Moore color spectrum, AKQA enticed consumers with questions such as, "What's the color of your imagination? And what about the color of wicked? Of rock 'n roll?"

With seven weeks from concept to live launch, AKQA had a lot to think about, particularly where cultural significance is involved. "Americans wear white to weddings. It means purity. Yet in China, this color represents death and mourning," the agency says. "The idea that colors have rich cultural and emotional meaning, and that this meaning is unique to each of us, drove the creative thinking. From a brand perspective, Benjamin Moore provides the largest assortment of colors in the market – and by extension, the greatest license to express personal style." With color product names ranging from descriptive to playful—"Icing on the Cake" and "Forget Me Not," to name a couple—AKQA drove the idea to develop a "word association" interface that invited users to think about their own ideas on color.

1

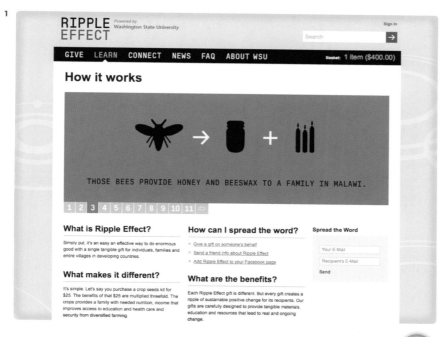

2

1 Creative Firm: Hornall Anderson Design Works - Seattle, WA **Creative Team:** Halli Theil - Executive Producer; Zak Menkel - Interactive Producer; Joseph King - Designer; Rachel Blakely - Designer; Don Kenoyer – Designer; Gordon Mueller – Developer **Client:** Washington State University Foundation **URL:** rippleeffect.wsu.edu **2 Creative Firm:** JPL - Harrisburg, PA **Creative Team:** Modesty Guarente - Project Manager; Chelsie Markel - Art Director; Matt Byers - Designer; Gabe Mariani – Flash Developer **Client:** The Hershey Company **URL:** www.twizzlers.coms

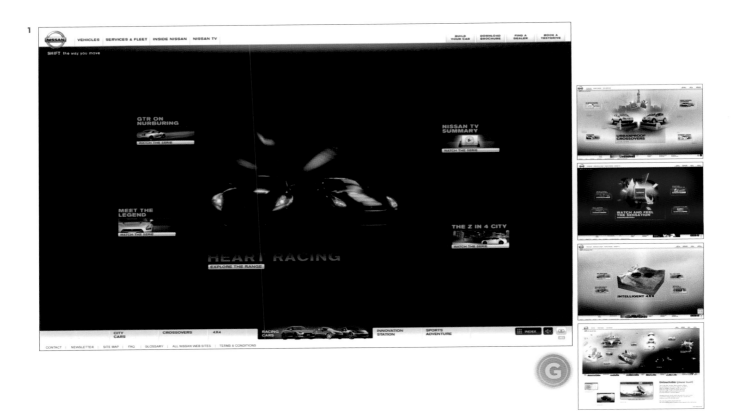

Print

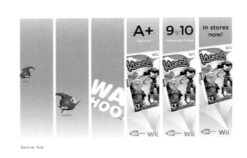

Banner Ads

Interactive

1 Creative Firm: DNA - Neuilly-sur-Seine, France **Creative Team:** Vincent Druguet - Senior Manager; Véronique Beaumont - Senior Manager; Olivier Delas – Creative Director **Client:** Nissan **URL:** http://www.nissaneurope.com **2 Creative Firm:** KNOCK inc. - Minneapolis, MN **Creative Team:** KNOCK inc. Design Firm; Todd Paulson - Creative Director; Sara Nelson - Design Director; Kat Townsend - Designer; Dan Armstrong - Writer; Soire – Design Programming **Client:** NAMCO BANDAI **URL:** www.klonoagame.com

1

2

3

1 Creative Firm: Agency Republic - London, England **Creative Team:** Gavin Gordon-Rogers - Creative Director; Jim Stump - Copywriter; Tim Gardiner - Director/ Editor/ Producer/ Music and Sound; Simon Maggs - Photographer; Carl Huber - Developer; Tom Danvers – Creative Technologist **Client:** Mercedes Benz UK **URL:** http://www. biginteractiveideas.com **2 Creative Firm:** BGT Partners - Miami, FL **Creative Team:** BGT Partners Interactive Team **Client:** FPL Group **URL:** http://www.generationclean.com **3 Creative Firm:** JPL - Harrisburg, PA **Creative Team:** Rick Carbo - Project Manager; Jessica Gieg - Art Director; Katy Bastas - Designer; Dan Leister - Front End and Flash Developer; Matt Byers - Flash Developer; Jason Beck – Back End Developer **Client:** The Hershey Company **URL:** http://www.hersheys.com/trickortreats

1

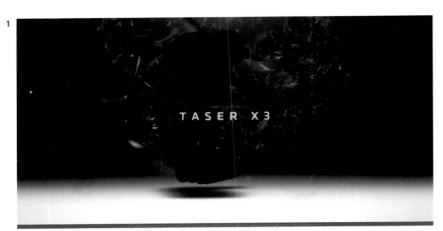

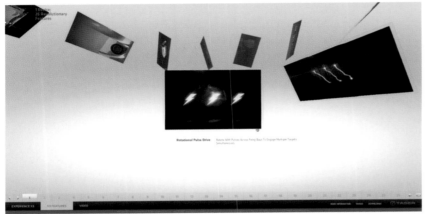

2

3

1 Creative Firm: Your Majesty - New York, NY **Creative Team:** Peter Karlsson - Account Director; James Widegren - Creative Director; Jens Karlsson - Creative Director; Heather Reddig - Executive Producer; Jonathan Pettersson - Developer; Michael Pelton – 3D **Client:** Taser International, Inc. **URL:** http://www.taserx3.com **2 Creative Firm:** Very Memorable Design - New York, NY **Creative Team:** Michael Pinto - Creative Director; Gwenevere Singley – Illustration **Client:** Scholastic Media **URL:** http://www.scholastic.com/goosebumps/videogame **3 Creative Firm:** Your Majesty - New York, NY **Creative Team:** Peter Karlsson - Account Director; James Widegren - Creative Director; Heather Reddig - Executive Producer; Caleb Johnson - Developer; Christian Johansson – 3D **Client:** Kirshenbaum Bond + Partners/Panasonic **URL:** http://www.vierapassions.com

1

2

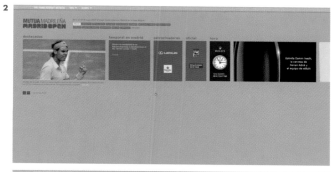

3

1 Creative Firm: The UXB - Beverly Hills, CA **Creative Team:** NancyJane Goldston - Creative Director; Daiga Atvara - Art Director; Hannah Cheadle - Account Executive; Kate Gaffney – Account Executive **Client:** Swatfame **URL:** www.swatfame.com **2 Creative Firm:** Internetria Interactive - Madrid, Spain **Creative Team:** Enrique Grandia - President; Angel Del Olmo - Designer; Jose Sopena – Content Supervisor **Client:** Madrid Trophy Promotion S.L. **URL:** http://www.madrid-open.com **3 Creative Firm:** Airside and With Associates - London, United Kingdom **Client:** Vitsoe **URL:** http://www.vitsoe.com

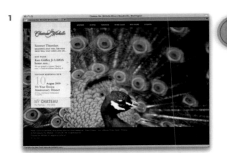

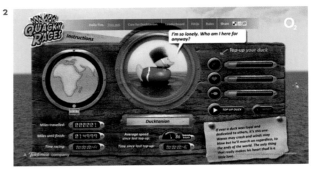

1 Creative Firm: FINE Design Group - San Francisco, CA **Creative Team:** Melissa Chan - Designer; Kenn Fine - Art Director; Lori Dunkin - Project Manager; Scott Brisko - Developer; Mark Hoffman - Developer; Mathias Baske – Developer **Client:** Saint Michelle Wine Estates **URL:** www.ste-michelle.com/ **2 Creative Firm:** Agency Republic - London, England **Creative Team:** Anders Gustavsson - Creative Director; Tarn Gordon-Rogers - Copywriter; Mick Charbonnel - Art Director; Jon Harris - Designer; Ben Heath - Designer; David Cox – Developer **Client:** O2 UK Ltd **URL:** www.biginteractiveideas.com **3 Creative Firm:** Campbell-Ewald - Warren, MI **Creative Team:** Bill Ludwig - Vice Chairman/Chief Creative Officer; Dennis Lim - EVP Executive Creative Director; Ann Phipps - EVP Executive Creative Director New & Alt Media; Kevin Omans - SVP Assoc Digital Creative Director; Bob Guisgand/ Duffy Patten - SVP Assoc Creative Director; Gustav Gerlach – Multi Media Art Director **Client:** Chevrolet **URL:** microsite.chevrolet.com/allnewcamaro/# **4 Creative Firm:** KNOCK inc. - Minneapolis, MN **Creative Team:** KNOCK inc. Design Firm; Kat Townsend - Designer; Todd Paulson - Creative Director; Jill Palmquist - Writer; Sandau – Creative Programming **Client:** Bee M.D/ BestSweet **URL:** www.sponsorabee.com

1

2

3

4

5

1 Creative Firm: Draftfcb Chicago - Chicago, IL **Creative Team:** Gigi Carroll - SVP/Creative Director; Suzanna Bierwirth - VP/Creative Director; Stu Thompson - Senior Copywriter; Steven Anderson – Agency Producer **Client:** Sharpie **URL:** www.sharpieuncapped.com/default.aspx **2 Creative Firm:** Sprokkit - Los Angeles, CA **Client:** Mimi's Cafe **URL:** www.mimiscafe.com **3 Creative Firm:** LBi - Atlanta, GA **Creative Team:** Lisa Harper - Client Partner; Thurston Yates - Executive Creative Director; Ivy Garcia - Associate Creative Director; Ali Harper - Senior Art Director; Mike Plymale - Senior Art Director; Maria Aguilar – Account Manager **Client:** Graco **URL:** www.gracobaby.com **4 Creative Firm:** LUON - Overijse, Belgium **Creative Team:** Onno Hesselink - Creative Director; Bart Verbeeren - Graphic Designer; Annemie Eyckerman - Graphic Designer; Sophie Baras - Account; Marjan Kegels – Account **Client:** Unilever **URL:** www.fermetteijs.be **5 Creative Firm:** LBi - Atlanta, GA **Creative Team:** Lisa Harper - Client Partner; Brad Hanna - Associate Creative Director; Chris Rebel - Senior Flash Developer; Jacob Warhaftig – Technical Director **Client:** Graco **URL:** www.readyfortheroadahead.com

1 Creative Firm: Quirk - Singapore **Creative Team:** Rina Lim – Creative Director **Client:** BreadTalk Group Limited **URL:** japantravelblog.breadtalk.com **2 Creative Firm:** Your Majesty - New York, NY **Creative Team:** Jens Karlsson - Creative Director; Heather Reddig - Executive Producer; Caleb Johnston - Developer; Erik Jonsson - Designer; Peter Karlsson - Account Director; Christian Johansson – Art Director **Client:** Strawberry Frog/TrueNorth-Frito-Lay **URL:** www.truenorthsnacks.com **3 Creative Firm:** JPL - Harrisburg, PA **Creative Team:** Mike Wilt - Project Manager; Chelsie Markel - Art Director; Matt Byers - Designer; Shane Hoffa - Flash Developer **Client:** Harrisburg Area Community College **URL:** apps.hacc.edu/admit **4 Creative Firm:** The UXB - Beverly Hills, CA **Creative Team:** NancyJane Goldston - Creative Director; Daiga Atvara - Art Director; Kate Gaffney - Account Executive; Hannah Cheadle – Account Executive **Client:** Swatfame **URL:** www.seethrusoul.com

1 Creative Firm: Baily Brand Consulting - Plymouth Meeting, PA **Creative Team:** Steve Perry - Creative Director; Gary LaCroix - Group Design – Director; David Kusiak – Designer; Todd Stare - Interactive Media Manager; Justin Thomas – Programmer/Developer; Jenna Ciacca - Interactive Specialist **Client:** Twinings USA **URL:** www.twiningsusa.com **2 Creative Firm:** The UXB - Beverly Hills, CA **Creative Team:** NancyJane Goldston - Creative Director; Daiga Atvara - Art Director; Kate Gaffney - Account Executive; Hannah Cheadle – Account Executive **Client:** Swatfame **URL:** www.kutdenim.com **3 Creative Firm:** Channel 1 Media Solutions Inc. - Toronto, ON, Canada **Client:** Los Angeles Kings **URL:** www.channel1media.com/kings/2009 **4 Creative Firm:** Ogilvy West - Culver City, CA **Creative Team:** Dan Burrier - Co-President/Chief Creative Officer; Vonnie Cameron - Group Creative Director; Peter Kang - Group Creative Director; Johann Conforme - Creative Director; Wendy Trilling - Associate Creative Director/Copywriter; Graham Simon – Senior Copywriter **Client:** Mattel Inc. **URL:** barbie.everythinggirl.com/grownups/web/anthem

1

2

3

4

1 Creative Firm: silver creative group - South Norwalk, CT **Creative Team:** Paul Zullo - Creative Director; Suzanne Petrow - Art Director; Susan Burghart - Illustrator; Scott Weiner - Programmer; Valerie Haboush – Copywriter **Client:** TF Cornerstone **URL:** 2goldstreet.com **2 Creative Firm:** Zeeland Oy - Helsinki, Finland **Creative Team:** Roy Gonzalez - Art Director; Tanja Kyynäräinen - Art Director; Timo Leskinen - Copywriter; Pia Gran - Project Manager; Juha-Matti Mäkelä - Planner **Client:** Puolustusvoimat // The Finnish Defence Forces **URL:** www.aliupseeriksi.fi **3 Creative Firm:** LUON - Overijse, Belgium **Creative Team:** Onno Hesselink - Creative Director; Annemie Eyckerman - Graphic Designer; Jordi Van Herck - Account; Tina Put – Account **Client:** Option **URL:** www.option.com **4 Creative Firm:** LUON - Overijse, Belgium **Creative Team:** Onno Hesselink - Creative Director; Lies Bosman - Graphic Designer; Alexis Masset - Account; Chris Dexters - Copywriter; Glenn Van Hoof – Strategic Planner **Client:** Fnac **URL:** www.gameismoney.be

1

2

3

4

1 Creative Firm: JPL - Harrisburg, PA **Creative Team:** Modesty Guarente - Project Manager; Jim Mitchell - Art Director; Matt Byers - Designer; Hollie Rudy – Flash Developer **Client:** The Hershey Company **URL:** www.hersheys.com/nightatthemuseum **2 Creative Firm:** Digitaria - San Diego, CA **Creative Team:** Daiga Atvara – Executive Creative Director **Client:** Shop Dreamy **URL:** www.shopdreamy.com **3 Creative Firm:** Hornall Anderson Design Works - Seattle, WA **Creative Team:** Michael Connors - Creative Director; Zak Menkel - Interactive Producer; Chris Monberg - Interactive Producer; Hans Krebs - Interactive Designer; Leo Raymundo - Designer; Alan Draper – Developer **Client:** PNB **URL:** www.pnb.org **4 Creative Firm:** Hornall Anderson Design Works - Seattle, WA **Creative Team:** Jamie Monberg - Interactive Director; Andrew Wicklund - Creative Director; Dana Kruse - Interactive Producer; Kevin Roth - Designer; Rachel Blakely - Designer; Matt Frickelton – Developer **Client:** Lovin' Scoopful **URL:** www.lovinscoopful.com

1

2

3

1 Creative Firm: Torre Lazur McCann - Parsippany, NJ **Creative Team:** Brett Nicols - VP/Director; Scott Sisti – Supervisor, Interactive Media; Jennifer Dee – VP/Executive Producer; Debra Feath - Assoc. Creative Director; Loretta Sohigian - Assoc. Art Director; Merissa Mayer - Sr. Copywriter; Clare Litx – Group Copy Sup; Al Mauriello – Copy Sup; Grace Thompson – Sr. Copywriter; Stacey Crowley - VP, Mgt Sup; Lisa Desbiens - Acct. Group Sup; Jessica Capozzolo - Account Exec. **Client:** Axcan Pharma **URL:** www.carefirstforlife.com **2 Creative Firm:** FiveHT Media Ltd - Victoria, BC, Canada **Creative Team:** Dave Arril – Web Director/Producer; Steven Zozula - Lead Design/Art Direction/Interface Design; Jake Ketchesen – Lead Programmer and Architect **Client:** The Condo Group Inc. **URL:** thecondogroup.com/ **3 Creative Firm:** FiveHT Media Ltd - Victoria, BC, Canada **Creative Team:** Dave Arril - Web Director/Producer; Mike Deas - Lead Illustrator and Animation; Steven Zozula - Design and Animation; Jake Ketchesen – Lead Programmer **Client:** The Great Canadian Dollar Store Inc **URL:** www.dollarstores.com

1

2

3

4

1 Creative Firm: Your Majesty - New York, NY **Creative Team:** Jens Karlsson - Creative Director; Emil Lanne - Creative Director; Peter Karlsson - Account Director; Sara Kayden - Producer; Kasper Kuijpers - Developer; Christian Johansson – Art Director **Client:** McCann Erickson/Nestle **URL:** your-majesty.com/nestle/ **2 Creative Firm:** BGT Partners - Miami, FL **Creative Team:** BGT Partners Interactive Team **Client:** Office Depot **URL:** www.officedepot.com **3 Creative Firm:** Bayshore Solutions - Tampa, FL **Client:** Florida Holocaust Museum **URL:** www.courageandcompassionexhibit.com/ **4 Creative Firm:** Kika Marketing & Communications Inc - Vancouver, BC, Canada **Creative Team:** Michael Mariano - Senior Graphic Designer; Enrico Cardenas – Senior Flash Designer & Developer **Client:** Michelange Panzini Architectes **URL:** www.panzini.com

1 Creative Firm: Targetbase - Irving, TX **Creative Team:** Kimberley Walsh - Executive Vice President/Creative Director; Jamie Thomas - Vice President/Group Creative Director; Rosalinda Reyes - Senior Project Manager; Rickey Brown - Senior Art Director; Jennifer Cowan - Senior Writer; Robbie Wilson – Senior Web Developer **Client:** Michaels Stores Inc. **URL:** www.wherecreativityhappens.com/home.aspx **2 Creative Firm:** Kas Design, LLC - Freehold, NJ **Client:** Pebble Creek Golf Club **URL:** www.pebblecreekgolf-club.com **3 Creative Firm:** Baily Brand Consulting - Plymouth Meeting, PA **Creative Team:** Steve Perry - Creative Director; Ken Cahill – Group Design Director; Todd Stare - Interactive Media Manager; Justin Thomas - Programmer/Developer; Jenna Ciacca – Interactive Specialist **Client:** Viridian Spirits **URL:** www.drinklucid.com

1

2

3

4

1 Creative Firm: Martin Williams - Minneapolis, MN **Creative Team:** Tom Moudry - Chief Creative Officer; Jeff Tresidder - Group Creative Director; Toby Balai - Art Director; Chris Gault - Copywriter; Andrea Allen - Interactive Production; Katie Krueger – Producer **Client:** Syngenta Crop Protection **URL:** www.avictacomplete.com **2 Creative Firm:** Liquified Creative - Annapolis, MD **Creative Team:** Shawn Noratel - Creative Director and Web Developer; Marc Regardie – Account Executive **Client:** Novo Development **URL:** www.coronadodc.com **3 Creative Firm:** LBi - Atlanta, GA **Creative Team:** Gina Jones - Account Manager; Matt Daly - Associate Creative Director; Alex Kurth - Senior Art Director; Chris Rebel - Senior Flash Developer; Mike Plymale – Art Director **Client:** Spectracide **URL:** www.spectracide.com/solutions **4 Creative Firm:** PacificLink iMedia Limited - Hong Kong **Creative Team:** Lennon Ho - Creative Director; Nancy Luk, Kong Lee - Interactive Designer; Chris Kong, Derek Chang - Programmer; Moski Mok, Sunny Ng, Yui Ng, Phoebe Li – Project Management **Client:** Ocean Park (Hong Kong) **URL:** www.oceanpark.com.hk

1 Creative Firm: LBi - Atlanta, GA **Creative Team:** Matt Daly - Associate Creative Director; Gina Jones - Account Manager; Brooke Buerkle, Chris Rebel - Senior Flash Developer; Mike Plymale - Art Director; Robert Boettcher – Senior Developer **Client:** The Home Depot **URL:** www.homedepotracing.com **2 Creative Firm:** Hitchcock Fleming & Associates Inc. - Akron, OH **Creative Team:** Nick Betro - Executive Creative Director; Greg Pfiffner - Writer; Patrick Ginnetti - Art Director; Jim Kiel - Web Developer; Rene McCann - Sr. Art Director/Interactive **Client:** Liquid Nails **URL:** www.liquidnails.com/diy/index.jsp **3 Creative Firm:** Creative Alliance - Louisville, KY **Creative Team:** Brendan Jackson - Director of Digital Services; Brian Phillips - Executive Creative Director; Zeke Snow – Account Executive **Client:** KFC **URL:** www.thebasement.tv/clients/KFCRocks **4 Creative Firm:** Alcone Marketing - Irvine, CA **Creative Team:** Carlos Musquez - Creative Director; Shivonne Miller - Sr. Art Director; Luis Camano - VP/Creative Director; Cameron Young – Copywriter **Client:** Seeds of Change **URL:** www.seedsofchangefood.com

PLATINUM

....
Creative Firm: Boston Interactive - Boston, MA
....
Creative Team: Chuck Murphy - Founder & CEO;
Scott Noonan - Chief Technical Officer; Jackie Roth
- Creative Director; Matt Berube - Senior Designer;
Lewis Goulden – Senior Developer
....
Client: ASPCA
....
URL: www.aspca.org

1 Creative Firm: Digitaria - San Diego, CA **Creative Team:** Daiga Atvara – Executive Creative Director **Client:** KCET **URL:** www.kcet.org/local/ **2 Creative Firm:** Torre Lazur McCann - Parsippany, NJ **Creative Team:** Christopher Bean - VP/Associate Creative Director, Art; Mark Oppici - VP/Group Creative Director, Copy; Brett Nichols – VP, Director; Scott Sisti – Supervisor, Interactive Media; Scott Kraus - Copywriter; Grace Thompson - Sr. Copywriter; Kristy Caraballo - VP, Management Supervisor; Lisa Desbien – Acct. Group Supervisor **Client:** OneGift/ Inc. **URL:** www.onegift.org/

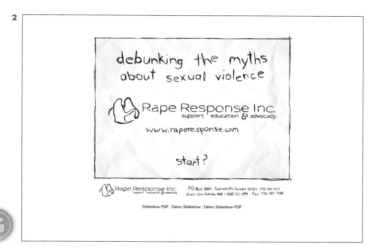

1 Creative Firm: Object 9 - Baton Rouge, LA **Client** Red Stick Festival **URL:** www.redstickfestival.org **2 Creative Firm:** Kelsey Advertising & Design - LaGrange, GA **Creative Team:** Brant Kelsey - Creative Director; Brian Handley – Developer/Designer **Client:** Rape Response **URL:** raperesponse.com/mythvsreality/index.php

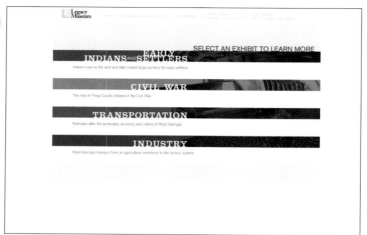

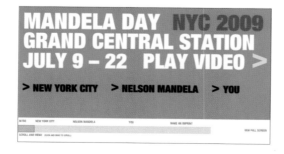
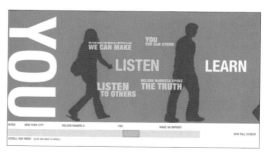

1 **Creative Firm:** Kelsey Advertising & Design - LaGrange, GA **Creative Team:** Brant Kelsey - Creative Director; Roman Alvarado – Designer/Developer **Client:** Troup County Historical Society **URL:** www.legacymuseumonmain.org/online_exhibit.php 2 **Creative Firm:** Ralph Appelbaum Associates - New York, NY **Creative Team:** Caroline Brownell - Art Direction/Graphic Design; Aki Carpenter - Graphic Design; Paul Williams - Writer; Andres Cleric - Director of Content and Media; Scott Edmonds - Director of Web Development; George Robertson – Media Editor **Client:** The Nelson Mandela Foundation **URL:** www.mandeladay.com/exhibition/nyc2009/

1

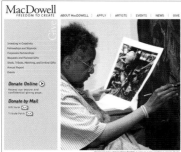

2

3

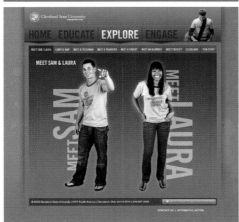

1 Creative Firm: Wetherbee Creative & Web llc - Derry, NH **Creative Team:** Wendy Wetherbee - Creative Director/Designer/Developer **Client:** The MacDowell Colony **URL:** www.macdowellcolony.org **2 Creative Firm:** CivicPlus - Manhattan, KS **Client:** Eureka Springs/AR **URL:** www.eurekasprings.org. **3 Creative Firm:** flourish, inc. - Cleveland, OH **Client:** Cleveland State University **URL:** www.engagecsu.com

1

2

3

4

5

6

1 Creative Firm: Collipsis Web Solutions - Broken Arrow, OK **Creative Team:** Nicholas Clayton - Web Designer; JP Jones – Graphic Designer **Client:** Nicholas Clayton **URL:** www.stillfollowingme.com **2 Creative Firm:** BGT Partners - Miami, FL **Creative Team:** BGT Partners Interactive Team **Client:** UHealth System **URL:** www.uhealthsystem.com **3 Creative Firm:** Crabtree + Company - Falls Church, VA **Creative Team:** Susan Angrisani - Creative Director; Rodrigo Vera - Art Director; William Weinheimer - Production Artist/Programmer; Lisa Suchy – Production Manager **Client:** YWCA **URL:** www.ywcaownit.org/ **4 Creative Firm:** Vision Internet - Santa Monica, CA **Client:** Calcasieu Parish Police Jury **URL:** www.cppj.net **5 Creative Firm:** Vision Internet - Santa Monica, CA **Client:** Eagle County School District, CO **URL:** www.eagleschools.net **6 Creative Firm:** INC Design - New York, NY **Creative Team:** Alejandro Medina - Senior Art Director; Martine Chepigin - Managing Partner; Jed Heuer - Senior Designer; Adam Leder – Web Programmer **Client:** International Securities Exchange **URL:** www.ise.com/regulatoryreform

1

2

3

4
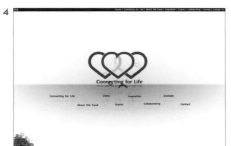  

5

6

1 Creative Firm: Vision Internet - Santa Monica, CA **Client:** City of Hamilton, OH **URL:** www.hamilton-city.org **2 Creative Firm:** Juno studio - Jersey City, NJ **Creative Team:** Jun Li - Creative Direction/Design/Flash Program; Ian Watson – Content Director **Client:** Rutgers University **URL:** andromeda.rutgers.edu **3 Creative Firm:** Fitting Group - Pittsburgh, PA **Creative Team:** Victoria Ravenstahl - Designer; Travis Norris - Creative Director; Tim Emanuel - Web Developer; Jeff Fitting – Interactive Director **Client:** Pittsburgh Mercy Health System **URL:** www.achildsplaceatmercy.org/ **4 Creative Firm:** FiveHT Media Ltd - Victoria, BC, Canada **Creative Team:** Dave Arril - Producer; Steven Zozula - Lead Design/Art Direction **Client:** The BC Adoption and Permanency Fund **URL:** www.connectingforlife.ca **5 Creative Firm:** Levine & Associates - Washington D.C. **Creative Team:** Lee Jenkins - Managing Director; Marco Javier - Creative Strategist; Jennie Jariel – Art Director **Client:** United Arab Emirates **URL:** www.uae-embassy.org/ **6 Creative Firm:** Gotham Inc. - New York, NY **Creative Team:** Marty Orzio - Chief Creative Officer; Corey Szopinski - Executive Producer; CORE (Digital Partner); Carl Ceo – CD/Art Director **Client:** 46664/ The Nelson Mandela Foundation **URL:** www.mandeladay.com

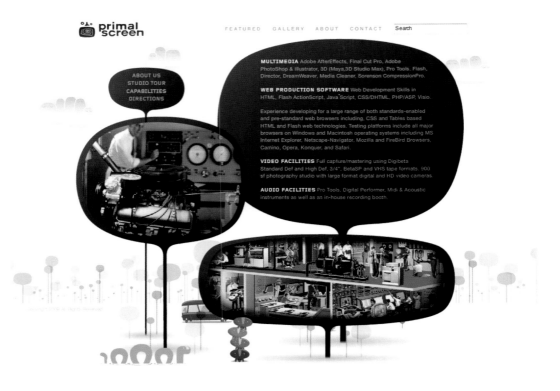

PLATINUM

Creative Firm: Primal Screen - Atlanta, GA
Creative Team: Doug Grimmett - Creative Director; Rick Newcomb - Art Director; Joe Kubesheski - Flash Animator; Dale Bradshaw - Director of Technology; Chris Silich - Programmer; Ciara Cordasco – Designer
Client: Primal Screen
URL: www.primalscreen.com

1

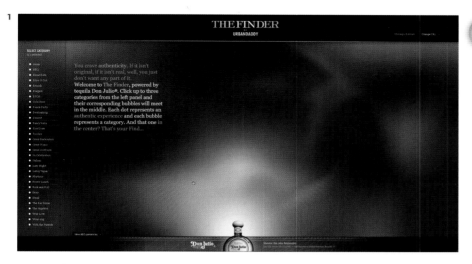

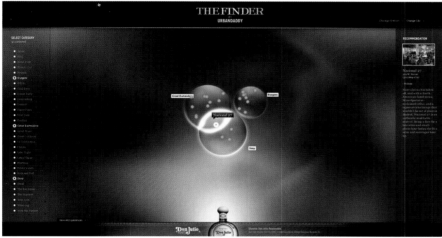

2

1 **Creative Firm:** Your Majesty - New York, NY **Creative Team:** Peter Karlsson - Account Director; Jens Karlsson - Creative Director; James Widegren - Creative Director; Vivian Sarratt - Producer; Chris Picheca - Developer; Johan Steen - Developer **Client:** Urban Daddy **URL:** thefinder.urbandaddy.com/ **2 Creative Firm:** LBi - Atlanta, GA **Creative Team:** Thurston Yates - Executive Creative Director; Brad Hanna - Associate Creative Director; Jason Hirthler - Senior Copywriter; Chris Rebel - Senior Flash Developer; Alex Kurth - Senior Art Director; Bryan Moss – Senior Art Director **Client:** LBi Atlanta **URL:** www.lbiatlanta.com

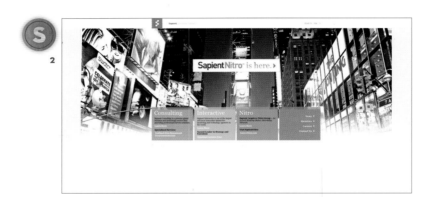

1 **Creative Firm:** Singularity Design - Philadelphia, PA **Creative Team:** Sean Trapani - Creative Director; Owen Linton - Art Director; Jeff Mills – Sr. Interactive Developer **Client:** Singularity Design **URL:** www.singularitydesign.com 2 **Creative Firm:** Sapient Interactive - Palmetto Bay, FL **Creative Team:** Sapient Brand – Team Internal Marketing **Client:** Sapient **URL:** www.sapient.com/ 3 **Creative Firm:** Your Majesty - New York, NY **Creative Team:** Peter Karlsson - Account Director; James Widegren - Creative Director; Jens Karlsson - Creative Director; Heather Reddig - Executive Producer; Christian Johansson - Art Director; Kasper Kuijpers – Developer **Client:** New York Times **URL:** www.nytimesconversations.com/

1

2

3

1 Creative Firm: Nexus Creative - Kuala Lumpur, Malaysia **Creative Team:** Pooi Fatt Wong – Music composer + Multimedia designer **Client:** Nexuscreative **URL:** www.nexuscreative.com **2 Creative Firm:** Digitaria - San Diego, CA **Creative Team:** Daiga Atvara - Executive Creative Director; Michael Jackson – Art Director **Client:** ATP World Tour **URL:** www.atpworldtour.com **3 Creative Firm:** Kelsey Advertising & Design - La Grange, GA **Creative Team:** Brant Kelsey - Creative Director; Niki Studdard - Designer; Brian Handley - Developer; Roman Alvarado – Developer **Client:** Kelsey Advertising & Design **URL:** www.kelseyads.com/

1

2

3

4

5
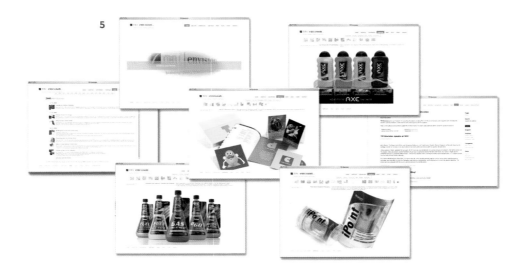

1 Creative Firm: Crabtree + Company - Falls Church, VA **Creative Team:** The Entire C+C Team **Client:** Crabtree + Company **URL:** www.crabtreecompany.com/
2 Creative Firm: Purple, Rock, Scissors - Orlando, FL **Creative Team:** Bobby Jones - Chief Creative Officer; Michael Parler - Information Architect; Shayne Bruno
- Creative Director; Zach Wood - Client-side Engineer; Rob Zienert - Lead Developer; Aaron Harvey – Copywriter **Client:** Purple, Rock, Scissors. **URL:** www.purplerock-
scissors.com **3 Creative Firm:** Kas Design, LLC - Freehold, NJ **Client:** Kas Design, LLC **URL:** www.kasdesign.com/ **4 Creative Firm:** Zeesman Communications, Inc. - Beverly
Hills, CA **Creative Team:** John Taylor - Creative Director; Ryan Powell - Sr. Graphic Designer; Chris Varosy – Interactive Designer **Client:** Zeesman Communications, Inc.
URL: www.zeesman.com **5 Creative Firm:** TFI Envision, Inc. - Norwalk, CT **Creative Team:** Elizabeth P. Ball **Client:** TFI Envision, Inc.

1

1 Creative Firm: Ripe Media - Los Angeles, CA **Creative Team:** Joe Hajek – Art Director; Merf Schultz – Flash Developer; Chris Simental – Technology & LMS Advisor; Heather Richman – Creative Director **Client:** Ford **URL:** www.ripetraining.com/bi/mkt/final/index.htm

commercials,
tv + radio

Thousands of cucumbers are assaulted every day.

Sara's Secret
EROTIC SHOP
sarassecret.com

 **PLATINUM**

Creative Firm: Dieste - Dallas, TX
Creative Team: Carlos Tourne – Executive Creative Director; Paty Martinez – Creative Director; Florencia Leibaschoff – Creative Director; Ernesto Fernandez – Copywriter; Sarai Gomez – Art Director; John Costello – Agency Producer
Client: Sara's Secret

A Plea From Your Vegetables

Sure, you could use a cucumber to satisfy your personal needs (and we're not talking hunger), but isn't that just asking too much of our produce? "Veggies give their lives for us, but enough is enough already," says Dallas agency Dieste. "We realized someone needed to speak on their behalf." This cheeky spot, which chronicles the adventures of a clearly traumatized cucumber (you can see it in its eyes!) making its escape from the bedroom ends with an image of a more durable alternative from local adult boutique chain Sara's Secret. "Someone needed to tell the world about the abuses [cucumbers] endure, and do something to put an end to it forever," Dieste says.

1

Do you accept Anna as your lawful wife?

Think about bacon.

Do you take this Bacon Club Chalupa to cherish and enjoy for the rest of your life?

I do!

BACON CLUB CHALUPA

Make it yours only at Taco Bell.

2

NUEVO PERDON DE ACCIDENTES

No one forgives like Nationwide.

3

YOUNG GIRL (OC): So, dad can I borrow the car?

DAD (OC): Where are you going?

YOUNG GIRL (OC): Just to the movies.
DAD (OC): Who's going?

YOUNG GIRL (OC): Cathy and Dylan...

DAD (OC): Dylan?

YOUNG GIRL (OC): Yes, dad, Dylan.

Please?

TEEN GIRL (OC): Thanks dad.

ANNCR (VO): She's growing up, weather you like it or not.

That's why State Farm created the Steer Clear Program. Teen's learn safe driving, you get lower rates.

Like a good neighbor, State Farm is there.

DAD (OC): Where are you going?
BOY (OC): Work.

1 Creative Firm: Dieste - Dallas, TX **Creative Team:** Carlos Tourne – Chief Creative Officer; Roberto Saucedo – Creative Director; Ignacio Romero – Copywriter; Saul Dominguez – Copywriter; Jesus Acosta – Art Director **Client:** Taco Bell **2 Creative Firm:** Dieste - Dallas, TX **Creative Team:** Carlos Tourne – Chief Creative Officer; Gabriel Puerto – Creative Director; Paty Martinez – Creative Director; Juan Daniel Navas – Sr. Copywriter; Jose Suaste – Art Director; John Costello – Executive Agency Producer **Client:** Nationwide Insurance **3 Creative Firm:** State Farm Insurance - Bloomington, IL **Creative Team:** Patty Dirker – Marketing Analyst; Mariana Rutledge – Marketing Analyst; Jim Stahly – Marketing Analyst; Shelia Law – Marketing Analyst; Tim Thomas – Marketing Analyst; Greg Sutter – Advertising Manager **Client:** State Farm Insurance

1

We all need someone to believe in.
To rely on. To trust.

Nothing's more important
than being there.

State Farm
Like a good neighbor, State Farm is there.

statefarm.com

2

I'm a clone.

But all that ended with one phone call.

Yes. I would like an insurance policy.

CLONE DISCOVERS PERSONALIZATION

MAURILIO MOYEDA
SECRETARY OF STATE:
"EVERYTHING IS UNDER CONTROL"

GERMAN LAB. BREAKING NEWS: CLONE RIOTS IN GERMAN LAB.

1 Creative Firm: State Farm Insurance - Bloomington, IL **Creative Team:** Patty Dirker – Marketing Analyst; Mariana Rutledge – Marketing Analyst; Jim Stahly – Marketing Analyst; Tim Thomas – Marketing Analyst; Shelia Law – Marketing Analyst; Greg Sutter – Marketing Analyst **Client:** State Farm Insurance **2 Creative Firm:** Dieste - Dallas, TX **Creative Team:** Carlos Tourne – Chief Creative Officer; Gabriel Puerto – Creative Director/Copywriter; Eduardo Duran – Senior Copywriter; Ana Carina Gallo – Art Director; Tony Sandoval – Agency Producer **Client:** Nationwide Insurance

355

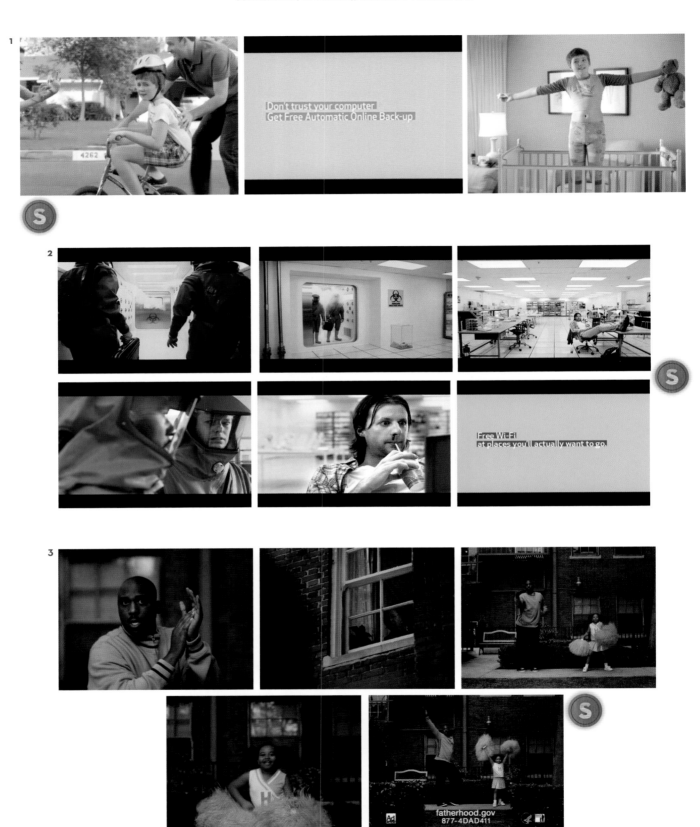

1 **Creative Firm:** Draftfcb - Chicago. IL **Creative Team:** Mary Knight – SVP/Group Creative Director; Tom O'Keefe – EVP/Executive Creative Director, North America; Sue Vering – VP/Creative Director; Greg Auer – Art Director; Tim Mason – Copywriter; Jennifer Bills – Copywriter **Client:** Qwest Communications **2 Creative Firm:** Draftfcb Chicago - Chicago, IL **Creative Team:** Mary Knight – SVP/Group Creative Director; Tom O'Keefe – EVP/Executive Creative Director, North America; Pat Durkin – SVP/Creative Director; Dave Gassman – VP/Creative Director; Karen (Snake) Roth – Agency Producer; Kelly Varga – Agency Producer **Client:** Qwest Communications **3 Creative Firm:** Campbell-Ewald - Warren, MI **Creative Team:** Bill Ludwig – Vice Chairman/Chief Creative Officer; Patrick O'Leary – SVP/Associate Creative Director; Craig Marrero –VP/Art Supervisor; Adam Van Dyke – Senior Producer; Bob Solano – EVP/Director Broadcast Services; Cristina Cecchetti/Dave Smith – Account Mgmt **Client:** National Fatherhood Inititative

356

1

2

3

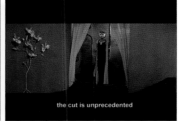
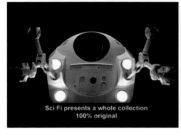

1 **Creative Firm:** Campbell-Ewald - Warren, MI **Creative Team:** Bill Ludwig – Vice Chairman/Chief Creative Officer; Michael Stelmaszek/Robin Todd – SVP/Creative Director; Bob Guisgand/Duffy Patten – SVP/Assoc Creative Director; Bob Solano/Jow Knisely – Production; Steve Majoros/ Liza Roach/Jill Bihler – Account Team **Client:** Chevrolet
2 **Creative Firm:** NBC Universal Global Networks Italia - Rome, Italy **Creative Team:** NBC Universal Global Networks Italia **Client:** NBC Universal Global Networks Italia
3 **Creative Firm:** NBC Universal Global Networks Italia - Rome, Italy **Creative Team:** NBC Universal Global Networks Italia **Client:** NBC Universal Global Networks Italia

1

 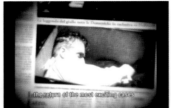 

2

 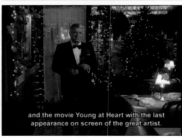 

3

1 Creative Firm: NBC Universal Global Networks Italia - Rome, Italy **Client:** NBC Universal Global Networks Italia **2 Creative Firm:** NBC Universal Global Networks Italia - Rome, Italy **Client:** NBC Universal Global Networks Italia **3 Creative Firm:** State Farm Insurance - Bloomington, IL **Creative Team:** Patty Dirker – Marketing Analyst; Tim Thomas – Marketing Analyst; Jim Stahly – Marketing Analyst; Mariana Rutledge – Marketing Analyst; Shelia Law – Marketing Analyst; Greg Sutter – Marketing Manager **Client:** State Farm Insurance

1

2

3

1 **Creative Firm:** State Farm Insurance - Bloomington, IL **Creative Team:** Patty Dirker – Marketing Analyst; Jim Stahly – Marketing Analyst; Shelia Law – Marketing Analyst; Mariana Rutledge – Marketing Analyst; Tim Thomas – Marketing Analyst; Greg Sutter – Marketing Manager **Client:** State Farm Insurance 2 **Creative Firm:** Inglefield, Ogilvy & Mather Caribbean Ltd. - Port of Spain, Trinidad & Tobago **Creative Team:** David Gomez – Executive Creative Director; Rory Moses – Associate Creative Director; Sara Camps – AV Production Director; Badger Smith – Director, Sasi Productions; Simone Camps – Producer, Sasi Productions; Richard Ahong – Music Composer/Producer, Da Crib **Client:** CARIB BREWERY 3 **Creative Firm:** Draftfcb Chicago - Chicago, IL **Creative Team:** Mary Knight – SVP/Group Creative Director; Tom O'Keefe – EVP/Executive Creative Director, North America; Sue Vering – VP/Creative Director; Greg Auer – Art Director; Tim Mason – Copywriter; Jennifer Bills – Copywriter **Client:** Qwest Communications

1

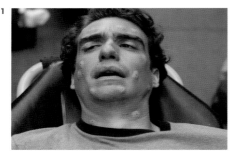

2

3

1 Creative Firm: Draftfcb Chicago - Chicago, IL **Creative Team:** Mary Knight – SVP/Group Creative Director; Tom O'Keefe – EVP/Executive Creative Director, North America; Pat Durkin – SVP/Creative Director; Dave Gassman – VP/Creative Director; Cary Pierce – EVP/Group Management Director; Sam Ciaramitaro – Agency Producer **Client:** Qwest Communications **2 Creative Firm:** Draftfcb Chicago - Chicago, IL **Creative Team:** Mary Knight – SVP/Group Creative Director; Tom O'Keefe – EVP/Executive Creative Director, North America; Pat Durkin – SVP/Creative Director; Dave Gassman – VP/Creative Director; Cary Pierce – EVP/Group Management Director; Sam Ciaramitaro – Agency Producer **Client:** Qwest Communications **3 Creative Firm:** Draftfcb Chicago - Chicago, IL **Creative Team:** Mary Knight – SVP/Group Creative Director; Tom O'Keefe – EVP/Executive Creative Director, North America; Pat Durkin – SVP/Creative Director; Dave Gassman – VP/Creative Director; Karen (Snake) Roth – Agency Producer; Kelly Varga – Agency Producer **Client:** Qwest Communications

1 **Creative Firm:** Martin Williams - Minneapolis, MN **Creative Team:** Tom Moudry – Chief Creative Officer; Julie Kucinski – Group Creative Director/Copywriter; David Richardson – Group Creative Director/Art Director; Stan Prinsen – Director of Production/Executive Producer; Jake Burns – Director, Stardust (Production Company) **Client:** Payless ShoeSource 2 **Creative Firm:** Ogilvy West - Culver City, CA **Creative Team:** Dan Burrier – Co-President/Chief Creative Officer; Bob Strickland – Group Creative Director/Copywriter; Jeff Compton – Group Creative Director/Art Director; Julie Salik – General Manager/Creative Production Services; Tarsem – Director; John Lennon – Composer **Client:** Cisco Systems, Inc. **URL:** www.ogilvywest.net 3 **Creative Firm:** Luminus Creative - Zagreb, Croatia **Creative Team:** Renato Grgic – Creative Director; Tonci Klaric – Copywriter; Željko Grgic – Art Director/Director **Client:** Croatian Government

1 **Creative Firm:** Campbell-Ewald - Warren, MI **Creative Team:** Bill Ludwig – Vice Chairman/Chief Creative Officer; Mark Simon/Debbie Karnowsky – EVP/Executive Creative Director; Mike Conboy/Neville Anderson/John Haggerty – Creative Team; Angela Zepeda/Jennifer Bittner/Matt Clark/Ali Forgeron – Account Team **Client:** Kaiser Permanente 2 **Creative Firm:** Campbell-Ewald - Warren, MI **Creative Team:** Bill Ludwig – Vice Chairman/Chief Creative Officer; Mark Simon/Debbie Karnowsky – EVP/ Executive Creative Officer; David Bierman/Keith McLenon – Creative Team; John Haggerty – Production; Angela Zepeda/Jennifer Bittner/Matt Clark/ Ali Forgeron – Account Team **Client:** Kaiser Permanente

 PLATINUM

Creative Firm: State Farm Insurance - Bloomington, IL

Creative Team: Patty Dirker – Marketing Analyst;
Jim Stahly – Marketing Analyst; Tim Thomas –
Marketing Analyst; Shelia Law – Marketing Analyst;
Mariana Rutledge – Marketing Analyst; Greg Sutter
– Marketing Analyst

Client: State Farm Insurance

A Good Neighbor

America is currently in a time of uncertainty, leaving people looking for things they can believe in, rely on, and trust. So there was no better time for State Farm® to remind consumers of the long standing promise of their brand, "Like a good neighbor, State Farm is there™". In fact, for State Farm, there's nothing more important than being there, as demonstrated in five television commercials produced by DDB Chicago and Alma DDB.

The anthem spot for the campaign, "I'll Be There", backed by the popular Jackson 5 track, is a tribute to the power of human connection. "It's people being there for people," explains DDB Chicago, "unwavering in their loyalty and support. Finding strength in the smallest of gestures, like clasped hands that won't let go..."

The other general market spots "One Day" and "The Door" further show the power of self sacrifice, be it working hard to build a bet-ter life for loved ones or supporting others no matter what the day may bring.

State Farm's "being there" message resonates especially strong within the Hispanic market, says Alma DDB, "Hispanics always turn to each other. They want a friend, a partner, an extended family member who will take the time to help them tackle the problems in becoming more established, while respecting where they're at right now. However, in a foreign system there are things they can't always help each other with." The two Hispanic spots, "Extra Room" and "First Kiss," illustrate "being there" through intergenerational relationships whether it's a family taking in an aging parent or a father coming to terms with his little girl going "de niña a mujer" (from girl to woman).

"[The stories] reinforce the notion that being there for those who matter most is what we do," says DDB Chicago, " A perfect picture of how State Farm is also there for you."

1

1 **Creative Firm:** State Farm Insurance - Bloomington, IL **Creative Team:** Patty Dirker – Marketing Analyst; Tim Thomas – Marketing Analyst; Shelia Law – Marketing Analyst; Mariana Rutledge – Marketing Analyst; Jim Stahly – Marketing Analyst; Greg Sutter – Marketing Analyst **Client:** State Farm Insurance

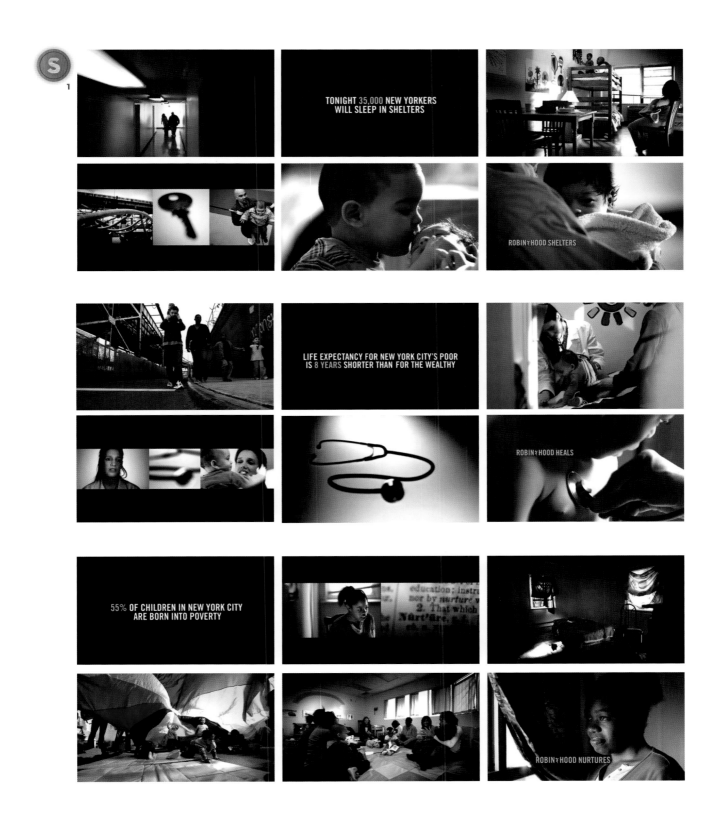

1 **Creative Firm:** Collective Production - New York, NY **Creative Team:** David McNamara – Director; Carin Zakes – Creative Consultant/EP; Arthur Bijur – Creative Consultant/CD; Jim Samalis – Managing Director/ Events at Robin Hood; Michael Garza – Executive Producer; Ivy Dane – Line Producer **Client:** Robin Hood Foundation

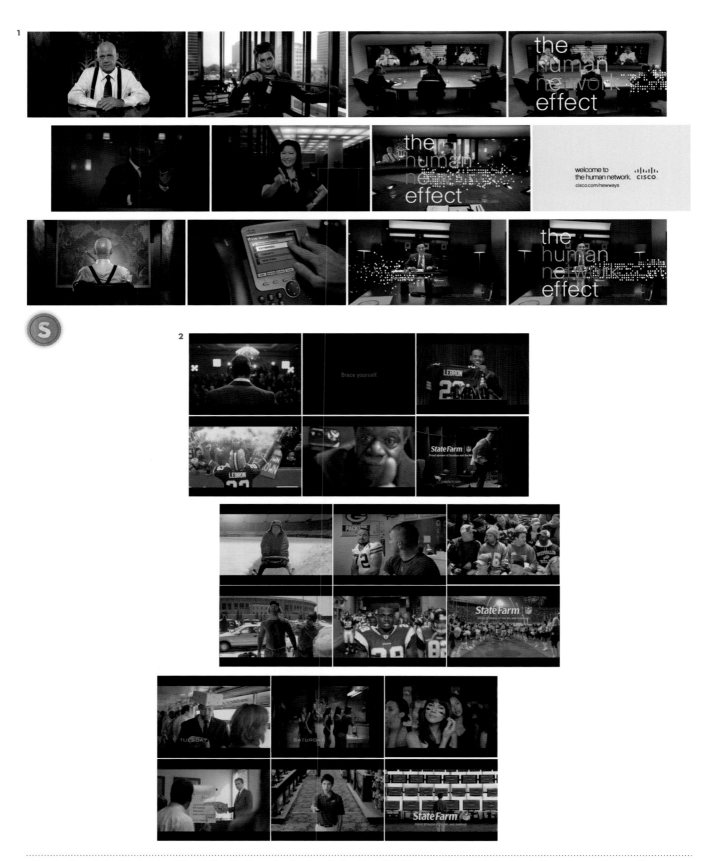

1 **Creative Firm:** Ogilvy West - Culver City, CA **Creative Team:** Dan Burrier – Co-President/Chief Creative Officer; Bob Strickland – Group Creative Director/Copywriter; Jeff Compton – Group Creative Director/Art Director; Graham Simon – Senior Copywriter; Ned Selover – Copywriter; Rob Anton – Art Director **Client:** Cisco Systems, Inc. **URL:** www.ogilvywest.net 2 **Creative Firm:** State Farm Insurance - Bloomington, IL **Creative Team:** Patty Dirker – Marketing Analyst; Tim Thomas – Marketing Analyst; Jim Stahly – Marketing Analyst; Shelia Law – Marketing Analyst; Mariana Rutledge – Marketing Analyst; Greg Sutter – Marketing Manager **Client:** State Farm Insurance

1

2

1 Creative Firm: Draftfcb Chicago - Chicago, IL **Creative Team:** Mary Knight – SVP/Group Creative Director; Tom O'Keefe – EVP/Executive Creative Director, North America; Sue Vering – VP/Creative Director; Greg Auer – Art Director; Tim Mason – Copywriter; Jennifer Bills – Copywriter **Client:** Qwest Communications **2 Creative Firm:** Draftfcb Chicago - Chicago, IL **Creative Team:** Mary Knight – SVP/Group Creative Director; Tom O'Keefe EVP/Executive Creative Director, North America; Pat Durkin – SVP/Creative Director; Dave Gassman – VP/Creative Director; Cary Pierce – EVP/Group Management Director; Sam Ciaramitaro – Agency Producer **Client:** Qwest Communications

1 Creative Firm: Ogilvy West - Culver City, CA **Creative Team:** Dan Burrier – Co-President/Chief Creative Officer; Bob Strickland – Group Creative Director/Copywriter; Jeff Compton – Group Creative Director/Art Director; Julie Salik – General Manager/Creative Production Services; Tarsem – Director **Client:** Cisco Systems, Inc.
URL: www.ogilvywest.net

1 Creative Firm: Zeeland Oy - Helsinki, Finland **Creative Team:** Migu Snäll – Creative Director; Riitta Bergman – Project Manager; Mikko Vaija – Art Director; Anna Korpi-Kyyny – Copywriter **Client:** Oy Kopparberg Finland Ab

PLATINUM

Creative Firm: Primal Screen - Atlanta, GA

Creative Team: Doug Grimmett - Creative Director; Rob Shepps - Director; Chuck Carlton - Director of Photography; Teresa Cloud - Production Coordinator/ Production Artist; Brandon Bentley - Digital Capture Technician; Steve Mank – Sound & Music

Client: Tombras Advertising

1 Creative Firm: Martin Williams - Minneapolis, MN **Creative Team:** Tom Moudry - Chief Creative Officer; Julie Kucinski - Group Creative Director/Copywriter; David Richardson - Group Creative Director/Art Director; Stan Prinsen - Director of Production/Executive Producer; Jim Gartner – Director **Client:** The Partnership for a Drug-Free America **2 Creative Firm:** Martin Williams - Minneapolis, MN **Creative Team:** Tom Moudry - Chief Creative Officer; Jim Henderson - Group Creative Director; Lyle Wedemeyer - Group Creative Director; Gabe Gathmann - Art Director; Nate Virnig - Copywriter; Andrea Eilers - Producer **Client:** Not For Sale **3 Creative Firm:** Martin Williams - Minneapolis, MN **Creative Team:** Tom Moudry - Chief Creative Officer; Randy Tatum - Group Creative Director; Steve Casey - Group Creative Director/Copywriter; Toby Balai - Art Director; Jennifer Cadwell - Producer; Sakona Kong – Director **Client:** Protect Minnesota **4 Creative Firm:** Casanova Pendrill - New York, NY **Creative Team:** Elias Weinstock - VP/Executive Creative Director; Alejandro Ortiz - Creative Director/Copywriter/Art Director; Gil Arevalo - Copywriter; Dámaso Crespo - Art Director; Keith Olwell - Editor (Proton); James Long – Post-production (Proton) **Client:** UNICEF

2010 // CREATIVITYAWARDS.COM

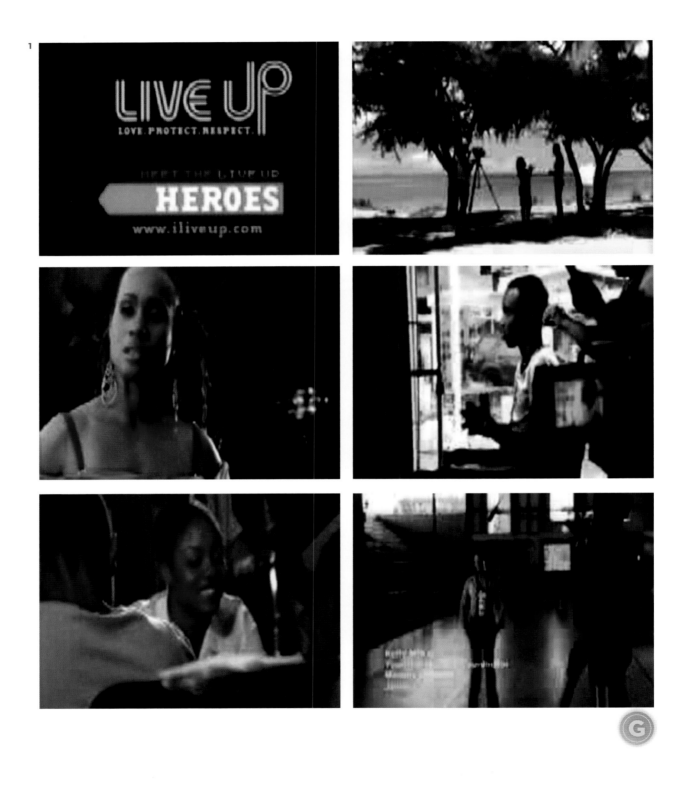

1 **Creative Firm:** Inglefield, Ogilvy & Mather Caribbean Ltd. - Port of Spain, Trinidad & Tobago **Creative Team:** David Gomez - Executive Creative Director; Sara Camps - AV Production Director; Paula Obe - Senior Copywriter; Badger Smith – Director, Sasi Productions; Simone Camps – Producer, Sasi Productions; Rrommel Best - Sound Design, fine tune media **Client:** Henry Kaiser Family Foundation

PLATINUM

Creative Firm: Draftfcb Chicago - Chicago, IL
Creative Team: Rob Sherlock - EVP/Chief Creative Officer; Chuck Rudnick - EVP/Group Creative Director; Berk Wasserman - VP/Associate Creative Director; Todd Durston - VP/Associate Creative Director; Brian Siedband - Copywriter; Larry Pecorella - Producer
Client: MillerCoors/Coors Light

COMMERCIALS, TV & RADIO // RADIO, SINGLE UNIT

Creative Firm: Clear Channel Creative Services Group - Atlanta, GA **Creative Team:** Liz Smith - Creative Director; Summer Mullins - Writer; Jason Phelps – Music Director **Client:** Computer Solutions & Repair

Creative Firm: Clear Channel Creative Services Group - Atlanta, GA **Creative Team:** Liz Smith - Creative Director; Terry Yormark - Senior Writer; Vito Gorinas – Senior Producer **Client:** Geico

Creative Firm: Clear Channel Creative Services Group - Atlanta, GA **Creative Team:** Liz Smith - Creative Director; Summer Mullins - Writer; Forrest Martin – Producer **Client:** Bayberry Uniform & Shoe

 **PLATINUM**

Creative Firm: Draftfcb Chicago - Chicago, IL

Creative Team: Rob Sherlock - EVP/Chief Creative Officer; Chuck Rudnick - EVP/Group Creative Director; Berk Wasserman - VP/Associate Creative Director; Todd Durston - VP/Associate Creative Director; Brian Siedband - Copywriter; Larry Pecorella – Producer

Client: MillerCoors/Coors Light

COMMERCIALS, TV & RADIO // RADIO, CAMPAIGN

Creative Firm: Draftfcb Chicago - Chicago, IL
Creative Team: Rob Sherlock - EVP/Chief Creative Officer; Chuck Rudnick - EVP/Group Creative Director; Berk Wasserman - VP/Associate Creative Director; Brian Siedband - Copywriter; John Bleeden - VP/Content Director; Marty Stock – EVP/Group Management Director **Client:** MIllerCoors/Coors Light

green marketing

9

39
CREATIVITY
AWARDS ANNUAL

 **PLATINUM**

Creative Firm: Eve Faulkes Design - Morgantown, WV
Creative Team: Eve Faulkes – Designer
Client: John Garlow

Design For The Times

West Virginia takes pride in its natural environment, right down to its nickname of the "Mountain State." EcoStructures, a Maidsville construction company, hired Eve Faulkes Design in nearby Morgantown to design directional signage that stands for its mission of building off-the-grid, custom-built, affordable homes. The resulting signs each keep two steel drum lids and a used tire out of the landfill— EcoStructures even uses recycled tires for some wall and floor surfaces—while the logo on the sign incorporates many of the client's green ideas.

"The inverted peace symbol represents the radiant heat water circulation through the house," Faulkes says. "The open wall of the cube stands for the south facing passive solar glass wall. The philosophy of the owner is summed up in the mantra, 'use it up, wear it out, make do or do without,' and the idea of making a tire 'do' as the carrier for the sign was too fun to pass up."

1

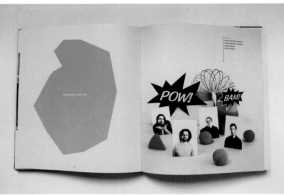

2

1 Creative Firm: Prattonia - Brooklyn, NY **Creative Team:** Meghan Forsyth - Creative Director/Designer; Kathryn Dreier - Creative Director/Designer; Alexander Driscoll - Photographer; David Nunez - Designer; Colin Matsui – Designer **Client:** Pratt Institute **URL:** www.meghanforsyth.com **2 Creative Firm:** STUDIO SONDA - Porec, Croatia **Creative Team:** Kristina Poropat - Creative Director; Jelena Simunovic - Art Director; Sean Poropat - Art Director; Ana Bursic - Designer; Tina Erman - Designer; Aleksandar Živanov – Designer **Client:** Gradska knjižnica Porec

Recycled paper using
30% post-consumer waste.
Printed with soy inks.

1 Creative Firm: Copia Creative, Inc. - Santa Monica, CA **Client:** IVIZE Group, LLC

 **PLATINUM**

Creative Firm: Airside - London, United Kingdom
Client: Greenpeace

Greenpeace Plots

The green of England resembles what many air travelers refer to as "flyover country." With this image in mind, London's Airside created a brand identity for Greenpeace's Airplot campaign opposing a third runway at Heathrow Airport, also in London. The modular green logos, based on the idea of fields viewed from the air, directly communicated Airplot's central strategy of purchasing land within the airport's proposed expansion zone while maintaining the concept of what Greenpeace is all about.

1

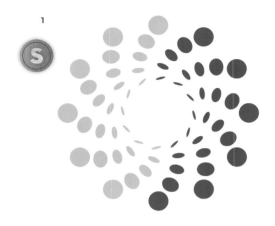

National Semiconductor SolarMagic Logo

The leading semiconductor company's advanced solar conversion technology
magically transforms solar energy into electric current by multiplying
the power of the sun. The progression of silicon wafers symbolizes
the transformative nature of the technology, using alternating yellow and blue
colors to represent solar input and electrical output.

2

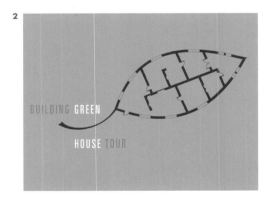

1 Creative Firm: Gee + Chung Design - San Francisco, CA **Creative Team:** Earl Gee - Creative Director/Designer/Illustrator **Client:** National Semiconductor Corporation
2 Creative Firm: Robin Horton Design - Old Greenwich, CT **Creative Team:** Robin Horton - Principal/Creative Director/Designer **Client:** League of Women Voters Greenwich

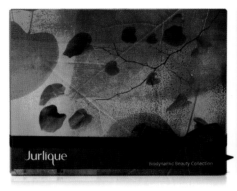
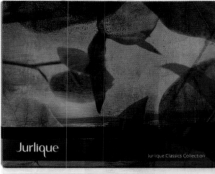

 PLATINUM

Creative Firm: Acosta Design Inc - New York, NY

Creative Team: Mauricio Acosta – Art Director;
Katarina Sjoholm – Creative Director;
John Dionaldo – Designer

Client: Jurlique

Earth Friendly Product & Packaging

The gift market is tough, but never as competitive as it is during the holiday gift-giving season. Skincare products brand Jurlique asked New York's Acosta Design to create a colorful holiday line as a departure from its traditional white packaging and also to reflect the "organic life force" of its plant-based products while also adhering to strict environmental requirements. Inspired by Jurlique's lavender, rose and tangerine ingredients sourced from a biodynamic farm in southern Australia, "we incorporated images and textures of the plant-based ingredients to create a rich, deeply colored painting-like effect, with each box set having its own vibrant color," the agency says. The producers then worked with a sustainable printing company to ensure the packaging was made according to certified sustainable forestry methods, with all recycled and recyclable materials, soy ink and 100% wind power. Acosta's elegant design and Jurlique's good scents combined to create, in the end, an effective and environmentally friendly gift.

1

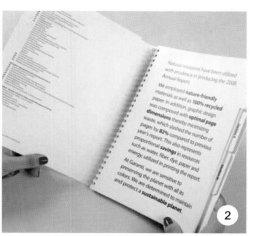

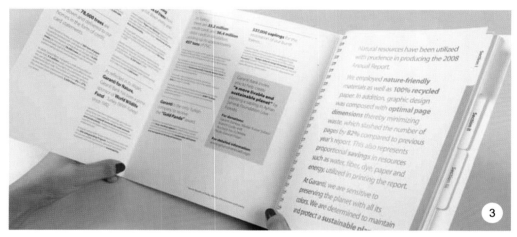

1 Creative Firm: Finar Kurumsal - Istanbul, Turkey **Creative Team:** Teoman Fiçicioglu – Art Director; Süheyla Acar – Copywriter; Mustafa Cosan – Assistant Copywriter; Özlem Firat – Illustrator; Grasiela Bardavit Giritli – Account Manager **Client:** Garanti Bank

1 Creative Firm: Sower & Seed Landscaping, LLC - Blacksburg, VA **Creative Team:** Mary Jaasma – Graphic Designer; Jonathan Bluey – Marketing Manager **Client:** Sower & Seed Landscaping, LLC

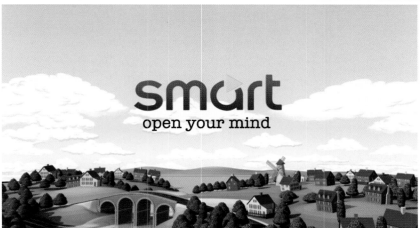

PLATINUM

Outside The Box

Creative Firm: Sticky Pictures - Brooklyn, NY

Creative Team: Michael Darmanin - Director; Nol Kittiampon - Lead Animator; Matt Choi – Designer

Client: Smart Car/Sticky Pictures

URL: vimeo.com/4768672?pg=transcoded_embed&sec=4768672

The Smart Car is just so... cute. But can it sell? Sticky Pictures pitched an inventive commercial to Smart Car USA based on the electric vehicle's playful aesthetic. "The experience of car ownership goes beyond sitting behind a steering wheel," the Brooklyn firm says. "We wished to express the concept of the environment outside of traditional definitions by opening peoples' eyes and minds to the world outside of the car." Inspired by the tagline, "Open Your Mind," and interpreted as a wakeup call to the world outside of our carsÐa place where one might find trees, happiness or even true love.

The commercial's animation conjures a trippy alternate world that may exist as far away as an idealized European countryside or as close as one's own head. "We wanted to express the narrative in the form of a question, 'What's on the mind of a Smart Car driver?'" the team says. To convey the consciousness of an owner of an environmentally friendly car, Sticky Pictures explored the idea of a tree being literally in the driver's mind, with the rest of the story unfolding within that framework. The viewer seamlessly travels inside the driver's mind "to a new state of reality, using a tree... doubling as his 'brain'" and then growing to encompass other tree motifs.

385

CREATIVE CATEGORY

student

1

2

3

4

1 Category: Annual Reports **Design Program/School:** Drexel University Graphic Design Program/AWCoMAD - Philadelphia, PA **Creative Team:** Joey Krietemeyer – Student Designer; Jody Graff – University Instructor **2 Category:** Annual Reports **Design Program/School:** Drexel University Graphic Design Program/AWCoMAD - Philadelphia, PA **Creative Team:** John Dunn – Student Designer; Jody Graff – University Instructor **3 Category:** Magazine Ad, Consumer, Campaign **Design Program/School:** The Creative Circus - Atlanta, GA **Creative Team:** Billy Simkiss - Art Director; Trey Tyler - Copywriter **4 Category:** Cross-Platform Campaign **Design Program/School:** Westerdals School of Communication - Oslo, Norway **Creative Team:** André Gidoin – Art Director; Markus Ivan Johansson, Aleksander Hoel – Copywriters **5 Category:** Show Openings, IDs, Titles **Design Program/School:** Art Center College of Design - Pasadena, CA **Creative Team:** Hyun Ju Yang – Student *Image Not Available

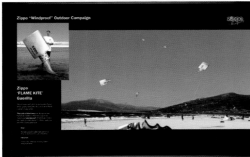

1 Category: Ambient Media, Campaign **Design Program/School:** Academy of Art University - Fremont, CA **Creative Team:** Jimin Halim, Chaichat Pilun-Owad – Art Directors **2 Category:** Ambient Media, Campaign **Design Program/School:** Academy of Art University - Fremont, CA **Creative Team:** Jimin Halim – Art Director **3 Category:** Ambient Media, Single Unit **Design Program/School:** School of Visual Arts - New York, NY **Creative Team:** Kenji Akiyama – Art Director/Copywriter/Photographer; Frank Anselmo – Instructor; Richard Wilde – Dept. Chair **4 Category:** Audio-Visual Presentation **Design Program/School:** School of Visual Arts - New York, NY **Creative Team:** Ori Kleiner – Instructor/Creative Director; Richard Wilde – Chair/Advertising/Graphic Design Department SVA

1

2

3

4

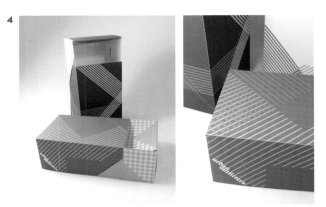

1 Category: Billboards, Single Unit **Design Program/School:** School of Visual Arts - New York, NY **Creative Team:** HyoJoo Kim - Student; Frank Anselmo – Professor
2 Category: Newspaper Ad, Consumer, Single Unit **Design Program/School:** European School of Design - Frankfurt, Germany **Creative Team:** Pavel Bondarenko – Art/
Photo/Idea **3 Category:** Audio-Visual Presentation **Design Program/School:** School of Visual Arts - New York, NY **Creative Team:** Graham Elliott – Instructor/Creative
Director; Richard Wilde – Chair/Advertising/Graphic Design Department SVA **4 Category:** Retail Packaging **Design Program/School:** Drexel University Graphic Design
Program/AWCoMAD - Philadelphia, PA **Creative Team:** Joey Krietemeyer - Student Designer; Sandy Stewart – University Instructor

1

2

3

4

1

4

WVU Creative Arts Center Calendar of Events Publication

Because theatre, dance, music and art performances reflect more genres than can be shown in a few images, this student used a silhouette of one genre as a mask for another. The silhouette is simple enough to carry still another background image from the discipline.

The cover used the same effect to bring in audience and facility using an applause silhouette.

2

3

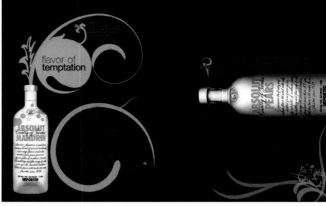

1 Category: Billboards, Campaign **Design Program/School:** The Creative Circus - Atlanta, GA **Creative Team:** Colin Gray - Copywriter; Kirsten Mohr – Designer
2 Category: Typography, Magazine **Design Program/School:** Art Institute of New York City - New York, NY **Creative Team:** Tjhang Steven - Student; Simona Prives - Instructor **3 Category:** Typography, Magazine **Design Program/School:** Art Institute of New York City - New York, NY **Creative Team:** Tjhang Steven - Student; Simona Prives - Instructor **4 Category:** Book Design, Interior **Design Program/School:** West Virginia University - Morgantown, WV **Creative Team:** Blake Stewart - Student Designer

From the Muddy Banks of the Monongahela

This publication is a catalog of a West Virginia University printmaking alumni show which will travel. Morgantown, home of West Virginia University, is a river town, hence the title. Since printmaking is the least known medium among non-artists, and because the making process is so important to the medium, the catalog pages reflect the love of ink and the look of draw-downs as part of the printmaker's color selection process.

1 **Category:** Book Design, Interior **Design Program/School:** Drexel University Graphic Design Program/AWCoMAD - Philadelphia, PA **Creative Team:** Sasha McCune - Student Designer; Don Haring Jr. - University Instructor 2 **Category:** Book Design, Interior **Design Program/School:** West Virginia University Studio 2453 - Morgantown, WV **Creative Team:** Bradford Robertson - Student Designer 3 **Category:** Book Design, Interior **Design Program/School:** Drexel University Graphic Design Program/AWCoMAD - Philadelphia, PA **Creative Team:** Anne Trencher - Student Designer; Jody Graff – University Instructor 4 **Category:** Book Design, Jacket **Design Program/School:** Art Institute of New York City - New York, NY **Creative Team:** Tatiana Bogdan - Student; Simona Prives – Instructor 5 **Category:** Catalog, Consumer **Design Program/School:** The Creative Circus - Atlanta, GA **Creative Team:** Larissa Brandao – Designer

1

2

4

3

WVU Health Sciences Graduate Programs Publication

This student-designed piece is intended to recruit college seniors in the sciences into graduate study at WVU. Graphic material from the output of science disciplines floats over the images which primarily include students in the programs, so that viewers might feel like peers. The school is situated in the mountains and the curves connote the rural geography of the area.

---

1 Category: Book Design, Interior **Design Program/School:** Drexel University Graphic Design Program/AWCoMAD - Philadelphia, PA **Creative Team:** Bryan Howell - Student Designer; Jody Graff – University Instructor **2 Category:** Book Design, Interior **Design Program/School:** School of Visual Arts - New York, NY **Creative Team:** Genevieve Williams - Creative Director; Richard Wilde – Chair/Advertising/Graphic Design Department SVA **3 Category:** Book Design, Interior **Design Program/School:** West Virginia University Studio 2453 - Morgantown, WV **Creative Team:** Lauren Lamb, Michael Todaro - Student Designers
4 Category: Public Service Film/Video **Design Program/School:** The Creative Circus - Atlanta, GA **Creative Team:** Matt Moore, Mark Adler - Art Directors & Copywriters; Christy Parry – Videographer

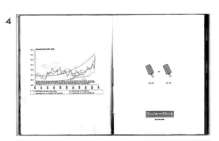

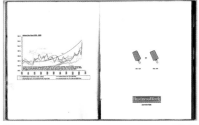

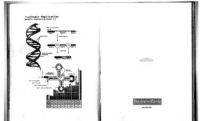

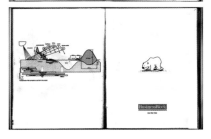

1 Category: Typography, Magazine **Design Program/School:** Art Institute of New York City - New York, NY **Creative Team:** Chin Yan Ng - Student; Simona Prives, Instructor **2 Category:** Cross-Platform Campaign **Design Program/School:** Forsbergs School of Graphic Design and Advertising - Stockholm, Sweden **Creative Team:** Peter Nylind - Copywriter/Art Director; Henry Stenberg - Copywriter **3 Category:** Collateral Material, Campaign **Design Program/School:** Drexel University Graphic Design Program/AWCoMAD - Philadelphia, PA **Creative Team:** Mike Valentine - Student Designer; E. June Roberts-Lunn – University Instructor **4 Category:** Collateral Material, Campaign **Design Program/School:** Academy of Art University - Fremont, CA **Creative Team:** Jimin Halim - Art Director **5 Category:** Book Design, Jacket **Design Program/School:** Drexel University Graphic Design Program/AWCoMAD - Philadelphia, PA **Creative Team:** Yesenia Perez-Cruz - Student Designer; E. June Roberts-Lunn – University Instructor

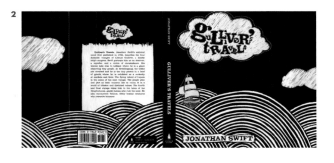

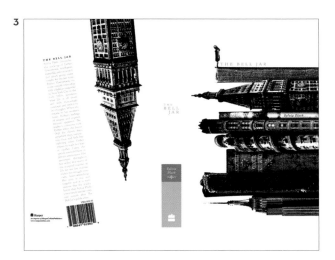

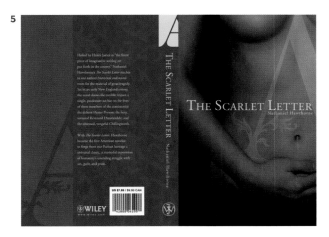

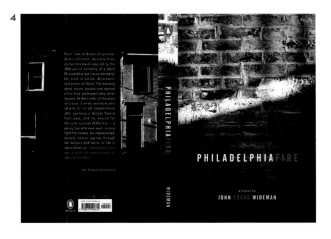

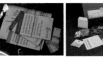

beneFIT: A service design project

The BeneFIT project was a fitness-program led by a graphic design graduate student for the WVU Community Medicine Department to be used in rural clinics for diabetes patients. To ensure more success than most programs that fail within 6 months, this is a service design plan, directing roles for doctors, clinics and patients, as well as families of the patients.

The doctors get a set of diagnostic cards which help patients communicate more effectively in short visits. It includes the design of a workbook, family and friend invitatiions to help support the patient, refrigerator progress chart magnets and wristbands for the patient.

The clinic gets conversation maps which is a group product like a game with cards that encourage patients to talk about issues related to the program and their health. they also get buddy invitations to allow them to find a partner within the group. The clinic is given encouragement cards to mail to patients during the course.

The design uses common proverbs for the steps of change, and images of real West Virginians to make the program more accessible to older rural patients. It also uses humor and animal personification to help the material feel friendly and not preachy or clinical.

1 Category: Typography, Magazine **Design Program/School:** Art Institute of New York City - New York, NY **Creative Team:** Rubio Camila - Student; Simona Prives – Instructor
2 Category: Book Design, Jacket **Design Program/School:** Drexel University Graphic Design Program/AWCoMAD - Philadelphia, PA **Creative Team:** Bryan Howell - Student Designer; E. June Roberts-Lunn – University Instructor **3 Category:** Book Design, Jacket **Design Program/School:** Drexel University Graphic Design Program/AWCoMAD - Philadelphia, PA **Creative Team:** Allison Fegan - Student Designer; E. June Roberts-Lunn – University Instructor **4 Category:** Book Design, Jacket **Design Program/School:** Drexel University Graphic Design Program/AWCoMAD - Philadelphia, PA **Creative Team:** Gary Brooks - Student Designer; E. June Roberts-Lunn – University Instructor **5 Category:** Book Design, Jacket **Design Program/School:** Drexel University Graphic Design Program/AWCoMAD - Philadelphia, PA **Creative Team:** Trissy Harding - Student Designer; E. June Roberts-Lunn – University Instructor **6 Category:** Collateral Material, Campaign **Design Program/School:** West Virginia University Studio 2453 - Morgantown, WV **Creative Team:** Emily Frye - Project Lead/Designer; Marcie Kent, Scott Taylor – Designers

1

2

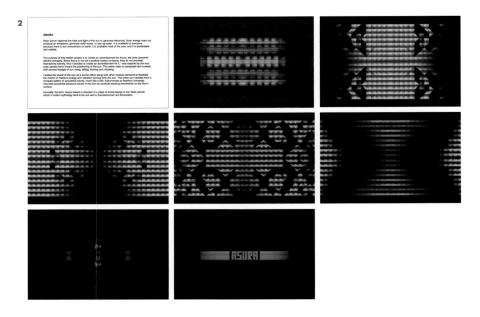

4

3

WVU Creative Arts Center Wayfinding

Two senior students in graphic design developed this signage system for the Creative Arts Center at WVU which is a round building that is a maze complicated by dual numbering systems.

In addition to solving the wayfinding needs, they wanted to make sure people were aware of being in a building about the arts. Not only does the signage reflect artistic license in typography, shape and color, but even the different divisions of the arts have specialized restroom signage. Main offices entryways have floor-to-ceiling stickers with the same curve system.

5

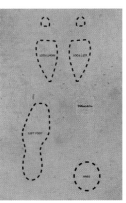

1 Category: Website, Public Service, Non-profit **Design Program/School:** Hyper Island - Stockholm, Sweden **Creative Team:** Dennis Rosenqvist - Art Director; Christian Söderholm – Copywriter **2 Category:** Creative Firm Film, Self-Promotion **Design Program/School:** Art Center College of Design - Pasadena, CA **Creative Team:** Hyun Ju Yang – Student **3 Category:** Environmental Graphics, Campaign **Design Program/School:** West Virginia University Studio 2453 - Morgantown, WV **Creative Team:** Matthew Carson, Xioli Guan, Alan Smith - Student Designers **4 Category:** Green Advertising, Single Unit **Design Program/School:** School of Visual Arts - New York, NY **Creative Team:** Kenji Akiyama - Art Director/Copywriter; Frank Anselmo - Instructor; Richard Wilde – Dept. Chair **5 Category:** Guerilla Marketing, Single Unit **Design Program/School:** School of Visual Arts - New York, NY **Creative Team:** Eunhaee Cho, HyoJoo Kim – Art Directors

1

2

3

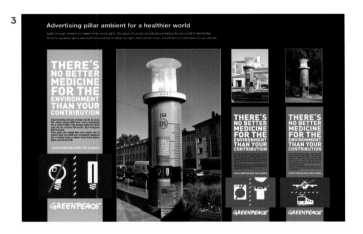

4

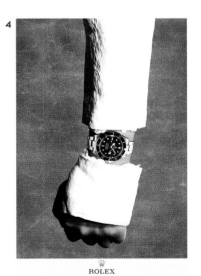

1 Category: Cross-Platform Campaign **Design Program/School:** The Creative Circus - Atlanta, GA **Creative Team:** TJ Walthall, Andrew DiPeri - Art Directors; Kyle Cavanaugh – Copywriter **2 Category:** Editorial Design, Single Spread **Design Program/School:** Art Institute of New York City - New York, NY **Creative Team:** Juan Chavarria Jr. - Student; Simona Prives – Instructor **3 Category:** Green Media **Design Program/School:** European School of Design - Frankfurt, Germany **Creative Team:** Pavel Bondarenko - Art/Photo/Illu/Idea; Stefan Mildner – Art/Photo/Text/Idea **4 Category:** Magazine Ad, Consumer, Single Unit **Design Program/School:** School of Visual Arts - New York, NY **Creative Team:** Kenji Akiyama - Art Director/Copywriter/Photographer; Jack Mariucci - Instructor; Richard Wilde – Dept. Chair

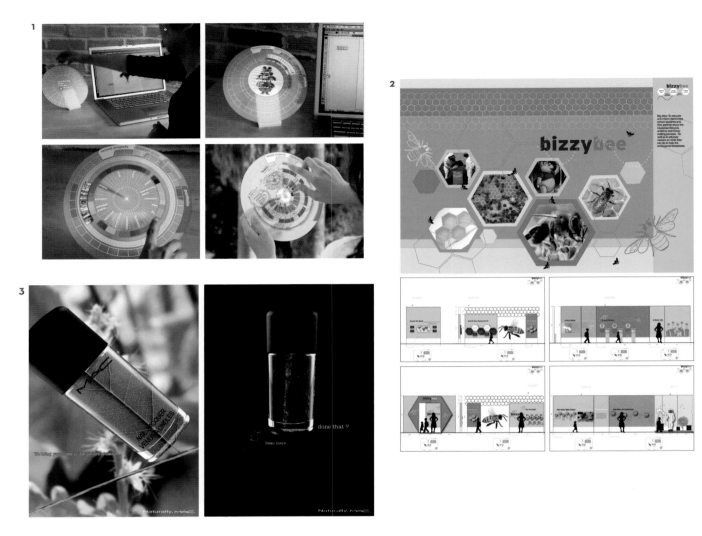

1 Category: Demo/Presentation Video **Design Program/School:** Art Center College of Design - Pasadena, CA **Creative Team:** Hyun Ju Yang – Student **2 Category:** Environmental Graphics, Single Unit **Design Program/School:** Drexel University Graphic Design Program/AWCoMAD - Philadelphia, PA **Creative Team:** Dorothy Lun, Brielle Weinstein, Sheena Lewoc - Student Designers; Alice Dommert – University Instructor **3 Category:** Magazine Ad, Consumer, Campaign **Design Program/School:** Mudra Institute of Communications Ahmedabad - Ahmedabad, India **Creative Team:** Nimisha/Arvindh/Chrisel – Students of Linda Conway Correll **4 Category:** Magazine Ad, Consumer, Campaign **Design Program/School:** Academy of Art University - San Francisco, CA **Creative Team:** Jun Ho Oh - Art Director; Jerry Kurniawan – Art Director

1

2

3

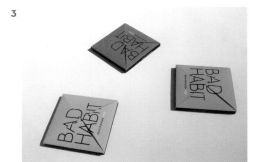

1 Category: Environmental Graphics, Single Unit **Design Program/School:** Iowa State University Graphic Design Program - Ames, Iowa **Creative Team:** Brooke Scherer - MFA Graduate Student - Graphic Design; Kim Topp - MA Graduate Student - Environmental Graphics; Thomas Grier - Senior - Architecture; Lisa Fontaine – Professor - Graphic Design **2 Category:** Food & Beverage Packaging **Design Program/School:** Drexel University Graphic Design Program/AWCoMAD - Philadelphia, PA **Creative Team:** Jenna Navitsky - Student Designer; E. June Roberts-Lunn – University Instructor **3 Category:** Food & Beverage Packaging **Design Program/School:** School of Visual Arts - New York, NY **Creative Team:** Yuna Kim – Student

1

2

3

4

5

6

1 Category: Letterheads & Envelope Sets **Design Program/School:** University of Baltimore - Baltimore, MD **Creative Team:** Simon Fong – MFA Integrated Design Student
2 Category: Magazine Ad, Consumer, Single Unit **Design Program/School:** School of Visual Arts - New York, NY **Creative Team:** Kenji Akiyama - Art Director/Copywriter/ Photographer; Jack Mariucci - Instructor; Richard Wilde – Dept. Chair **3 Category:** Health & Beauty Packaging **Design Program/School:** Drexel University Graphic Design Program/AWCoMAD - Philadelphia, PA **Creative Team:** Yesenia Perez-Cruz - Student Designer; Sandy Stewart – University Instructor **4 Category:** Magazine Ad, Consumer, Single Unit **Design Program/School:** School of Visual Arts - New York, NY **Creative Team:** Kenji Akiyama - Art Director/Copywriter; Jack Mariucci - Instructor; Richard Wilde – Dept. Chair **5 Category:** Illustration, Commercial, Single Unit **Design Program/School:** Drexel University Graphic Design Program/AWCoMAD - Philadelphia, PA **Creative Team:** Allison Chang - Student Designer; Bill Rees – University Instructor **6 Category:** Magazine Ad, Consumer, Single Unit **Design Program/School:** School of Visual Arts - New York, NY **Creative Team:** Kenji Akiyama - Art Director/Copywriter; Jack Mariucci - Instructor; Richard Wilde – Dept. Chair

1

2

3

4

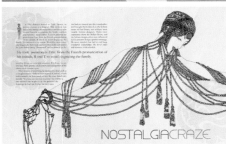

5

1 Category: Health & Beauty Packaging **Design Program/School:** Drexel University Graphic Design Program/AWCoMAD - Philadelphia, PA **Creative Team:** Cariese Bartholomew - Student Designer; Jody Graff – University Instructor **2 Category:** Home & Garden Packaging **Design Program/School:** Drexel University Graphic Design Program/AWCoMAD - Philadelphia, PA **Creative Team:** Courtney Remm - Student Designer; Sandy Stewart – University Instructor **3 Category:** Typography, Magazine **Design Program/School:** Art Institute of New York City - New York, NY **Creative Team:** Tatiana Bogdan - Student; Simona Prives – Instructor **4 Category:** Magazine Ad, Consumer, Campaign **Design Program/School:** The Creative Circus - Atlanta, GA **Creative Team:** Ben Salas - Art Director; Lauren Spoto - Copywriter **5 Category:** Logos & Trademarks **Design Program/School:** University of Baltimore - Baltimore, MD **Creative Team:** Simon Fong – MFA Integrated Design Student

1

2

3

4

5

1 Category: Magazine Ad, Consumer, Campaign **Design Program/School:** The Creative Circus - Atlanta, GA **Creative Team:** Evan McAlister - Art Director; David Zandman – Copywriter **2 Category:** Magazine Ad, Consumer, Campaign **Design Program/School:** Academy of Art University - San Francisco, CA **Creative Team:** Jun Ho Oh, Chung Han Chou - Art Directors **3 Category:** Magazine Ad, Consumer, Campaign **Design Program/School:** The Creative Circus - Atlanta, GA **Creative Team:** Chris Araujo - Art Director; Rich Ford – Copywriter **4 Category:** Magazine Ad, Consumer, Campaign **Design Program/School:** The Creative Circus - Atlanta, GA **Creative Team:** Evan McAlister - Art Director; Kim Healy – Copywriter **5 Category:** Magazine Ad, Consumer, Single Unit **Design Program/School:** School of Visual Arts - New York, NY **Creative Team:** Kenji Akiyama - Art Director/Copywriter; Jack Mariucci - Instructor; Richard Wilde – Dept. Chair

1

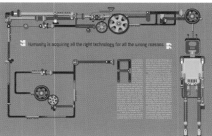
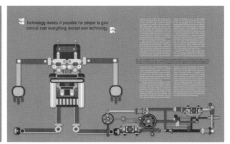

2

3

4

1 **Category:** Typography, Magazine **Design Program/School:** Art Institute of New York City - New York, NY **Creative Team:** Elen Winata - Student; Maurizio Masi - Instructor 2 **Category:** Typography, Magazine **Design Program/School:** Art Institute of New York City - New York, NY **Creative Team:** Ricardo Rodo - Student; Simona Prives – Instructor 3 **Category:** Magazine Ad, Consumer, Campaign **Design Program/School:** School of Visual Arts - New York, NY **Creative Team:** Kenji Akiyama - Art Director/Copywriter; Vinny Tulley - Instructor; Richard Wilde – Dept. Chair 4 **Category:** Show Openings, IDs, Titles **Design Program/School:** Drexel University Graphic Design Program/AWCoMAD - Philadelphia, PA **Creative Team:** Mike Valentine - Student Designer; E. June Roberts-Lunn – University Instructor

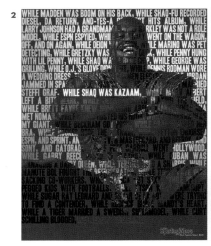

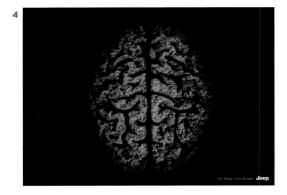
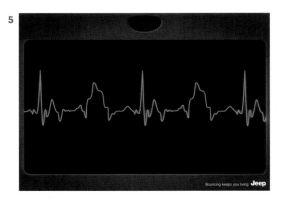

1 Category: Magazine Ad, Consumer, Campaign **Design Program/School:** The Creative Circus - Atlanta, GA **Creative Team:** Brandon Rapert - Art Director; Andy Pearson - Copywriter; Bobby Prokenpek – Photographer **2 Category:** Magazine Ad, Consumer, Campaign **Design Program/School:** The Creative Circus - Atlanta, GA **Creative Team:** Andrew Harper - Art Director; Lauren Silva – Copywriter **3 Category:** Magazine Ad, Consumer, Campaign **Design Program/School:** The Creative Circus - Atlanta, GA **Creative Team:** Kasia Haupt - Art Director; Trey Tyler – Copywriter **4 Category:** Magazine Ad, Consumer, Single Unit **Design Program/School:** University of the Arts London - Daegu, South Korea **Creative Team:** Tae Jay Lee – Art Director/Copywriter **5 Category:** Magazine Ad, Consumer, Single Unit **Design Program/School:** University of the Arts London - Daegu, South Korea **Creative Team:** Tae Jay Lee – Art Director/Copywriter

1

2

4

3

5

1 Category: Poster, Campaign **Design Program/School:** European School of Design - Frankfurt, Germany **Creative Team:** Pavel Bondarenko – Art/Photo/Idea
2 Category: Magazine Ad, Public Service, Single Unit **Design Program/School:** School of Visual Arts - New York, NY **Creative Team:** Kenji Akiyama - Art Director/
Copywriter; Jack Mariucci - Instructor; Richard Wilde – Dept. Chair **3 Category:** Poster, Campaign **Design Program/School:** European School of Design - Frankfurt,
Germany **Creative Team:** Pavel Bondarenko – Art/Photo/Idea **4 Category:** Magazine Design, Complete **Design Program/School:** The Art Institute of California
- Orange County - Santa Ana, CA **Creative Team:** Nicole Blaschke; Jeremy Godinez; Reggie Hidalgo - Art Director; Victor Lam **5 Category:** Web Games & En-
tertainment **Design Program/School:** Westerdals School of Communication - Oslo, Norway **Creative Team:** André Gidoin - Art Director; Markus Ivan Johansson,
Aleksander Hoel – Copywriters

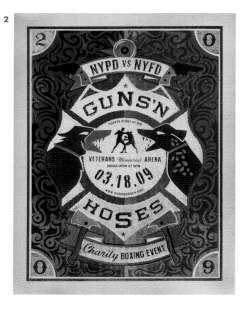

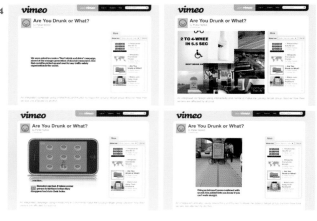

1 Category: Magazine Design, Complete **Design Program/School:** The Art Institute of California - Orange County - Santa Ana, CA **Creative Team:** Tristan Cruz - Art Director/Illustrator; Chase Van Huysen - Photographer/Designer; Danny Hunsaker - Photo Director/Designer; Hannah Yoon – Designer/Writer **2 Category:** Poster, Single Unit **Design Program/School:** The Creative Circus - Atlanta, GA **Creative Team:** Meredith Callaway – Designer **3 Category:** Photography, Book, Campaign **Design Program/School:** The Creative Circus - Atlanta, GA **Creative Team:** John Robert Ward II – Photographer **4 Category:** Cross-Platform Campaign **Design Program/School:** Forsbergs School of Graphic Design and Advertising - Stockholm, Sweden **Creative Team:** Petter Nylind - Copywriter/Art Director; Henry Stenberg – Copywriter **5 Category:** Mobile Device, Advertising **Design Program/School:** Westerdals School of Communication - Oslo, Norway **Creative Team:** André Gidoin – Art Director; Markus Ivan Johansson, Aleksander Hoel – Copywriters

1

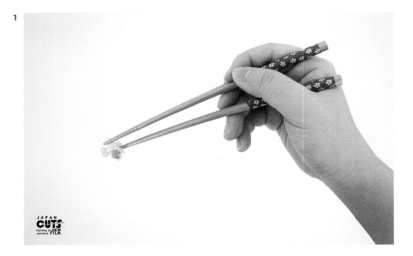

2

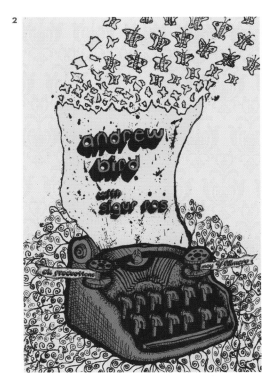

3

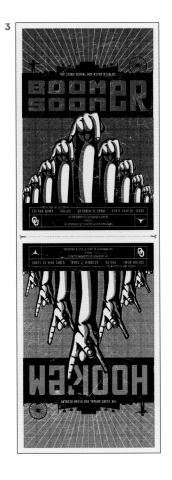

4

5

1 Category: Poster, Single Unit **Design Program/School:** School of Visual Arts - New York, NY **Creative Team:** Kenji Akiyama - Art Director/Copywriter/Photographer; Vinny Tulley - Instructor; Richard Wilde – Dept. Chair **2 Category:** Poster, Single Unit **Design Program/School:** The Creative Circus - Atlanta, GA **Creative Team:** Josh Kessler – Designer **3 Category:** Poster, Single Unit **Design Program/School:** The Creative Circus - Atlanta, GA **Creative Team:** Chris Araujo – Designer **4 Category:** Poster, Single Unit **Design Program/School:** The Creative Circus - Atlanta, GA **Creative Team:** Jill Brunner – Designer **5 Category:** Retail Packaging **Design Program/School:** Drexel University Graphic Design Program/AWCoMAD - Philadelphia, PA **Creative Team:** Mike Valentine - Student Designer; Jody Graff – University Instructor

1

2

3

4

5

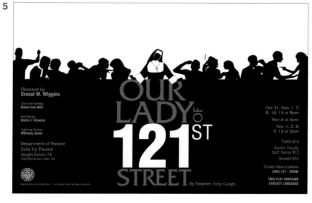

6

1 Category: Poster, Campaign **Design Program/School:** Art Institute of New York City - New York, NY **Creative Team:** ChinYan Ng - Student; Simona Prives - Instructor
2 Category: Poster, Single Unit **Design Program/School:** School of Visual Arts - New York, NY **Creative Team:** Eunhaee Cho – Art Director **3 Category:** Poster, Single Unit
Design Program/School: Art Institute of New York City - New York, NY **Creative Team:** Elen Winata - Student; Maurizio Masi – Instructor **4 Category:** Poster, Single Unit
Design Program/School: Art Institute of New York City - New York, NY **Creative Team:** Tatiana Bogdan - Student; Simona Prives – Instructor **5 Category:** Poster, Single
Unit **Design Program/School:** The Design Studio at Kean University - Union, NJ **Creative Team:** Jamie Maimone - Designer and Illustrator; Steven Brower - Art Director;
Dawnmarie McDermid – Associate Art Director **6 Category:** Poster, Campaign **Design Program/School:** European School of Design - Frankfurt, Germany
Creative Team: Pavel Bondarenko , Reinhard Obinger – Art/Photo/Idea

index

by creative firm

index

index

by client

index

index